Western Images of China

of China

REVISED EDITION

Colin Mackerras

OXFORD
UNIVERSITY PRESS

OXFORD
UNIVERSITY PRESS

Oxford University Press is a department of the University of Oxford.
It furthers the University's objective of excellence in research, scholarship,
and education by publishing worldwide in

Oxford New York

Athens Auckland Bangkok Bogotá Buenos Aires Calcutta
Cape Town Chennai Dar es Salaam Delhi Florence Hong Kong Istanbul
Karachi Kuala Lumpur Madrid Melbourne Mexico City Mumbai
Nairobi Paris São Paulo Singapore Taipei Tokyo Toronto Warsaw

with associated companies in Berlin Ibadan

Oxford is a registered trade mark of Oxford University Press

British Library Cataloguing in Publication Data
Data Available

Library of Congress Cataloguing in Publication Data
Data Available

ISBN 0-19-590738-8

Printed in Hong Kong
Published by Oxford University Press (China) Ltd
18th Floor, Warwick House East, Taikoo Place, 979 King's Road, Quarry Bay
Hong Kong

Books are to be returned on or before
the date before below.

**7 Day
Loan**

LIBREX —

WESTERN IMAGES OF CHINA

Preface

As one long fascinated by China, both past and present, I have often been struck by the contrasting attitudes which different and equally competent specialists have adopted towards matters relating to China. The controversial nature of Western images of China was borne in on me with particular strength when from 1964 to 1966 I got what was, at that time for a Westerner, the most unusual opportunity of teaching English in the People's Republic of China, at the Beijing Institute of Foreign Languages. I was able to compare and contrast what Westerners were saying about China in their home media and elsewhere, with my own interpretation of what I saw and heard going on around me. Images are an important area of study because they bear on how people of one culture perceive and relate to those of another.

In the first half of 1986 I was invited to give a series of lectures on Western images of China at the same Beijing Institute of Foreign Languages where I had taught twenty years before. Although I had long been very interested in this subject, I had never before set down ideas and information about it in a coherent form. The first edition of the present book, which was published in 1989, derived in large measure from the lectures I gave.

This second edition differs vastly from the first. One major difference is the addition of two completely new chapters, covering the crises of 1989 and the 1990s. The events of 1989 had a tremendous impact on Western images of China, the results of which are still evident as the twentieth century yields to the twenty-first. Besides this task of updating, I have made many other changes, taking into account new research and ideas. In addition, I have omitted all the material from the first edition which concerned images of the medium to distant past—in fact, anything more than thirty years before the author of the image being discussed. Other changes are mainly concerned with pruning the material and sharpening its focus.

I should like to thank those various people with whom I have discussed the ideas and material in this book. These include colleagues and students, both at the Beijing Institute of Foreign Languages and Griffith University in Brisbane, Australia. I have learned an enormous amount from them. I should also like to thank the Oxford University Press for the opportunity to undertake this second edition, and my wife Alyce for her encouragement to research and complete this book.

Colin Mackerras
1999

Contents

1

Introduction

Marco Polo has become legendary both in the West and much of the rest of the world as an early representative of one major civilization who lived and worked in another, who took the trouble to understand and appreciate what he saw and heard. Although doubt has been cast on whether Marco Polo ever went to China at all, it does not alter the fact that he was the first major formulator of Western images of China.

The aim of this book is to present and analyse such images; to trace how they have changed from era to era, and to relate both the images and the changes they underwent to the politics and intellectual environment in the West. The real subject of this study is the West, and China is the object. Though the theme of cross-cultural relationships is never far from the surface, this is primarily a study of one aspect of the intellectual history of the West.

An image is a view or perception held by a person or group. In the present context, however, it is more specifically a perception which holds sufficient priority with the viewer to impinge upon the consciousness. Under this definition, a completely trivial perception is not an image at all. But what is important for one viewer may not be that at all for another. In this book the concern is only with part of the range of views of China, in particular those that are not trivial but relate to general Western preoccupations with China.

One aim not within the scope of this book is the presentation of the reality of China. In general, there is no comment on who is 'right' or 'wrong' when observers present rival or conflicting views. Images are not and have never been necessarily the same as reality. At all times there is an infinity of realities. What all observers of China appear to have done is to filter what they see through the spectacles of their own backgrounds, ideologies, biases, and experiences, and they cannot avoid the impact of the period and place in which they live. It is nearly universal, and perfectly understandable and natural, that observers of another people remain firmly planted in their own culture. Some make more attempts at understanding, even appreciation, than others. Some are quicker to draw comparisons with their own civilization than others. Some are by temperament more eager to expose weaknesses or criticize, or alternatively admire and exult in what is foreign. But while there can be common ground between images and realities, they rarely overlap completely.

None of this means that the present author has no point of view. On the contrary, like the Western observers who are the subject of the book, I am bound by my own culture, times, upbringing, training, and temperament. Here, as elsewhere, phraseology and the selection of material inevitably reveal a point of view or sympathy. My aim is to be fair to all, including the presentation of images which may be extremely contentious, while acknowledging that what appears fair to one person may not seem so to another.

Two related theories have been suggested, which bear on knowledge and interpretation and are of great relevance to a study of images. Both are by well-known scholars and have exerted considerable influence, including on the formulation of my own position. It may be possible to determine their applicability in the light of the Western images discussed in the following chapters.

The author of the first of these theories is the distinguished French historian and philosopher Michel Foucault (1926–84), one of the most influential thinkers of the second half of the twentieth century. He has described his theory simply as 'power/knowledge' (*pouvoir–savoir*). In a book published first in 1980, one scholar of Foucault's ideas stated that this concept 'constitutes the strategic fulcrum of his recent work'.[1] In essence it argues that knowledge or 'truth' is in effect a function of power. Those who hold power can and do use it to further their own interests, to exercise power, or to keep themselves in power. Foucault says:

> Truth is a thing of this world: it is produced only by virtue of multiple forms of constraint. And it induces regular effects of power. Each society has its régime of truth, its 'general politics' of truth: that is, the types of discourse which it accepts and makes function as true; the mechanisms and instances which enable one to distinguish true and false statements ... the status of those who are charged with saying what counts as true.[2]

Foucault defines this 'régime of truth' in the following famous sentence: '"Truth" is linked in a circular relation with systems of power which produce and sustain it, and to effects of power which it induces and which extend it'.[3] According to this theory, images of China would tend to become a bulwark for a particular set of policies towards that country, or even for a more general policy. Information would be carefully selected and propagated to justify that policy or set of policies. The relationship between knowledge and reality dwindles in importance beside that between knowledge and power.

The other theory is that of Edward Said, who in quite a few places acknowledges his debt to Foucault.[4] Said designates his theory simply as 'Orientalism'. Although designed specifically as a critique of the Western study of West Asian civilizations, its main points are equally applicable to the study of China. Said argues that Western scholars have misinterpreted or produced distorted accounts of Eastern civilizations because of their ethnocentric attitudes.

> If it is true that no production of knowledge in the human sciences can ever ignore or disclaim its author's involvement as a human subject in his own circumstances, then it must also be true that for a European or American studying the Orient there can be no disclaiming the main circumstances of his actuality: that he comes up against the Orient as a European or American first, as an individual second.[5]

Said's study is a passionate attack on Western scholarship for its lack of sensitivity to the value systems of the people studied, for its general inability to examine Asian countries in their own terms. He believes 'too close a relationship between the scholar and the state' to be inadvisable and a feature of Orientalism. This is one of the respects in which Said is clearly heavily influenced by Foucault's 'power/knowledge' concept. Said calls for an emphasis on *discipline* as opposed to areas studies: 'Interesting work is most likely to be produced by scholars whose allegiance is to a discipline defined intellectually and not to a "field" like Orientalism, defined either canonically, imperially, or geographically'.[6] In other words, despite his passionate attacks on Western scholarship, he is quite specific in recognizing the possibility of 'decolonizing' knowledge, in acknowledging 'that there is scholarship that is not as corrupt, or at least as blind to human reality'[7] as the 'Orientalist' type he castigates in such strong terms. Clearly the two theories just outlined are related to each other, because Said's notion that the West 'colonized' knowledge about Asia means that the West devised the construct of 'the Orient' as part of the process of enhancing the power of the West over Asian peoples.

The term 'China' can be understood in a number of ways. It denotes a geographical entity, a nation, a history, a society, and a people. While it is true that the geographical entity which is China and the people who inhabit it are separate, they are related closely to each other. The focus of the present book is on images of the people and what they have created, rather than on the physical country. The particular images chosen tend to be social and political, but some attention is also given to economic and historical matters. In view of the enormity of the subject, certain important topics have been specifically omitted or treated only very sparsely. These include China's literature and arts and its minority nationalities. An exception is made for Tibet in the 1990s, because of the way in which images of China's treatment of Tibetans have impinged on images of the country as a whole.

The time-frame of this book is deliberately comprehensive. It covers Western images from the very beginnings of contact between China and the West to the present time. The early centuries from the time of Ancient Rome until the thirteenth century are covered extremely briefly, for the very simple reason that images then were vague and not extensive. It is with Marco Polo's account that detailed Western images of China begin. Unlike a drama or novel, history does not end, and so an image that one culture has of another can reach no final conclusion. Nevertheless, it is necessary to place a limit on this study, and the one I have chosen is the middle of 1998. Again, the reason is simple: this is the time that the typescript for this book was completed.

Given the number of 'Western' countries and the range of areas within each, the place-frame also needs definition. In this book the 'West' as a broad generalization is the countries of Western Europe, North America and Australasia. Such a definition will require refinement depending on the period under discussion. So North America and Australasia are irrelevant to this book until the nineteenth century.

Over the centuries there has been a strong tendency for one country to dominate the West's perception of China. In the eighteenth century it was France, in the nineteenth Britain, and for most of the twentieth, unquestionably, it was the United States. Foucault's power/knowledge relationship is relevant here, because dominant powers also tend to be able to dominate in the field of ideas.

It follows that for any given period, examples from one country are likely to predominate. There are some parts of the West which figure but rarely in this study, as total comprehensiveness is impossible and certainly not my aim here. What I have tried to do is to allude to 'images' which are most important in the West at any one time.

The concept of the 'West' takes on meaning mainly if juxtaposed to the 'East', and the boundary between the two fluctuates according to the political, economic, and cultural circumstances of the day. One area which is in this book excluded from the 'West' is eastern and most of central Europe. There are occasional references to the Austro-Hungarian Empire and, for the period since World War I, to Austria. But countries such as Czechoslovakia, Romania, and Greece are not covered here at all. The most important omission is Russia and the former Soviet Union. Although these countries, or in the case of Russia or the Soviet Union a major portion of it, are unquestionably part of Europe, it is a moot point whether they should be considered part of the 'West'. The main reason for excluding them is scale. It appears to me that 'Central and Eastern European images of China' are an entirely different topic from the one central here. It would be an important field of research and include such major matters as Soviet Marxist attitudes towards China, but it is not one covered in this book.

Images do not exist in a vacuum. Within those countries and areas considered as the 'West', it is worth considering just who or what groups hold the images that are the topics of the following chapters. The answer will vary with the period. Probably few people at any time in any Western country have held clear images about China. But both images and information have filtered more extensively to the millions without specialist knowledge or experience of China since the middle of the eighteenth century. Not only more and more people in absolute terms have held images of China with the passage of time, but also a higher proportion of them. In the early centuries few Westerners other than the educated held images of China, but the groups have expanded as the numbers have done so. Increasingly since the nineteenth century, and especially since World War II, the holders of 'Western images of China' have come to include 'ordinary people', students, journalists, business people, members of religious or political groups, workers, farmers, and so on. But the identity of these 'ordinary people' is extremely unclear, let alone their depth of knowledge and how they perceive China. Of course I can, and to some extent will, appeal to opinion surveys for the recent period when they exist, but these probably do little more than refer to a particular place and time and consequently are not central to this study.

Putting the question the other way round, one can ask who are the formulators or creators of images. Some are specifically *not* China specialists, including those who simply used China as a background for an adventure story. A case in point is Captain W. H. Johns, the author of the 'Biggles' books. Novels or films set in China create images of that country, even if they are totally incidental to the story at hand.

While Johns would not rate a mention in a treatment of serious literature, let alone of sinology, he does figure in the chapter on contemporary images of China from 1949 to 1966. Despite such examples, most image-formulators about China are specialists, or have a deep interest in the country. They are travellers, missionaries, priests, diplomats, merchants, business people, government personnel, novelists, journalists, and academics, among others. The priority one suggests in this list depends upon the age. In the days of Marco Polo the traveller clearly took precedence, while the diplomats and academics mattered not at all and the journalists did not exist. In the nineteenth century, diplomats and missionaries made significant contributions, probably greater for contemporary studies than academics, but less in the field of history and literature. Since 1949, the influence of missionaries as a source of images of China has declined drastically. For immediately current images it is journalists who matter most, but they obtain a great deal of their information and perceptions from diplomats. For images of the past academics take priority. A scholarly work refers to the past by the time it is published, even if it is intended to concern the present, and the same is true of a television documentary. Journalists tend to be specialists less on China than on reporting. Thus it is that advisers to the creators of television documentaries are more often academics than journalists or diplomats.

In some ages there is overlap among the professions that contribute most to formulating images. In the nineteenth century some diplomats and missionaries went on to become distinguished academics. Since World War II, academics have often moved to government service or journalism, and vice versa. There is overlap also within the list suggested. Priests can be academics and anybody can be a traveller. The overwhelming majority of image-creators have been intellectuals in the sense of being literate people capable of constructing images in written form.

The function of travel to China among image-formulators is problematic. In the eighteenth century, not many Westerners either resided or travelled in China. J. B. du Halde, the greatest author of the age on China, never visited the country. In the 1950s and 1960s much was written about China by journalists and academics, and said by government spokespersons, who did not visit China. Yet travel is at all times one important part of image formulation; its priority, *how* important it is by comparison with other sources, depends on circumstances.

Another variable among image-formulators is language. Some of the greatest works on China in the past were written by people who did not know Chinese at all. Most journalists both of the past and present know little or no Chinese. Especially in the 1950s and 1960s, quite a few academics were in the same position. On the other hand, many of those with the greatest mastery over the classical or contemporary language have either been or have become academics.

Looking at the China specialists over the centuries, one can see that knowledge of the Chinese language has been useful, but by no means necessary to become an image-formulator.

Images may be conceptual, visual, aural or olfactory, or a mixture of these. Due to the constraints of the print medium, the images discussed in this book belong to the first two kinds. Until the present century, those Westerners who did not actually visit China derived the overwhelming majority of their images of China from reading books or magazines, either with or without pictures. Nowadays, people derive their ideas about China from television programmes, films or pictures, listening to radio items, stories from friends, or lectures from people who claim to know something about the country. They may read books, newspaper or magazine articles, or travel to or live in China itself. Print remains important for imparting images, but to nothing like the extent of the age before the spread of radio, and especially television. As the twenty-first century dawns, the Internet is becoming an increasingly important formulator of images, but in the terms of this book, such images are not too different from those found in other forms.

The images discussed in this book are those presented in books or magazines that were or are widely read, or contain important or path-breaking ideas. For the recent period it is necessary to add films or popular television programmes. Books, articles, films, and television programmes may be documentary, and aim to represent actuality, or they may be fictional. Either way they are sources for images. The assumption is made that such works, whether by China specialists or not, exert an impact on the way people perceive China. In other words, it is valid to cite what is written or screened about China as an 'image' of China, even if I can offer no evidence on how many people actually read or saw the relevant work, or remembered or believed it if they did.

Finally, why write such a book as this? There are both negative and positive reasons. There already exist treatments of Western attitudes towards China covering particular periods or the people of one country. But there is room for a new evaluation of old ideas and a need for an account of the period since the crisis of June 1989. So far the first edition of this book remains the only consolidated general treatment of Western images of China from the earliest to the most recent times, and it became sorely out of date following the effect of the June 1989 crisis on these images.

A positive reason for researching Western images of China is that the country and its people have been for centuries, and remain, controversial in the West. This is partly because China is so large and populous and consequently so important, and because its tradition is so long and grand. In addition, Western images gain additional significance because they bear upon the West's relations with China, how one major civilization relates to another. Though the images have tended to fluctuate, the West has been concerned about China for a very long time. The signs are that this situation will continue into the indefinite future.

At certain times, particular dominant groups have designated China in a range of ways, as worthy of admiration, sympathy, curiosity, fear, ridicule, hostility, conversion to Christianity, or as a means of profit. Western images of China are both interesting and an active part of a series of power relationships. They are consequently an important area of study well worth exploring.

Notes

1   Gordon, 'Afterword', in Gordon (ed.), *Power/Knowledge*, p. 233.
2   Foucault, 'Truth and Power', in Gordon (ed.), *Power/Knowledge*, p. 131.
3   Ibid., p. 133.
4   Said, *Orientalism*, p. 23.
5   Ibid., p. 11.
6   Ibid., p. 326.
7   Ibid., pp. 325–6.

Part I

Western Images of China
until 1949

2
Early Western Images of China

The ancient Romans knew of the existence of China; they called it Serica and its people the Seres or Sinae. The term Seres derives from the clearest image in their extremely hazy knowledge of China: that it traded silk. The famous *Historia Naturalis* (*Natural History*) of Pliny the Elder (AD 23–79) mentions the labour involved in making silk fabrics: 'so has toil to be multiplied; so have the ends of the earth to be transversed: and all that a Roman dame may exhibit her charms in transparent gauze'.[1] However, he was unaware that silk was produced by silkworms. Like Virgil (70–19 BC) and many other Roman poets down to Claudian (*c.* 370–*c.* 404),[2] he believed silk was combed from the leaves of the forest.

It is possible that Chinese traders entered Roman territory from the first century BC, but no official Chinese missions visited the city of Rome itself. Pliny believed the Seres to be 'inoffensive in their manners indeed'. They keep to themselves, he adds, and do not seek trade with other people, but are prepared to engage in it if others seek it.[3]

The first Western writer to discuss China coherently in detail extending beyond a paragraph or so is the Egyptian Greek Theophylactus Simocatta, whose work dates from the early seventh century. He calls the Chinese Taugas and names their ruler as *Taissan*, identified as the great Tang emperor Taizong (reigned 626–49). We are now in the era when Christianity had become dominant in the Byzantine Empire, so it is not surprising to find Theophylactus Simocatta raising the criticism that 'the nation practises idolatry'. On the other hand, his comments are broadly positive. The Chinese 'have just laws, and their life is full of temperate wisdom'. This is a large, powerful, and rich country with a thriving commerce. The emperor is said to have 700 concubines. 'The king's women go forth in chariots made of gold, with one ox to draw them', while the women of the chief nobles use silver chariots. Already China comes over as a rich and exotic marvel, an idea which was to dominate Western images for many centuries. And, of course, Theophylactus praises the Chinese for their 'skill and emulation' in raising silkworms and producing silk filaments of various colours.[4]

Theophylactus's work was not particularly influential in his own time. Despite his remarks on Chinese silk production, the silk trade between Byzantium and China had fallen on bad times simply because Nestorian monks had smuggled silkworm eggs from China to the West and Byzantium had begun its own silk industry. Theophylactus Simocatta was roughly contemporary with Mohammed and not long afterwards Islamic power placed a curtain between China and the West because the peoples of Western and Central Asia, dominated by Islam, were not in any position to form any kind of bridge between China and Europe. Europe more or less forgot about China. It was not until the medieval crusaders began returning from the east 'with their tales' that 'the store of factual knowledge' was again increased.[5]

The First Great Age of Sino-European Contact

Although stories about the magnificent Christian ruler of the East, Prester John—in fact a legendary figure—began to circulate in the middle of the twelfth century, the medieval era of European consciousness of Eastern Asia reached its height about a century later. In 1206 Genghis Khan (1162–1227) founded his great Mongol Empire, which followed an expansionary policy in succeeding decades, including towards the west. In the early 1240s, Mongol troops scored substantial victories in Poland, Silesia, and Hungary. In the spring of 1242 they were within a few miles of Vienna and were about to attack it when news reached them of the death of the Great Khan Ögödei on 11 December 1241. 'The presence of all the princes and military leaders was immediately required for the convocation' which elected the new khan.[6] Central and Western Europe's escape was indeed a narrow one.

Yet for Western Europe there could have been advantages in the Mongol conquest. Up to this point it had done incomparably more damage to Russia, not to mention the arch-enemy Islam, than to Western Europe. Why not attempt to convert the Mongols to Christianity and use them as allies against Islam? Pope Innocent IV (reigned 1243–54) despatched two embassies to Mongolia. One of them was never heard of again. The other, led by the Franciscan friar John of Plano Carpini, returned to Europe in 1247 after a voyage to Mongolia of over two years, becoming, according to one writer, 'the first European on record to proceed east of Baghdad and return to tell his tale'.[7] Although thus historically important, he succeeded neither in converting the Mongol khan nor in persuading him to cooperate with the Christians against Islam.

John of Plano Carpini wrote extensively of his travels but, while he heard about China, he did not actually visit it. The image he conveyed of the Chinese was of an affable, kind, and hard-working people, fine craftsmen, with a language of their own. He believed they worshipped one God, and honoured Jesus Christ, but needed to be baptized. China itself he believed 'very rich in corn, in wine, gold, silver, silk, and in every kind of produce that tends to the support of mankind'.[8] His was an idealized view, which included a measure of wishful thinking. Yet he appears to be the first Western writer to mention China who had actually seen a Chinese. He is also the first to call them Cathayans (normally used to refer to north Chinese).

John of Plano Carpini was followed by others. William of Rubruquis, a Flemish Franciscan, stayed eight months at the Mongol capital of Karakorum from December 1253 to August 1254. Like John, he did not visit China. However, he did meet many Chinese in Karakorum and was generally impressed with them. 'They are first-rate artists in every kind of craft, and their physicians have a thorough knowledge of the virtues of herbs, and an admirable skill in diagnosis by the pulse', he writes. And later he continues, 'they do their writing with a brush such as painters paint with, and a single character of theirs comprehends several letters so as to form a whole word'.[9] Although William was struck by several of the same features mentioned by his predecessor John, he does not make the mistake of seeing the Chinese as quasi-Christians.

In 1264 the Mongols extended their control south of the Great Wall and made Khan-balik (Beijing) their capital. In 1279 they completed the reunification of China by conquering the last remnants of the former Southern Song dynasty. Meanwhile the first visitors from Europe were arriving in China itself, including the Polo brothers Niccolo and Maffeo from Venice. Khublai Khan received these two in audience and asked them about Europe. When they proved unable to satisfy his curiosity, he despatched them to request the Pope to send him 100 learned men who could teach his court about Europe and debate there with people from other countries.

The Polos were appointed apostolic delegates to the Khan's court and left Europe again for Khan-balik in 1271. This time they took with them Niccolo's seventeen-year-old son Marco. They went overland through Persia and what is today the Xinjiang Autonomous Region;

they crossed the Gobi desert, passed Chang'an (now Xi'an) and arrived in the capital in 1275.

The Polos left China in 1292 with the task of taking a Mongolian princess by sea to marry a Mongol ruler in Persia. The intended husband had actually died in 1291, even before they left China, so instead she married his son. The Polos pressed on to Italy, arriving back in Venice in 1295. Marco was later a naval officer and was taken prisoner during a naval skirmish in the Mediterranean between Venice and Genoa, major rivals at the time. He remained in gaol for nearly a year in 1298 and 1299. It is said to have been during his imprisonment that he dictated to a fellow captive, Rustichello of Pisa, an account of his experiences in China. One contemporary scholar comments as follows on his historical importance:

> Other Europeans lived and worked in China during the thirteenth century, but Marco Polo was the only one, so far as is known, to travel and work there and to write an account of his experiences. For the first time in history Europe possessed a detailed narrative about China and its neighbours based upon more than hearsay and speculation.[10]

The book he dictated is usually called in English *The Description of the World* or *The Travels of Marco Polo*. Probably Rustichello's original manuscript was destroyed, but well over 100 copies survive, in various languages. The book was immediately popular and consequently influential as a source of images of the China of its time. It should be added here that one contemporary scholar has argued a case that Marco Polo never actually visited China,[11] and he did not always command belief, because of his reputation as a storyteller. There are signs that Rustichello was not above embellishing what Marco Polo had told him if he thought the romance of the story demanded it. For example, recent scholarship suggests that stereotyped descriptions of battles and other events may have come from Rustichello's hand, rather than Polo's. There are also some curious omissions, such as any mention of the Great Wall, tea cultivation or foot-binding. For the present purposes, however, what matters is not so much its accuracy as the view of China it imparted to Europe.

Khublai Khan comes out of Marco Polo's account very well; there are no criticisms of his policies. The overall thrust of *The Description* is immensely laudatory of China and its civilization, but not so positive about relations between the Mongol rulers and the Chinese people.

Marco Polo was very impressed by China's prosperity. Indeed, because of his account, Cathay, as he called North China, 'became for over two centuries synonymous with Eldorado—a fabulous land of wealth on the far side of the world'.[12] Marco Polo was also much struck with the flourishing commerce and interregional trade he found in China. In particular, he admired the emperor's personal concern for his people's well-being. The Great Khan 'sends emissaries and inspectors throughout all his dominions' to find out if there has been a crop failure anywhere. 'And if he finds that any have lost their harvest, he exempts them for that year from their tribute and gives them some of his own grain to sow and to eat'. Marco Polo calls this 'a magnificent act of royal bounty'.[13] It is but one of a whole list of imperial kindnesses to the people, which gave Marco Polo the impression of a happy country indeed.

Polo was completely amazed by the grandeur of the Chinese cities. Kinsai (Hangzhou) he states flatly is 'without doubt the finest and most splendid city in the world'.[14] He describes the West Lake in the city: 'And all round it are stately palaces and mansions, of such workmanship that nothing better or more splendid could be devised or executed. These are the abodes of the nobles and magnates'.[15] It is also a very prosperous city with numerous and well-stocked market places.

Khan-balik is nearly as magnificent and prosperous. Palaces and fine houses abound. 'The streets are so broad and straight' that 'you can see along the whole length of the road to the gate opposite'. There is much traffic but all is well controlled. 'The whole interior of the city is laid out in squares like a chess-board with such masterly precision that no description can do justice to it.'[16] Strong words indeed. Polo does not dwell on the poverty he must have seen around him, perhaps because it was not as bad as what he was used to at home.

Polo records the use of coal, which was apparently new to him and not in use in his native Italy, although it was certainly used in Britain in his time. All over the country of Cathay 'there is a sort of black stone, which is dug out of veins in the hillsides and burns like logs'. Wood exists in plenty also but the stones burn better and cheaper.

> But the population is so enormous and there are so many bath-houses and baths continually being heated, that the wood could not possibly suffice, since there is no one who does not go to a bath-house at least three times a week and take a bath, and in winter every day, if he can manage it. And every man of rank or

means has his own bathroom in his house, where he takes a bath. So it is clear there could never be enough wood to maintain such a conflagration.[17]

In the manner of Europeans of his day, Marco Polo categorized people according to religion. Given the circumstances of Europe in his time, it is not surprising to find him extremely hostile towards Islam. Yet towards the Buddhists he was very tolerant, even admiring. Although he called them 'idolators', the term was clearly not intended as insulting. He gave to the 'sages of the idolators' credit for the fact that the Great Khan provided alms to the poor.[18] He marvelled at the 'huge monasteries and abbeys, of such a size that I assure you that some resemble small cities inhabited by more than 2,000 monks'. The feasts they made for their 'idols' were magnificent and accompanied by 'the most magnificent hymns and illuminations that were ever seen'.[19]

On the other hand, Polo was not oblivious to certain political problems. He was well aware that the Mongols were overlords in someone else's country. 'The Great Khan had no legal title to rule the province of Cathay, having acquired it by force'. For that reason he put authority not in the hands of Chinese, but those of 'Tartars, Saracens, and Christians'. Polo recognized that, because the Chinese did not like the domination of foreigners, 'all the Cathayans hated the government of the Great Khan'.[20] He is also quite open about the savage punishments meted out to rebels, such as being flayed alive, and about the dreadful beatings suffered by criminals.[21] His wording, however, everywhere suggests support for Mongol rule and the assumption that the Great Khan's opponents are in the wrong.

The Polos were travellers, merchants, and servants of the Mongol government, and there were others like them. Italian merchants, especially from Genoa, remained active in China up to the middle of the fourteenth century. Trade existed and Chinese silk was still sold in Europe, even though by this time there were also thriving silk industries in Sicily, Spain, and other places nearer to home than China.

Franciscan friars travelled in China for missionary and other religious work. Among them the one to leave the most detailed record was Odoric of Pordenone (c. 1286–1331), who lived in China for some three years in the 1320s. Like Marco Polo he was much impressed with the splendour of Chinese cities; he described Hangzhou as 'the greatest city in the whole world'[22] and shared Polo's awe at Khanbalik and the Great Khan's court.[23] Unlike Polo, he drew attention to the custom of foot-binding, being the first Westerner to write of it: 'And with the women the great beauty is to have little feet; and for this reason mothers are accustomed, as soon as girls are born to them, to swathe their feet tightly so that they can never grow in the least.'[24] The lack of any criticism of China's government or customs, even of so unfamiliar and cruel a custom as foot-binding, is symptomatic of Odoric's extremely positive attitude towards China. If anything, he is even more enthusiastic than Marco Polo. Constantly he uses superlatives—the biggest or finest—to describe the things he has seen. It is true that some people in the fourteenth and later centuries refused to believe Odoric's story. Yet he became extremely famous in his own day. Indeed, among the various medieval travelogues of the monks, which, of course, do not include Marco Polo's narrative, Odoric's was 'the only one that enjoyed great popularity throughout the ages',[25] and that is ample testimony to its importance as a creator of images.

In the middle of the fourteenth century, China and Europe again became cut off from one another. The collapse of the Mongol dynasty in China made the overland route to the west much more difficult to pass. Trade and interest in Europe or its religion dried up. The Black Death, which killed about a third of Europe's population between 1348 and 1351, had a disastrous impact on the economy and stopped European merchants or missionaries from travelling to far-off places. The first great era of Sino-European contact was over.

The Century of Discovery

In 1508 the Portuguese King Manuel I sent Diogo Lopez de Sequeira to reconnoitre Malacca and gave him the specific instruction to inquire about the Chinese. For the next century or so, a revived interest in China centred on Portuguese and Spanish authors.

Three men produced eyewitness accounts of parts of southern China which formed the basis of sixteenth-century European knowledge and images of China. Galeote Pereira was a Portuguese soldier, sailor, and merchant adventurer who was captured off the coast of Fujian for smuggling in 1549 and held under arrest for several years. Gaspar da Cruz was a Portuguese Dominican, doing missionary work in China, while Martin de Rada was a Spanish Augustinian priest whose writing reports his visit to Fujian in 1575. All three wrote accounts of their stays in China, but only the first two were printed in their own day,

Pereira's in Italian translation in 1565 and da Cruz's in its original Portuguese in 1569–70. Pereira's work covered not only China but other places as well and circulated fairly widely in its time. Da Cruz's book, on the other hand, remained rather rare, possibly because it was published in Portugal during a plague epidemic, a time when not many people would be interested in reading books about China (or about anything, for that matter). Being in Portuguese it could not hope to achieve as wide a readership as Pereira's account anyway.

Pereira emphasizes the large size and population of China. He has quite a bit to say about the officials who 'are served and feared'. He describes them as 'an idle generation, without all manner of exercises and pastimes, except it be eating and drinking'.[26] Having been closely involved with it himself, Pereira also describes the legal system in great detail. He notes the beatings with bamboo whips, which make 'the standers-by tremble at their cruelty',[27] and the effect they produce on the sufferer, as well as the severe prisons from which escape is impossible. At the same time, Pereira's experience made him believe the Chinese law system fair. The public trials rendered false testimony out of the question. His summation is that the Chinese are better than Christians 'in doing justice' and 'more bounden than they to deal justly and in truth'.[28] Clearly Pereira's favourable verdict resulted from the outcome of his own case. Viceroy Zhu Wan, who was initially responsible for his arrest, committed suicide after losing a power struggle over his strong enforcement of anti-smuggling and foreign-trade laws. Though he may not have known it, Pereira's own trial probably functioned to gain incriminating evidence against Zhu Wan.

Gaspar da Cruz's *Treatise in which the Things of China are Related at Great Length* 'may fairly be claimed as the first book devoted to China which was printed in Europe'.[29] Unlike Marco Polo's book, much of which is about other countries, da Cruz's is about 90 per cent directly concerned with China. It thus occupies an important place in the history of Western literature on China, even if its relatively narrow circulation (see earlier) puts it lower on the scale of sixteenth-century Western image-formulators of China than Pereira's account.

Gaspar da Cruz spent only a few months in China altogether, and much of his work is based on Pereira, a debt which he frankly acknowledges. Yet da Cruz was a most observant and honest traveller and his book contains many interesting and perceptive comments. Like many others he was impressed with China's prosperity, and while he saw poverty he could state that 'these poor people notwithstanding do not live so poorly and beggarly in their apparel as do those who live poorly in Portugal'.[30] He also commented favourably on Chinese agriculture, and on the industriousness of the people. 'China is almost all a well husbanded country', he observed, where the people 'are great eaters' and 'every one laboureth to get a living, and every one seeketh ways to earn their food'. But they are not so kind to the underdog or the lazy: 'A great help . . . is that idle people be much abhorred in this country, and are very odious unto the rest, and he that laboureth not shall not eat, for commonly there is none that do give alms to the poor.'[31]

The only chapter to be designated 'notable' in its title is that which deals with those 'who are sentenced to death, and . . . other matters that pertain to justice'. Although it is at least partly based on Pereira's experience, the overall impression it gives the reader is in fact very much more critical. While da Cruz follows Pereira in suggesting that open trials made false testimony very rare, he has more to say in more gruesome language about the savagery of the penal and prison system obtained in the China of the sixteenth century.[32]

As is to be expected, Gaspar da Cruz suffered from the religious intolerance of his age. Yet in some respects he was remarkably, even extraordinarily, broadminded. For instance, he was the first, and for quite a long time the only, European writer to remark upon Chinese music. Moreover, he took the trouble to understand some of the various musical instruments and singing styles, and did so not to condemn but to appreciate. He describes the Chinese as 'commonly very ingenious and cunning with their hands' and comments on their achievements in the arts, with 'many inventions in every kind of work', especially masonry and painting.[33] In fact, Gaspar da Cruz's *Treatise* was a remarkable achievement, which deserved a wider readership in its own day than it got.

About 1583, in response to considerable and growing interest in China among educated Europeans, Pope Gregory XIII ordered the composition of a comprehensive history of China. The chosen author was the Augustinian priest Juan Gonzalez de Mendoza. Basing himself on Pereira's, da Cruz's, as well as de Rada's and other accounts, he produced the best-selling and path-breaking *Historia de la cosas mas notables, ritos y costumbres del gran Reyno de la China*, which means literally 'History of the Most Notable Things, Rites and Customs, of the Great Kingdom of China', published in Rome in Spanish in 1585 and later translated into English under the title *The History of the Great and Mighty Kingdom of China*. He never realized his dream to visit China, and stands at the head of a number of great European scholars whom circumstances prevented from setting foot in the country that fascinated them so much.

Mendoza tried, and largely succeeded, in bringing together in one volume everything which was known in the West about China, the first man ever to attempt such a task. This alone makes his *History* very important. It was also very successful, and consequently influential. No book created images of China in late sixteenth-century Europe as this one did. By the end of the sixteenth century it had been reprinted forty-six times in seven European languages: Spanish, German, Dutch, Italian, French, English, and Latin. As the scholar C. R. Boxer aptly writes: 'It is probably no exaggeration to say that Mendoza's book had been read by the majority of well-educated Europeans at the beginning of the seventeenth century'.[34] Its authority was so great that 'it became the point of departure and the basis of comparison' for all later works on China written in Europe before the eighteenth century.[35]

Like Marco Polo and other early writers, Mendoza is much impressed by the size of China. It is 'the most biggest and populous that is mentioned in all the world'.[36] The title of the book itself, with its reference to 'the great and mighty kingdom', already shows the thrust of Mendoza's view of China. The cities he writes of in exuberant terms, emphasizing the magnificence of their walls, and the splendour of their streets, which are 'very well paved, and so broad that 15 horsemen may ride together in them'.[37] The highways everywhere in China are, according to Mendoza, 'the best and gallantest paved that ever hath been discovered'. Both in their streets and their houses, the Chinese are 'marvellous clean'.[38]

Mendoza writes of the central and local bureaucracy in much detail and with admiration. The highest officials he says 'generally have a marvellous moral virtue, and that is, they be all very patient in hearing any complaint'.[39] He is aware of the examination system by which men entered the public service and describes it in enthusiastic terms.[40]

On the other hand, Mendoza is harshly critical of the legal system. He notes the very savage punishments given out by the courts and describes in great detail the 'cruel torments' used to extract confessions. Admittedly, he is defensive even here: 'yet do they execute none of them [the tortures] except first they have good information',[41] as if innocent people hardly ever confessed under torture, but the picture is pretty grim all the same. The prisons are 'as terrible and as cruel' as the punishments, and since the population is so large, 'so have they many prisons and very great'. In this way the officials can 'keep in peace and justice this mighty kingdom'.[42] Like most other relevant writers of his time, Mendoza was very favourably impressed by the Chinese family system. The women are not only attractive but virtuous, 'secret and honest',[43] meaning that one does not often see them in public. And foot-binding he discusses in some detail, without criticism. 'She who hath the least feet is accounted the gallantest dame', he says. The reason for the custom he believes to be to immobilize women, both in the home and outside it,[44] almost certainly a very incomplete analysis.

Finally, Mendoza treats the subject of religion in China with spectacles rose-tinted by his own Christian beliefs. He does not appear to have understood Confucian rationalism at all and his accounts of monastic life read like descriptions of Christian monasticism. He states directly that the Chinese believe in the immortality of the soul: the soul of a virtuous person 'shall live eternally with great joy, and shall be made an angel' but, on the other hand, that of an evil one 'shall go with the devils into dark dungeons and prisons'.[45]

Mendoza's book was strongly attacked by the Constable of Castile, Juan Fernández de Velasco, soon after it was published. The basic ground was that Mendoza's account extolled China's greatness too much.[46] What is most important is that Mendoza appears to have carried the public with him, and European images of China followed his version rather closely. In other words, they remained dominantly positive and more detailed than at any earlier time.

It is necessary to remember that what Mendoza and many others were most concerned with was the conversion of the Chinese to Christianity. There were even some who wished to impose Christianity on China by military force. In 1576, the governor of the Philippine Islands, Dr Francisco de Sande, formally proposed a military attack on China but King Philip II of Spain rejected the suggestion the next year, and instead suggested 'good friendship' with the Chinese. Mendoza was clearly in the 'peace camp', but the eyes with which he viewed China were just as dedicated to Christianity nonetheless.

The sixteenth century was, for Europe, the age of discovery. Although India, the East Indies and the Philippines had loomed larger in Europe's consciousness in the first half, China and Japan replaced them in the dominant place from about 1550 on. Most of the authors and readers on China were not only genuinely interested in it, but also very favourably disposed towards it. Their aim to convert it to

Christianity was senseless and futile but not yet imperialistic. At the end of the sixteenth century, Europe may have believed it could teach the Chinese, but it was still prepared to admire them.

Notes

1   See Yule and Cordier, *Cathay and the Way Thither*, Vol. I, p. 197.
2   Ibid., pp. 20–1.
3   Ibid., p. 198.
4   Ibid., pp. 29–32, 232–3.
5   Lach, *Asia in the Making of Europe*, Vol. I, p. 22.
6   De Rachewiltz, *Papal Envoys to the Great Khans*, p. 81.
7   Lach, *Asia in the Making of Europe*, Vol. I, p. 32.
8   Yule and Cordier, *Cathay and the Way Thither*, Vol. I, pp. 157-8.
9   Ibid., pp. 159, 161.
10 Lach, *Asia in the Making of Europe*, Vol. I, p. 35.
11 Frances Wood's *Did Marco Polo go to China?* has cast doubt on whether Marco Polo ever travelled much further than the Black Sea or Constantinople and argues that his work was based on hearsay. She concedes, however, that it remains 'a very rich source' (p. 150), and in particular for the city of Beijing, and does not doubt its influence in Europe.
12 Humble, *Marco Polo*, p. 35.
13 Latham (trans. and introduced), *The Travels of Marco Polo*, p. 155.
14 Ibid., p. 213.
15 Ibid., p. 218.
16 Ibid., pp. 128–9.
17 Ibid., pp. 156–7.
18 Ibid., p. 158.
19 Ibid., p. 111.
20 Ibid., p. 133.
21 Ibid., pp. 134, 101.
22 Yule and Cordier, *Cathay and the Way Thither*, Vol. II, 192–3.
23 See the lengthy description ibid., Vol. II, 215–26.
24 Ibid., p. 256.
25 De Rachewiltz, *Papal Envoys*, p. 18.
26 Boxer (ed.), *South China in the Sixteenth Century*, pp. 13, 15.
27 Ibid., p. 18.
28 Ibid., p. 17.
29 Ibid., p. lxii.
30 Ibid., p. 115.
31 Ibid., p. 118 .
32 Ibid., p. 175.
33 Ibid., p. 146.
34 Ibid., p. xvii.
35 Lach, *Asia in the Making of Europe*, Vol. I, Two, p. 744.

36   Mendoza, *The History of the Great and Mighty Kingdom of China*, Vol. I, Two,
     p. 20. This edition is reprinted from the English translation from Spanish of R.
     Parke, published first in 1588. I have retained the original words in quotations,
     but changed the spelling to conform to contemporary, not sixteenth-century, usage.
37   Ibid., I, p. 25.
38   Ibid., I, p. 27.
39   Ibid., I, p. 103.
40   Ibid., I, p. 124–8.
41   Ibid., I, p. 111.
42   Ibid., I, p. 116.
43   Ibid., I, p. 32.
44   Ibid., I, p. 31.
45   Ibid., I, p. 53.
46   See Lach, *Asia in the Making of Europe*, Vol. I, Two, pp. 791–2.

3
Jesuit Missionaries and the Philosophers

While Mendoza was working on his great book about China, other developments were occurring in Catholic Europe which were to lead on to the first great age of European Sinology. In 1540 the Society of Jesus was founded by Ignatius of Loyola (1491–1556). Part of the Catholic Reformation of the sixteenth century, the Society saw the conversion of non-Christians to Catholicism as part of its brief. Among Loyola's earliest followers was Francis Xavier (1506–52) who in 1534, even before the Jesuits' formal establishment, had pledged himself to missionary work in Loyola's service.

Xavier went to Goa in India in 1541 and to Japan in 1549. He was enthusiastic about the Japanese and their culture. Although he had heard about China as early as 1546, it was in Japan that he came to realize China's importance if he was to succeed in his aim of Christianizing Eastern Asia. He wrote of China as 'an immense empire, enjoying profound peace'. Portuguese merchants had informed him that it was 'superior to all Christian states in the practice of justice and equity'. The Chinese themselves he believed very wise. Those he had met in Japan were 'acute, and eager to learn' and 'in intellect, they are superior even to the Japanese'.[1] These latter held 'a very high opinion of the wisdom of the Chinese,' he wrote on several occasions. 'They used to make that a principal point against us, that if things were as we preached, how was it that the Chinese knew nothing about us?'[2]

Xavier died in Macao while waiting for a Chinese merchant he had bribed to take him to China to fulfil their joint plan. He never realized his dream of going to the Chinese empire.

Xavier's policy had been that 'to win converts a missionary had to become an "integral part" of a particular civilization'.[3] Such a broad-minded concept was extraordinarily contentious in his day. Yet it was followed also by Alessandro Valignano, who succeeded Xavier as the head of the Jesuit missions in East Asia. Valignano was extremely impressed by the Chinese. He encouraged his followers to learn their language. It was at his command that Matteo Ricci learned as much as possible of the language, society, politics, and culture of China from 1582 on. In 1601 Ricci actually reached the Chinese capital Beijing, the first European on record to do so for eighty years, and lived there until his death in 1610. Later Jesuits built on the foundations which Ricci had laid. At the end of the Ming dynasty, the Jesuit Johann Adam Schall von Bell gained the favour of the imperial court itself by his knowledge of astronomy and the manufacture of cannon. The new Qing dynasty retained his services in charge of the Department of Astronomy (*Qin tian jian*). It is true that he was disgraced at the death of the Emperor Shunzhi (reigned 1644–61), but Emperor Kangxi (reigned 1662–1722) rehabilitated him posthumously and appointed another Jesuit, the Belgian Ferdinand Verbiest, to head the Department of Astronomy.

The Manchu emperors forbade the Jesuits to involve themselves in politics and appear to have trusted them only because they came from a remote civilization and were not part of the system. One scholar has called them 'unbiased sources of information' and 'impartial witnesses from outer space'.[4] However, it is important to remember that only a small number operated at court and the vast majority of missionaries never went near so exalted a place.

In the seventeenth century, missionaries of other Catholic orders, especially the Dominicans and Franciscans, began working in China. All orders became embroiled in a sharp controversy over the 'rites'. The Jesuits believed that ceremonies in honour of Confucius and one's ancestors were compatible with Christianity under certain circumstances, while the Dominicans and Franciscans adopted the alternative attitude. The matter was taken to Rome and involved several subsequent popes.

In 1715 Pope Clement XI condemned the tolerant missionary practices of the Jesuits, insisting on European forms of Christian practice in China and forbidding the use of Chinese rites. In 1742, Pope Benedict XIV not only reaffirmed the ban, but even prohibited further debate on the matter. After Kangxi's death the decline of Jesuit influence gathered momentum. Most were expelled from China; the final blow came when, in 1774, news of the decree dissolving the Society of Jesus reached Beijing. Writing in an inscription for the Jesuit cemetery at the time, the most famous of the last generation of Jesuits in China, Joseph-Marie Amiot (1718–93), recognized that this event marked the effective end of the Society's influence at the Chinese court and in the country as a whole. By the end of the eighteenth century there were only about thirty European missionaries left in the whole of China.

The policy of 'integration' that Xavier had originated was thus a permanent one for the Jesuits in China. It meant that, in order to convert the Chinese to Catholicism, the Jesuits must learn as much as they could about the land and its people. Certainly they must speak the language. Ricci had aimed at the top; in other words he began by trying to convert the mandarinate and made a practice of adopting their dress. This approach was in sharp contrast with the Dominicans, whose policy was to try and convert the ordinary people first, the ruling groups later. Adam Schall, Verbiest, and other Jesuits worked at the court itself. Otto van der Sprenkel sums up the results of Jesuit policy thus:

> The fact that so many of the missionaries, from Ricci at the beginning to Amiot at the end, were as indefatigable in scholarship as they were devoted in religion, ensured that while they failed in their mission to interpret Christianity to the Chinese, they were brilliantly successful in interpreting China to the West. In letters, pamphlets, and folios, in travel notes, translations, and learned monographs, they sent back a flood of information to Europe on every aspect of China's past history and present condition.[5]

These voluminous writings include two particularly famous series. The first and more important is the *Lettres édifiantes et curieuses écrites des missions étrangères par quelques missionaires de la Compagnie de Jésus* or *Edifying and Curious Letters of Some Missioners, of the Society of Jesus, from Foreign Missions*, which began publication in 1703 and continued until 1776, about one-third of them dealing with China. The other is the *Mémoires concernant l'histoire, les sciences, les arts, les mœurs, les usages, etc., des chinois, par les missionaires de Pékin* (*Memoirs on the History, Sciences, Arts, Manners and Customs etc. of the Chinese, by the Missionaries of Beijing*), which ran for seventeen volumes from 1776 to 1814.

The Dominicans took a very different, and much more negative view of China and its society than did the Jesuits. And although the net political result of the Rites Controversy was defeat for the Jesuits, in terms of images of China conveyed to Europe, the Jesuits were incomparably more important and influential during the seventeenth and eighteenth centuries than any of the rival religious orders.

Matteo Ricci

The first of the major Jesuit works on China was, of course, that of Ricci. His diaries were taken to Rome by Father Nicholas Trigault, a fellow Jesuit, who translated them from Italian into Latin and had them published in Augsburg in 1615.[6] In the next decade or so the work was reprinted four times in Latin and translated into German, Spanish, French and Italian, and excerpts into English. Like Mendoza's work, Ricci's was widely read and popular. It is likely, as claimed by one scholar, that the diary 'is not reliable as evidence for Ricci's own view' of the Jesuit interpretation of Confucianism,[7] but there is no reason to doubt that it was an extremely influential source of images of China in its day.

Ricci appears to have been the first European to become fully aware of the Chinese intellectual tradition and transmit that knowledge to the West. His book describes their achievements in mathematics, astronomy, and medicine, as well as the importance of the Confucian classics in Chinese society. He had a good deal of contact with the mandarins (officials) who ran the Chinese empire. He thus knew a good deal about the system of official examinations through which these officials entered the public service. There were numerous levels of these examinations, all of them based on Confucian ideology. Ricci described them in great detail, including their various levels and their Confucian contents, probably being the source for the knowledge, still new in Europe, that the Chinese examinations were written.[8]

Ricci recognized the place of rationalistic and this-worldly moral philosophy in Chinese society. He also tried to come to grips with Neo-Confucianism, and he shows some understanding, albeit rudimentary, of the complicated philosophy that it entailed. The reason was not so much broad-mindedness as his attempt to convert the literati to Christianity. He could see that it was necessary for him to gain some idea of how they thought his efforts were to bring any success, and it was his conscious policy to interpret any ambiguities in Confucius' writings to suit Catholic Christianity.[9] Ricci was not impressed with China's various other religions; and astrologers, fortune-tellers and such people he regarded as 'the blind leading the blind'.[10] As one scholar has aptly commented: 'For tactical purposes Ricci wished an alliance with the Confucians against the Buddhists'.[11]

The earliest reference to Confucianism in Trigault's version of Ricci's diaries is the following passage:

The only one of the higher philosophical sciences with which the Chinese have become acquainted is that of moral philosophy, and in this they seem to have obscured matters by the introduction of error rather than enlightened them. They have no conception of the rules of logic, and consequently treat the precepts of the sciences of ethics without any regard to the intrinsic co-ordination of the various divisions of this subject. The science of ethics with them is a series of confused maxims and deductions at which they have arrived under guidance of the light of reason.

The most renowned of all Chinese philosophers was named Confucius. This great and learned man was born five hundred and fifty-one years before the beginning of the Christian era, lived more than seventy years, and spurred on his people to the pursuit of virtue not less by his own example than by his writings and conferences. His self-mastery and abstemious ways of life have led his countrymen to assert that he surpassed in holiness all those who in times past, in the various parts of the world, were considered to have excelled in virtue. Indeed, if we critically examine his actions and sayings as they are recorded in history, we shall be forced to admit that he was the equal of the pagan philosophers and superior to most of them. He is held in such high esteem by the learned Chinese that they do not dare to call into question any pronouncement of his and are ready to give full recognition to an oath sworn in his name, as in that of a common master.[12]

The condemnatory first paragraph of this passage is actually not from Ricci's hand at all. It is Trigault's embellishment of Ricci's observations that dialogue, not logic, is the form Chinese philosophers use to present their views.[13] Just as Ricci's views on Confucianism had taken on a political twist in China to favour his missionary work, they immediately began to become enmeshed in theological debate in Europe itself after his death.

Like many of his European predecessors, Ricci was much impressed by China's size and variety of produce. He was also struck by its prosperity: 'everything which the people need for their well-being and sustenance, whether it be for food or clothing or even delicacies and superfluities, is abundantly produced within the border of the kingdom'.[14] The reasons for this prosperous life he believed to have been the fertile soil, the mild climate, and the industry of the people. As far as the first two are concerned it is necessary to note that he was referring to south China, not the north; this is clear from his reference to two or even three harvests a year.

Another point that struck Ricci very favourably was how peace-loving China appeared. He regarded it as remarkable that, though China possessed a well-equipped army and navy, 'neither the King nor his people ever think of waging a war of aggression'. They are content with what they have and lack any ambition for conquest. 'In their respect they are much different from the people of Europe', Ricci observes.[15] However, Ricci also dwelled on several of the most abhorrent aspects of Ming China. These included slavery, female infanticide, and the castration of 'a great number of male children' in northern China so that they could serve the emperor. Above all, he was horrified by the power of the magistrates. Although he found the penal laws of the country 'not too severe', he describes in some detail the frightful beatings that certain people suffered. He notes specifically that 'as many are illegally put to death by the magistrates as are legally executed'. Because of the magistrates' 'lust for domination', Ricci believed that 'everyone lives in continual fear of being deprived of what he has, by a false accusation'.[16]

Ricci's picture is thus only partly a favourable one and he pulls no punches in criticizing. It is to be noted that he lived in China when the Ming dynasty was in decline. Hardly more than a decade after Ricci's death China was in the grip of the notoriously tyrannical eunuch Wei Zhongxian (1568–1627). Not long afterwards the dynasty itself collapsed. Perhaps what is striking under these circumstances is how positive Ricci's impression was. It is by no means to cast doubt on his honesty or withhold credit for his achievement to suggest that his aim to Christianize China influenced his view of that country.

The Jesuits after Ricci

The Jesuits were tremendously impressed by the early Manchu emperors. In the second half of the seventeenth, and all of the eighteenth centuries they presented Europe with an extremely, indeed unduly, flattering picture of China.

It is worth remembering that Loyola had specifically ordered full reporting of their activities by Jesuit missionaries in the field, but had distinguished those that might be published from those which only the Society's superiors might see. The editors omitted sections which could undercut the value of Jesuit missionary work, or show differences of opinion about China that rival orders could exploit. Since the Jesuits had chosen to work from the top down it was in their interests to show the ruling classes as effective and to get on well with them. Hence there was a tendency to downplay criticism of China in public statements. In 1687 there appeared in Paris a book entitled *Confucius Sinarum Philosophus* (*Confucius, Philosopher of the Chinese*). It was the first full translation into any European language of any of the Confucian classics to be published in Europe, and included the *Lunyu* (*Analects*), the *Zhong yong* (*Doctrine of the Mean*), and the *Da xue* (*Great Learning*). The Jesuit translator claimed his work to be a literal rendering of the original, but in fact there is also a considerable infusion of European moral philosophy. In places 'Confucius speaks not only in the language, but also with the thoughts of the medieval scholastic philosophers and theologians'.[17] The reason was partly the conviction of the Jesuits of Christian veracity. But it is much more important to note that the translator was in fact imputing to the Chinese a knowledge of truth irrespective of Christian revelations. Indeed the introduction to the translations asserts specifically that the ancient Chinese must have had knowledge of the true God and worshipped him.

Among the earliest Jesuit missionaries in China to publish an account of the country in his own lifetime was Louis Daniel Le Comte (1656–1729), whose *Nouveaux mémoires sur l'état présent de la Chine* appeared in Paris in 1696. It was immediately translated into several languages and widely read, and in the context of its time it was certainly an image-formulating work. In fact it was somewhat too influential for the Catholic authorities of the day. Le Comte was very impressed with Chinese government and law. 'As if God himself had been the legislator, the form of government is hardly less perfect in its origin than it is at present after the more than 4,000 years that it has lasted'.[18] More dangerous still from the point of view of certain Catholic superiors was his view of Chinese religion and morality. The Chinese may be heathens, but 'I have everywhere noticed a chosen people who adore in spirit and in truth the Lord of heaven and of earth',[19] by implication a direct challenge to the exclusiveness of the Judaeo-Christian divine revelation. He even thought that the Chinese worship of the true God could serve as an example for Christians. Issues of this sort had been under debate in Catholic circles for some time. In 1700, the theological faculty of the Sorbonne investigated several books—including that of Le Comte—and ordered them to be burned.

By far the most important of works on China in the seventeenth and eighteenth centuries is Jean-Baptiste Du Halde's *The General*

History of China, which, according to part of its immensely long subtitle, contains 'a geographical, historical, chronological, political and physical description' of China, Chinese Central Asia, Korea, and Tibet. Du Halde edited Volumes IX to XXVI of the *Lettres édifiantes et curieuses* (1709–43) and they are his most important source; his work is in a sense a digest of what they say. Du Halde himself was among the great sinologists never to have visited China. Du Halde's work, in four volumes, is the largest and most comprehensive single product of Jesuit scholarship on China. It is a truly spectacular accomplishment and in all senses a major landmark in the history of sinology. Among the many in Europe who referred to China and relied on Du Halde as a principal source of information were Montesquieu, Joseph De Guignes, the Encyclopedistes, Rousseau, Voltaire, Hume, and Goldsmith. It is clearly of major importance as a source of Western images of China in its day.

Du Halde was immensely positive about China. He praises virtually every aspect of its people and society, and where he offers criticism it is in a defensive tone, as if he regarded himself as an advocate for China. He frequently makes comparisons with Europe, mostly to show better conditions in China. Du Halde and other editors of the *Lettres* apparently made a conscious policy of selecting and publishing material favourable to China in order to refute their opponents' image of an atheistic culture.

The work is so comprehensive that it is not easy to select points needing mention. The following are illustrative only.

Du Halde believed China very well governed. He could see the power of the mandarins, but believed it generally benign. 'They would not be able to maintain themselves in their offices,' he wrote, 'if they did not gain the reputation of being the fathers of the people, and seem to have no other desire than to procure their happiness.'[20]

China is extremely prosperous, says Du Halde. It is 'one of the most fruitful countries in the world, as well as the largest and most beautiful'. He ascribes this 'plenty' to the industry of the people and to the large number of lakes, rivers, and canals.[21]

Du Halde's view of the Chinese people was favourable. They 'are mild and peaceable in the commerce of life', although they can be 'violent and vindictive to excess when they are offended'.[22] He found their modesty 'surprising' in that 'the learned are very sedate, and do not make use of the least gesture but what is conformable to the rules of decency'. As for the women, decency 'seems to be born' with them, as shown by the fact that 'they live in a constant retirement' and 'are decently covered even to their very hands'.[23] Du Halde seems to have been impressed by the demeanour and even social position of women. He is not shocked even by foot-binding. 'Among the charms of the sex the smallness of their feet is not the least,' he writes.

> When a female infant comes into the world, the nurses are very careful to bind their feet very close for fear they should grow too large. The Chinese ladies are subject all their lives to this constraint, which they were accustomed to in their infancy, and their gait is slow, unsteady and disagreeable to foreigners. Yet such is the force of custom, that they not only undergo this inconvenience readily, but they increase it, and endeavour to make their feet as little as possible, thinking it an extraordinary charm, and always affecting to show them as they walk.[24]

Clearly Du Halde was aware of some shortcomings in Chinese society. Despite the 'plenty' to which he draws attention, he knew there was also great poverty. He was perceptive enough to attribute this partly to overpopulation. 'Yet it must be owned that, however temperate and industrious these people are, the great number of inhabitants occasions a great deal of misery,' he writes. Some people expose their children to die because they cannot afford an upbringing.[25]

Finally we may note Du Halde's rather positive view even of the Chinese law system of his day. The 'prisons are neither so dreadful nor so loathesome as the prisons of Europe, but are much more convenient and spacious, and are built in the same manner almost throughout the empire'.[26] The generally favourable judgment, even in comparison with Europe, is quite characteristic of Du Halde's work. Although he was aware of the use of torture he goes some way towards excusing it by stating that 'the Chinese have remedies to diminish, and even to destroy the sense of pain, and after the torture they have others to make use of to heal the criminal'.[27] He appears to have believed that punishments meted out were usually well deserved.

The Jesuit writings on China, at the pinnacle of which Du Halde's stands, were much read and produced a big impact on Europe. The Society's scholars were, in a real sense, the fathers of Western sinology, and the earliest secular writers on Chinese history—to be discussed in a separate chapter—owe their learning to the Jesuit efforts. The net result was that eighteenth-century Europe knew quite a lot about China.

The Philosophers

Many philosophers of the day admired the Confucian rationalism that contrasted very strongly, they believed, with the religious conflict so prevalent in Europe. In Germany, the famous Lutheran logician and mathematician Gottfried Wilhelm Leibniz (1646–1716) was appalled at the immorality of his own time and country and argued that China ought 'to send missionaries to us to teach us the purpose and use of natural theology, in the same way as we send missionaries to them to instruct them in revealed theology'. He believed China and Europe, at the opposite ends of the vast Eurasian continent, to be the greatest of the world's civilizations.[28] Leibniz worked much of his life for cultural interchange between China and Europe, and his efforts bore some fruit.

Among the thinkers of the French Enlightenment, the most influential of those positive about China was Voltaire. Most impressed with Chinese government, he departed from a view widely held in his time that China was an 'enlightened despotism' and denied that it was a despotism at all. Such a view he believed to be false and based on the external factor of prostration. Voltaire's contrary opinion was that China's governance was based on morals and law, and the respect of children for their fathers. The educated mandarins were the fathers of the cities and provinces, and the king that of the empire.[29]

One of the points which struck Voltaire most positively about China was the secular nature of Confucianism. The religion of the emperors and tribunals he claims 'has never been troubled by priestly quarrels'. He praised Confucius for claiming to be not a prophet but simply a wise magistrate who taught old laws. This was a doctrine of virtue, which preached no mysteries and taught that mankind was naturally good. At the same time, Voltaire rejected utterly the charge that the Chinese were atheists, although he did see their religion as primarily concerned with the present world, not that which follows death, and appears to have regarded their approach as a point in their favour.[30]

Voltaire was much impressed by China's large population, which he estimated at some 150 million and much more than all of Europe, where he believed there were some 100 million people. He comments on the large cities and the considerable prosperity of the country as well as on the range of foods and fruits available there. He was aware that the Chinese had known about printing long before the Europeans did.[31]

Almost exactly contemporary with Voltaire was François Quesnay (1694–1774), the leader of the first systematic school of political economy known as the physiocrats. Quesnay's *Le despotisme de la Chine* (*Despotism in China*) was published in Paris in 1767. It is enthusiastic about China, even though, as its title shows, its author sees that country's government as despotic. Quesnay regarded China's despotism as benign, in contrast to that of his own country.

> The Emperor of China is a despot, but in what sense is that term applied? It seems to me that, generally, we in Europe have an unfavourable opinion of the government of that empire; but I have concluded from the reports about China that the Chinese constitution is founded upon wise and irrevocable laws which the emperor enforces and which he carefully observes himself.[32]

Quesnay considered agriculture as by far the most economically productive activity, and China was his model. Here was a rich and prosperous nation with fertile soil and a multiplicity of rivers, lakes, and well-maintained canals, where peasants were free and ran no risk of 'being despoiled by arbitrary impositions, nor by exactions of tax collectors'.[33] Yet Quesnay did recognize much poverty in China. Like Du Halde he attributed it largely to overpopulation: 'in spite of ... the abundance that reigns, there are few countries that have so much poverty among the humbler classes. However great that empire may be, it is too crowded for the multitude that inhabit it'.[34]

Though China was of less importance for the great Scottish political economist and philosopher Adam Smith (1723–90) than for Voltaire or Quesnay, he does merit mention here because of the supreme importance and enormous influence of his work *The Wealth of Nations* in the history of political economy.

For Smith, China had for a long time been 'one of the richest, that is, one of the most fertile, best cultivated, most industrious, and most populous countries in the world'.[35] Smith to some extent shared Quesnay's enthusiasm for Chinese agriculture but in contrast saw the large population as a positive factor. He praises China for not going backwards and its 'lowest class of labourers' for making shift 'to continue their race so far as to keep up their usual numbers'. On the other hand, Smith was keenly aware of the 'poverty of the lower ranks of people in China' which, he claims, 'far surpasses that of the most beggarly nations in Europe'. So bad is this poverty that in the great towns several children 'are every night exposed in the street, or drowned like puppies in the water'.[36]

The other point to strike Adam Smith most strongly is the extent of domestic, but lack of foreign, trade. Because of its agricultural wealth, its enormous extent, its large population, the variety of its climate, 'and consequently of productions in its different provinces, and the easy communications by means of water-carriage between the greater part of them', the domestic market is perhaps 'not much inferior to the market of all the different countries of Europe put together'. But Smith regarded the resultant lack of foreign trade as a serious drawback for the Chinese political economy. Foreign trade would open the possibility of learning about the machines and industry of other parts of the world, and 'could scarce fail to increase very much the manufactures of China, and to improve very much the productive powers of its manufacturing industry'.[37]

Despite trenchant and perceptive criticisms, Smith's view of China was basically positive. A very different and very negative image of China came from Charles Louis de Secondat Montesquieu (1689–1755). He agreed with Quesnay that China was a despotism, but saw little benign about it.

Montesquieu was famous for his division of governments into three types: republic, based on virtue; monarchy, based on honour; and despotism, based on fear. He argued, further, that the natural environment was the main social determinant. Climate takes pride of place, but terrain is also important. Montesquieu believed that in hot climates, people were weak, lazy, and cowardly, so despotism was the norm, but in cold places people were courageous and free. Montesquieu posed a dichotomy between free Europe, where the temperate zone was large, and Asia, where it hardly existed at all. In China the cold north had conquered the hot south and inflicted despotism everywhere. China seems unable to win; even though some of it is in fact cold, none of it is free.

Despite the fear by which as despots they rule, the Chinese emperors are not without saving graces: they have and are themselves subject to very good laws. Moreover, they are forced to govern well because they know that otherwise revolutionaries will rise up to attempt their overthrow. This is no doubt a reference to the doctrine of the mandate of heaven (*tianming*).

Montesquieu knew of the strong family system in China and apparently admired it. The relationship between rulers and people was that of father and children. The legislators required the people to be submissive, peaceful and industrious. 'When everyone obeys, and everyone is employed, the state is in a happy situation.'

Unfortunately, however, 'by the nature of the soil and climate, their subsistence is very precarious'. As a result the Chinese, Montesquieu believed, were 'the greatest cheats on earth', despite their good laws. 'Let us not then compare the morals of China with those of Europe', he writes.[38] So whatever good points he may have found in China's society, he was hostile to its people, whom their environment had driven to deceit.

Conclusion

Montesquieu leads on to a much bleaker picture of China in the imperialist nineteenth century. Yet despite the existence of men such as he, it is almost certainly fair to see European images of China from about the middle of the seventeenth to the middle of the eighteenth century as more positive than at any other time before or since.

This was the period of the passion for chinoiserie in artistic tastes, which extended from products of craftsmanship and architecture to literature and the theatre. The most famous example of the last was Voltaire's *Orphélin de la Chine*. First produced in 1755, it was based on a translation by the Jesuit J. Prémare of the Chinese drama *Zhaoshi guer* (*Orphan of the Zhao Family*), which was included in Volume III of Du Halde's great work.

There were some strange political consequences of the sinomania, with the Chinese emperor even being held up as a model for Europe. In 1764 Mirabeau's *Philosophie rurale* bore as its frontispiece a picture of the Chinese emperor ploughing a small piece of ground to set a good example to his subjects. In 1768 the French dauphin and in 1769 the Emperor Joseph of Austria copied him.

It is of course true that the first half of the Qing was a relatively stable and prosperous period of China's history. Yet the images that the West came to accept were somewhat more flattering to China than the realities could warrant. The transmission of these images to Europe was primarily the work of the Jesuits. It is ironical that they should have been so successful in such a job, but so unsuccessful in the primary task they had set themselves, namely to convert the Chinese educated classed to Christianity.

The political and ideological dimensions of these images remain significant, despite the sincerity and pioneering work of these thinkers and sinologists. Du Halde and others had political and theological points to score through presenting Chinese society in a favourable light. For Voltaire, a splendid China was at the heart of a new and original view of civilization and its history. For several important philosophers China was a model constructed to criticize their own society. Both the Jesuits and the philosophers were like the great majority of people in all ages. What mattered most to them was not so much the foreign culture—in this case China—as home. Meanwhile the main European centres of interest in China had moved north. Marco Polo was Venetian, Rada and Mendoza Spaniards. Ricci, the founder of the Jesuit mission, was Italian, but it was France that led the way in informing Europe about China from the middle of the seventeenth century to the late years of the eighteenth century. The reign of the great French 'sun-king' Louis XIV (reigned 1643–1715) was contemporaneous with Emperors Shunzhi and Kangxi, and made France politically dominant in Europe. In any case, the countries of southern Europe, which had led the way up to the time of Ricci, never again became the West's main centre of the study of China.

Notes

1   Coleridge (ed.), *The Life and Letters of St. Francis Xavier*, Vol. II, p. 347.
2   Ibid., Vol. II, p. 300–1.
3   Young, *Confucianism and Christianity The First Encounter*, p. 23.
4   Paul Rule, 'Jesuit Sources', in Leslie, Mackerras and Wang (eds.), *Essays on the Sources for Chinese History*, p. 185.
5   Otto Berkelbach van der Spenkel, 'Western Sources', in Leslie, Mackerras and Wang (eds.), *Essays on the Sources*, p. 156.
6   For a translation into English see Ricci, *China in the Sixteenth Century*.
7   Rule, *K'ung-tzu or Confucius?*, p. 27.
8   Donald Lach claims in his *Asia in the Making of Europe*, Vol. I, Two, p. 804, that 'the first European writer to make clear that the examinations were written exercises' was the Jesuit Giovanni Pietro Maffei, who published a history of the Society of Jesus in 1588; the section on China was based largely on Ricci, who had been providing information to his order since earlier in the decade.
9   See Rule, *K'ung-tzu or Confucius?*, p. 1.
10   *China in the Sixteenth Century*, p. 85.
11   Rule, *K'ung-tzu or Confucius?*, p. 28.
12   *China in the Sixteenth Century*, p. 30.
13   See Rule, *K'ung-tzu or Confucius?*, p. 27.
14   *China in the Sixteenth Century*, p. 10.
15   Ibid., p. 55.
16   Ibid., pp. 85–8.
17   Rule, *K'ung-tzu or Confucius?*, p. 120.
18   Le Comte, *Nouveaux mémoires sur l'état présent de la Chine*, Vol. II, pp. 2–3.

19 Ibid., Vol. I, p. 129.
20 Du Halde, *Description géographique, historique, chronologique, politique, et physique de l'empire de la Chine et de la Tartarie chinoise*, Vol. II, p. 37. The translation is that of R. Brookes in *The General History of China*, Vol. II, p. 49.
21 Du Halde, *Description*, Vol. II, p. 163, as translated in *The General History*, Vol. II, p. 236.
22 Du Halde, *Description*, Vol. II, p. 89. The translation is my own.
23 Ibid., II, 90, as translated in *The General History*, II, 131.
24 Du Halde, *Description*, Vol. II, p. 95, as translated in *The General History*, Vol. II, p. 139. Note that Du Halde's original French says 'désagréable à nos yeux Européans' (disagreeable to our European eyes). 'Disagreeable to foreigners' is a loose translation.
25 Du Halde, *Description*, Vol. II, p. 87, as translated in *The General History*, Vol. II, p. 126.
26 Du Halde, *Description*, Vol. II, p. 154, as translated in *The General History*, Vol. II, p. 224.
27 Du Halde, *Description*, Vol. II, p. 162, as translated in *The General History*, Vol. II, p. 235.
28 Quoted from Franke, *China and the West*, p. 62.
29 Voltaire, *Essai sur les mœurs et l'esprit des nations*, pp. 215–16.
30 Ibid., pp. 69–71.
31 Ibid., pp. 209–13.
32 Quesnay, *Depotism in China*, translated by Maverick in *China, A Model for Europe*, pp. 141–2.
33 Ibid., p. 170.
34 Ibid., p. 168.
35 Smith, *An Inquiry into the Nature and Causes of the Wealth of Nations*, Vol. I, p. 80.
36 Ibid., Vol. I, pp. 80–1.
37 Ibid., Vol. I, 80–1.
38 Montesquieu, *The Spirit of the Laws*, pp. 303–4.

4
Nineteenth-Century Imperialism and China

Just like earlier centuries, the nineteenth century produced a variety of views in the West about China. However, the balance between positive and negative images shifted decisively away from the former and towards the latter.

There were various reasons for this. The cults of chinoiserie and sinophilism that characterized the Enlightenment 'had run their natural course and completely lost their impetus'.[1] The Chinese empire itself was declining quite rapidly from the late years of Qianlong's reign onwards, and even more so throughout the nineteenth century. But by far the most important reason was the rise of European, and especially British, imperialism from the time of the Industrial Revolution towards the end of the eighteenth century. For the first time Britain became a leader as a formulator of Western images of China.

The beginning of the change from the dominantly positive images of the eighteenth century towards the negative of the nineteenth century occurred in the middle of the eighteenth century. Baron George Anson returned from a long voyage around the world in 1744 and his account was published by his chaplain, Richard Walter, in 1748. It was the first full-scale attack on the rosy images of China that the French Jesuits were trying to convey. For a variety of domestic reasons, which had little to do with China, opinion both in France and England moved strongly against China in the second half of the eighteenth century. After the rupture of relations occasioned by the withdrawal of the Jesuits from China in the 1770s, the event which brought about the beginning of a new wave of interest in China was the embassy of Lord Macartney in 1793. On the whole, the newly industrializing and supremely confident West now observed a declining China with eyes totally different from those with which their predecessors of not long before had viewed an empire that appeared to be at the height of its glory.

In his diary recording his embassy to China, Lord Macartney remarked of its political system that its aim was apparently 'to persuade the people that they are themselves already perfect and can therefore learn nothing from others'. Macartney thought this an unwise approach: 'A nation that does not advance must retrograde, and finally fall back to barbarism and misery.'[2] This brief observation clearly illustrates three points which were to assume very great importance in the formulation of Western images of China in the nineteenth century. One is the assumption that China would be learning from the West in future; China would no longer be the model which Voltaire and others had seen in it. The second is the belief in change. Macartney expressed a view typical of nineteenth-century Europe when he stated that if China refused to change it would sink back into misery.[3] He was right in his perception that Chinese ideology at the time was intensely conservative and thus eschewed change. Finally, Macartney's implication that change meant progress brimmed over with the optimism that was characteristic of nineteenth-century Europe.

Macartney put forward yet another view, which was in contrast to these assumptions. One of the last remarks he makes in his diary under its final day, 15 January 1794, is that 'nothing could be more fallacious than to judge of China by any European standard'. But his next sentence says: 'My sole view has been to represent things precisely as they impressed me',[4] and that seems perfectly fair. Yet it raises and bypasses the issue of by what standards he himself judged China, if not the European ones with which he had been brought up. Macartney was aware of the problem and his diary on the whole suggests that he coped with it honestly according to his own lights. Yet the whole tone of nineteenth-century writings on China shows that realistic attempts to take account of non-European, for example Chinese, standards grew fainter and rarer as the century wore on and the military, economic, political, and social impact of Western imperialism strengthened. This was the period when Edward Said's 'orientalist' approach to China, explained in Chapter 1, reached its height, when Europe colonized not only parts of China, but also knowledge about it.

Macartney's journal was not published in full until 1962. However, John Barrow, who was a member of Macartney's suite, published selections from his writings in 1807 and several members of the party wrote and published their own accounts of the embassy. The 'official' version was that of Sir George Leonard Staunton,[5] who was Macartney's deputy and Minister Plenipotentiary in his absence. One twentieth-century writer has written of Staunton that he 'interlards his description of the embassy with occasional unqualified eulogies of Chinese society which are reminiscent of the reactions of earlier ages'.[6] He maintains the generally uncritical attitude that had characterized Du Halde, the physiocrats, or Voltaire.

More interesting, as representative of a new and very different point of view on China, is John Barrow's *Travels in China*, published first in 1804. Based on his travels there, this book focuses less on the embassy itself than on Barrow's comments on Chinese life and society. Before Chapter I there is an 'advertisement' in which Barrow declares his strong disagreement with 'the almost universally received opinion' and pleads his own comments as 'the unbiassed conclusions of his own mind, founded altogether on his own observations'.[7] He seems to be excusing himself for differing so basically with Staunton. It was, after all, through Staunton's patronage that he had gone to China in the first place; moreover, after returning to England he lived in London with Sir George and helped him write the official version of the embassy. He feels called on to warn his readers that, in contrast to the bland 'authentic version', his own book will represent a blistering attack on China, its government, institutions, society and people.

Barrow saw a country with a bad government, describable only in 'terms of tyranny, oppression, and injustice', exciting feelings of 'fear, deceit, and disobedience' from the governed.[8] The laws are so cruel as to 'exclude and obliterate every notion of the dignity of human nature'.[9] The murder and exposure of infants are common, induced by the 'extreme poverty and hopeless indigence, the frequent experience of direful famines, and the scenes of misery and calamity occasioned by them'.[10] As for the people themselves, they are dirty and 'their bodies are as seldom washed as their articles of dress';[11] they are cunning cheats and thieves and their 'general character . . . is a strange compound of pride and meanness, of affected gravity and real frivolousness, of refined civility and gross indelicacy'.[12] The reference to refined civility shows Barrow's willingness to allow relieving features in the Chinese and it is necessary to point out, in fairness to him, that he blames for the evils of China not 'the nature and disposition of the people' but rather the 'system of government', including the Manchus' failure to change either the 'forms' or 'abuses' of the previous ancient and stagnant political structures.[13] But the overall picture and images that emerge from Barrow's account, both of China and the Chinese, are very grim indeed.

Protestant Missionaries

The embassy of Lord Macartney in 1793 foreshadowed the rise of British and other encroachments on China, but these did not begin for several decades. On the other hand, the British Protestant missionaries of the early nineteenth century followed Macartney rather quickly. As it happened, they created very little impact in China at first and there were less than a hundred converts in 1840. They encountered great difficulty in gaining admission to China and their contact with the people was very sparse indeed. It was British gunboats that gave them the impetus they needed to make greater headway in China. The irony is that whereas their initial progress in converting the Chinese to their religion was negligible, their impact on Britain and the West was substantial in that it was they who played the major role in changing Europe's attitude towards China.

The contrast between the slight impact on China and the considerable one on the mind of the West recalls the experience of the Jesuits. However, the British Protestant missionaries of the early nineteenth century were 'narrow-minded, conservative and unimaginative', quite unlike the humanism of the Jesuits.[14]   England was in the throes of a general conservatism that resulted, at least in part, from a reaction against the doctrines of the French Revolution of 1789. At the same time its mood was, ironically, expansive as regards the missions. The last years of the eighteenth and first of the nineteenth centuries saw the establishment of quite a few new missionary societies by several Protestant denominations.

One of them was the London Missionary Society, set up in 1795, which was to provide the first of the British Protestant missionaries in China, Robert Morrison (1782–1834), who arrived in Guangzhou in 1807. Morrison made few Chinese friends and hardly any converts, but spent his time on a dictionary and Chinese translations of the Bible, the latter published in 1818. In addition, he wrote on the Chinese language itself and among his works are a Chinese grammar, printed in 1815. Morrison believed that the clue to converting the Chinese was to know their language. His overwhelming, more or less exclusive, interest in them was their conversion to Christianity.

Other early Protestant missionaries included the Englishman W. H. Medhurst (1796–1857), and the Americans David Abeel (1804–46) and Samuel Wells Williams (1812–84). All three wrote substantially on China. The Protestant missionaries regarded China mainly as a country of heathens 'who lacked the light of God and must be rescued from eternal damnation',[15] and the images they conveyed to the West were correspondingly condescending and negative.

Abeel was very caustic about conditions in China and also about its people. He writes that 'there is probably no other space upon earth so filled with real wretchedness as China'. It is a land known not only for the injustice and oppression of its government, but also for 'the indigence and depravity of the populace'. Worst off are the women, the condition of whom is evidence 'of the real barbarity and misery of the nation'. Abeel's overall verdict on the treatment of women is damning in the extreme:

> Without education, crippled from infancy, closely immured, married without their consent—in some instances even sold by their parents—and often treated most unfeelingly by the relatives and other wives of their husbands, we cannot wonder at the frequent suicides among them, nor at their attempts to poison those by whom all their happiness and hopes are spoiled.

The only relief, if it can be called that, is that women of the lower classes are exempt 'from the barbarous custom of compressing the feet . . . and [are] thus escaping the imprisonment to which their superiors are doomed'.[16]

S. Wells Williams was the author of the famous general work *The Middle Kingdom*, first published in 1848. It was in its day, and remains, the best known of the many nineteenth-century compendiums about China and Chinese life in general. It can certainly claim to be image-formulating, and in view of its importance as a general account of China it may be worth looking at more closely.

The Middle Kingdom is extraordinarily broad in its coverage, in scope very similar to Du Halde's monumental work. There are chapters on geography, population, natural history, law, government, education, language, classical and 'polite' literature, architecture, diet, social life, science, history, religion, commerce, foreign relations, and other matters.

Williams took the trouble to learn Chinese. Indeed, he believed that 'the contempt which the people feel for their visitors, and the restricted intercourse' that had characterized the last century, were due to the deplorable ignorance of foreigners of the Chinese language. And, of course, 'far above all in importance', knowledge of the language can help missionaries convert the people and 'accept the proferred grace of their Redeemer'.[17]

Williams believed himself sympathetic to China and the Chinese people. In his preface he states it as one of his objects in writing his work 'to divest the Chinese people and civilization of that peculiar and almost undefinable impression of ridicule which is so generally given them; as if they were the apes of Europeans; and their social state, arts, and government, the burlesques of the same things in Christendom'. Williams knew well of the *de haut en bas* attitude that Westerners of his own time held towards China. He himself was trying to be fair. For him China was 'the most civilized pagan nation in her institutions and literature now existing'.[18]

Yet Williams describes these same institutions as 'despotic and defective, and founded on wrong principles'. 'They may have the element of stability', he goes on, 'but not of improvement'. They do not make people 'honourable, truthful, or kind'. In short, 'this civilization is Asiatic and not European, pagan and not Christian'. What is surprising for Williams is 'that this huge mass of mankind is no worse'.[19]

As far as Chinese literature is concerned, S. Wells Williams regards it as worth looking at for its curiosity value and because it is 'the literature of so vast a portion of the human species'. Yet he also denies that it contains 'much to repay investigation . . . to one already acquainted with the treasures of Western science'.[20]

Despite the obvious ethnocentrism in such views, there are even sharper barbs reserved for the people themselves. His summation of 'the moral traits of Chinese character' is devastating. It is true that he does find some points to praise, such as that 'industry receives its just reward of food, raiment, and shelter, with a uniformity which encourages its constant exertion'. But the people themselves he found 'vile and polluted in a shocking degree'. 'Brothels and their inmates occur everywhere on land and on water' and 'young girls going abroad alone' risk 'incarceration in these gates of hell'. Williams has a solution, though only one: 'As long as they love to wallow in this filth, they cannot advance, and all experience proves that nothing but the gospel can cleanse and purify its fountain.'

The Chinese, according to Williams, are ungrateful and mendacious. This is no small matter: 'their disregard of truth has perhaps done more to lower their character in the eyes of Christendom than any other fault'. They are avaricious and deceitful. He quotes Abeel— whose portrait, incidentally, appears at the front of Volume II of Williams' book—as trusting a servant, whom he 'had taken to be peculiarly honest for a heathen', only to find him guilty of fraud.

Williams found that 'thieving is exceedingly common', and 'public and private charity is almost extinct'.

Williams concludes that the Chinese 'present a singular mixture' of virtue and vice. But 'if there is something to commend, there is more to blame'. The list of virtues is short, of vices long. The result is 'a full unchecked torrent of human depravity . . . proving the existence of a kind and degree of moral degradation, of which an excessive statement can scarcely be made, or an adequate conception hardly be formed'.[21] This is actually even a much more damning indictment than Barrow's overall conclusion.

Another and somewhat later American missionary was Arthur H. Smith, who lived in China for twenty-two years and in 1890 published what one authority as late as 1979 described as still 'the most comprehensive survey of Chinese characteristics'.[22] Its functions as image-formulator and reflector are obvious from the fact that it went through five editions within a decade of its first publication. By the nature of its subject, it concerns not China as an abstract entity but the Chinese as people. Much narrower in its scope than Williams' great work, it covers some of the same ground and is in general only slightly less damning and patronizing, but in some respects it can be even more so.

Smith devotes a chapter to each of twenty-six characteristics, beginning with 'face' and continuing with others, including economy, industry, politeness, the disregard for accuracy, intellectual turbidity, contempt for foreigners, the absence of public spirit, conservatism, filial piety, benevolence, mutual suspicion, and the absence of sincerity. These 'characteristics', a mixture of positive and negative, are embellished to include others and garnished with illustrative stories giving artistic verisimilitude. Smith claims that 'many old residents of China', presumably meaning Westerners, are 'in substantial agreement' with his views about the Chinese,[23] and there is no reason to doubt that most ordinary readers accepted his ideas as well.

One 'characteristic' was 'the absence of nerves' and its concomitant, the ability to endure physical pain. 'Those who have any acquaintance with the operations in hospitals in China, know how common, or rather how almost universal, it is for the patients to bear without flinching a degree of pain from which the stoutest of us would shrink in terror'.[24] The Chinese can sleep anywhere and under any conditions. They do not need or want peace and quiet when sick. Smith does not present these features as condemnation, indeed he even quotes with approval a letter of George Eliot to the effect that the ability to bear pain betokens 'the highest calling and election', but to this reader at least his style is so condescending as to imply criticism.

A chapter exemplifying an attempt at balance but with an exceedingly grim overall thrust is the one entitled 'the absence of sympathy', among the longest chapters in the book. It begins with an explanation of the Chinese absence of sympathy through their poverty. Smith also praises the Chinese as a people of mild disposition and acknowledges he has seen many instances of devotion by Chinese towards the sick, even when total strangers.[25] On the other hand, he gives far more space to proving his point that the Chinese lack sympathy and are cruel. Their 'whole family life' illustrates their lack of sympathy. The worst relationship of all is mother to daughter-in-law. 'Cases of cruel treatment which are so aggravated as to lead to suicide, or to an attempt at suicide' on the part of the son's hapless wife 'are so frequent as to excite little more than passing comment'.[26] Either inside or outside the family, the overall indifference of the Chinese to the suffering of others 'is probably not to be matched in any other civilised country'.[27] Not surprisingly, one of his main examples in support of this contention is the punishments meted out by the legal system. Since the time Gaspar da Cruz had praised Chinese justice, European law had progressed enormously while China's had, if anything, worsened. Smith was quite typical of his time in his utter condemnation of China's punishment system. While this is a perfectly reasonable point of view, Smith is less fair in suggesting that the punishments are cruel because that is the Chinese national character. A footnote spells out what the rest of the chapter implies: 'the Chinese being what they are, their laws and their customs being as they are, it would probably be wholly impracticable to introduce any essential amelioration of their punishments without a thoroughgoing reformation of the Chinese people as individuals'.[28] Barrow had blamed bad Chinese national characteristics on the government, Smith implies the reverse causation.

Although he has some praise for the Chinese people, Smith's overall evaluation of their characteristics is extremely harsh. Their needs are few. 'They are only Character and Conscience. Nay, they are but one, for Conscience *is* Character.'[29] This castigation that the Chinese lack any character leads Smith to a discussion of how this serious defect can be overcome. Experience shows that no solution can be found within the people themselves or their country, so obviously reform must come from without: 'To attempt to reform China without "some force from without", is like trying to build a ship in the sea; all the laws of air and water conspire to make it impossible'.[30] The force from without clearly means the West, or more specifically Christianity. China 'needs a new life in every individual soul, in the family, and in society'. These many needs boil down to 'a single imperative need. It will be met permanently, completely, only by Christian civilization'.[31] In its essentials, Smith's judgment of Chinese national characteristics is the same as that of S. Wells Williams before him.

This peroration concludes the book and thus emphasizes its importance for its author. Smith is justifying the twenty-two years he spent in a country he did not particularly like. It would be easy to accuse him of self-righteous bigotry. Of course, it would be an accurate charge but perhaps one that misses the point. He looked at China with eyes very strongly moulded by his own beliefs, a common and natural phenomenon, but with no attempt at all to consider any Chinese point of view. An eminent historian from the period since World War II considers that Smith 'expressed the tolerant but sometimes acerbic frustration of missionaries who found the Chinese villager impervious to progress and the gospel',[32] a charitable interpretation. Smith happened to publish at the beginning of the decade that probably represents the acme of imperialism in China, as shown by the scramble for the concessions in 1898 and the eight-power invasion in 1900. The effect of the images he portrays is support for cultural, even military intervention.

Raymond Dawson has argued that the missionaries became more liberal towards Chinese civilization in the second half of the nineteenth century, owing to the development of Darwin's theory of natural selection and other scientific ideas that challenged the fundamentalist interpretation of the Christian scriptures.[33] In support of this view one could point to James Legge, who after many years as a missionary in China went on to become the first Professor of Chinese at Oxford University. He prepared a translation of the Chinese classics which even today is regarded as authoritative. He was prepared to see elements of true religion in the Chinese religions and in Confucianism, and his style lacks the haughtiness of Williams. Moreover, his own mind broadened substantially as he grew older.

Dawson's is a fair view but should not be overstated. If Williams is a reasonable representative of missionary opinion in the middle of the century and Smith towards the end, then the change in attitude can be seen as no more than marginal. The same point emerges from a comparison between the mid-century edition of Williams' great work with one published in 1883, somewhat over three decades later. By that time Williams had become Professor of Chinese Language and Literature at Yale College. The preface of the later version has been more or less completely rewritten. He opens it by affirming that 'a greater advance has probably been made in the political and intellectual development of China than within any previous century of her history'. He also claims to have tried to show the better traits in their national character.[34] There are, indeed, substantial changes made. The reference to Chinese literature that it contains little to repay investigation 'to one already acquainted with the treasures of Western science' is qualified by the rider that 'in fairness, such a comparison is not quite just'.[35] Yet he has not for that reason eliminated the comparison. Moreover, all the caustic comments earlier quoted about the national characteristics of the Chinese remain essentially unchanged—their mendacity, dishonesty, moral vileness, and pollution, even the statement that the vices of the Chinese prove 'the existence of a kind and degree of moral degradation of which an excessive statement can scarcely be made, or an adequate conception hardly be formed'.[36]

Images Conveyed by Non-Missionaries

The imperialist onslaught on China brought with it the opening of consular diplomatic missions not only in Guangzhou and Beijing but in other cities as well. The staffs of these missions included many people with a serious attitude to the study of China. Many learned the language and produced studies on general and particular aspects of China, some of them pioneering works.

One of the earliest official missions to China was the French one of 1884, led by Théodose de Lagrené, the aim of which was to conclude a commercial and navigation treaty. On the staff were several people who later wrote much on China. An example is Natalis Rondot, author of a substantial work on French textile trade with China and many aspects of Chinese society, such as infanticide.

Among the Dutch Gustaaf Schlegel (1840–1903) and Jan Jacob Maria de Groot (1854–1921) stand out. Both worked in China (and Java) as interpreters in the government service, though Schlegel left in 1872 and later took up a chair at Leiden University especially created for him. Both wrote widely on Chinese society. Schlegel's area was law, and he also wrote a pioneering essay on prostitution. De Groot is the author of a major work on religion in China. Published in Leiden in six volumes from 1892 to 1910, it is extremely thorough but very condescending in tone. This is already clear from the work's first sentence, where he refers to the Chinese as a 'barbarous and semicivilized' people.[37] Nevertheless, the diplomatic missions of the nineteenth century do signal the first major Dutch contributions to the Western scholarly study of China.

British missions also produced writers of note. One well-known author is Thomas Taylor Meadows, an interpreter in the British consulate in Guangzhou with over a decade's personal experience in China in the 1840s and 1850s. He wrote a book called *The Chinese and their Rebellions*, published in 1856, which covers many aspects of China, such as philosophy, law, and administration. A substantial portion is given to the Taipings, whose rebellion began and expanded while Meadows was in China. There is also a long essay on 'civilization', with comparisons of China and the West.

The tone of Meadows' book is decidedly self-important. He gives much space to attacking the views of other China specialists, including both British and French. But what is striking is that he usually puts himself in the minority view of defending Chinese characteristics, customs, and ideas against criticism.

An illustrative case in point concerns the relationship between the intellect, morality, and progress in the physical sciences. Meadows denounces the French explorer and sinologue Evariste Régis Huc (1813–60) for his criticisms of the Chinese as 'destitute of religious feelings and beliefs' and 'pursuing only wealth and material enjoyments with ardour'. He describes such accusations, all too common in his own day, as 'baseless calumny of the higher life of a great portion of the human race'.[38] Again, he attacks T. F. Wade, whom he describes as 'one of our official sinologues' and who later became British Minister in China, for his description of the Chinese as 'short-sighted utilitarians, industrious and gain seeking' with an 'infinitely vicious' national mind. Meadows' conclusion on all this is worth quoting.

> The chief reason why the Chinese have made so little progress in the physical sciences is not a mental 'incapacity', or 'tenuity of intellect', of which Mr Wade accuses them, but a disregard or even contempt for things material as opposed to things intellectual or moral. In war, which is more especially a fight of physical or material forces, they paid the just penalty of this undue contempt when they became involved in a contest with the possessors of the highest material civilization the world has yet seen: the British people.[39]

Meadows attacks what he appears to perceive as outright racism. Yet his own ethnocentrism is evident from his criticism of the Chinese contempt for the material as 'undue', and his dubbing of the penalty for it as 'just'. And no defence of China weighs against the ringing nationalism of the last sentence.

Other than missionaries and diplomatic personnel, another category of those with experience in China are explorers or travellers, some with special purposes. The nineteenth century in the West saw a self-confident and prosperous middle class, which spawned people with the time, money and inclination to travel, even under the most uncomfortable of conditions. An example of a scientific traveller is Robert Fortune (1813–80) who went to China in 1843 as Botanical Collector to the Horticultural Society of London. In that capacity he travelled in China and wrote a book on his experiences, not only scientific but general.

The number of travellers grew as the century progressed. The Frenchman Jules Léon Dutreuil de Rhins (1846–94) was a sailor, who travelled in Africa, Siam, and China and was murdered by Tibetan villagers near Xining. The Australian George Ernest Morrison, whom President Yuan Shikai was to appoint as political advisor in 1912, travelled up the Yangtze River and overland through Sichuan and Yunnan to Burma in 1894. There were also women in this company, the outstanding one being Isabella Lucy Bishop (1831–1904). Despite poor health she travelled all over the world, including China. In the late 1870s, she travelled to South-East Asia, including South-East China, and in the 1890s she went up the Yangtze, roamed in Sichuan, and to Tibet; she covered about 11,000 kilometres in over a year, much of it alone and on horseback.

The tone of Fortune's book on his 'three years' wanderings in the northern provinces' is very high-handed towards the Chinese. Although he does sometimes make a favourable judgment about them, it is always based on the assumption of the superiority of British and Western civilization over Chinese. He claims to be 'far from having any prejudice against the Chinese people'.[40] On the other hand, he scoffs at the suggestion that the Chinese are 'for a moment to be compared with the civilised nations of the West' in agriculture. His summation is that the Chinese 'are not entitled to the credit of being equal to, much less in advance of the nations of the West in science, in the arts, in government or in laws.'[41] However, he does consider them 'considerably in advance of the Hindus, Malays, and other nations who inhabit the central and western portions of Asia'.[42] Sweeping generalizations ranking the peoples of Asia—below those of the West of course—was a typical characteristic of nineteenth-century Orientalism.

The Australian Morrison in his younger days was more tolerant and definitely saw himself not only as a friend of the Chinese but one who had undergone something of a conversion. 'I went to China possessed with the strong racial antipathy to the Chinese common to my countrymen, but that feeling has long since given way to one of lively sympathy and gratitude.' He recalls his journey with great pleasure and claims to have met everywhere with 'uniform kindness and hospitality, and the most charming courtesy'.[43] Isabella Lucy Bishop found China 'intoxicating' and 'enchanting'. After being carried around all day in Guangzhou she wrote that she had for the first time drunk of that water 'of which it may truly be said that who so drinks "shall thirst again"—true Orientalism',[44] by which term she obviously means something desirable and expressing a powerful image of exoticism. Though she understood by 'Orientalism' something quite different from Edward Said, her work no doubt falls under the pejorative sense of the word, as he has defined it.

The travellers quite naturally cover a vast range of topics and though their works probably reached a wider readership than did the scholarly or diplomatic literature, the images portrayed by the writers of the various callings do not necessarily differ essentially. Two perennial themes suffice as illustrations of the travelogues: the law, and females.

Fortune criticizes China not so much for the barbarity of its system of punishments, but rather because 'the government is powerless, and has not the means of punishing those who break the laws'. As a result, 'the only thing which keeps the country together is the quiet and inoffensive character of the people'.[45] Morrison atacks the problem from the opposite end. He is appalled at the shocking cruelty of the punishments and the widespread use of mutilation. While this is a reasonable view and an image justly very common in the literature, he has drawn a less justifiable conclusion about the Chinese people, one we have already seen in the work of the missionary A. H. Smith: that the Chinese are physically insensitive. 'The sensory nervous system of a Chinaman is either blunted or of arrested development. Can anyone doubt this who witnesses the stoicism with which a Chinaman can endure physical pain.' Another curious comment on the Chinese punishment system is Morrison's suggestion that the Chinese practice of compelling a culprit who has just been beaten to thank the magistrate for correcting his morals 'might with good effect be introduced into

England'.[46] Morrison seems to be looking for factors which mitigate his horror at the mutilations he has just been describing in grim detail. Isabella Bishop dwells at length on a prison and law court in Guangzhou. Her summative image is uncompromising and to the point: 'If crime, vice, despair, suffering, filth and cruelty can make a hell on earth, this is one.'[47]

Fortune attacked China for its treatment of women: 'The females here, like those of most half civilised or barbarous nations,' which presumably include China, 'are kept in the background, and are not considered on an equality with their husbands'. To prove his point he cites an example that 'they do not sit at the same table'.[48] This is a reasonable point, but to include it yet ignore foot-binding or concubinage shows a curious set of priorities.

Isabella Bishop was impressed with Chinese women. In contrast to Fortune, foot-binding does loom large as an image of their treatment of women for her, but she is strikingly defensive about it. Her comments are worth quoting in detail:

> I like the faces of the lower orders of Chinese women. They are both strong and kind, and it is pleasant to see women not deformed in any way ... The small-footed women are rarely seen out of doors; but the serving-woman at Mrs Smith's has crippled feet, and I have got her shoes, which are too small for the English baby of four months old! The butler's little daughter, aged seven, is having her feet 'bandaged' for the first time, and is in torture, but bears it bravely in the hope of 'getting a rich husband'. The sole of the shoe of a properly diminished foot is about two inches and a half long, but the mother of this suffering infant says, with a quiet air of truth and triumph, that Chinese women suffer less in the process of being crippled than foreign women do from wearing corsets! To these Eastern women the notion of deforming the figure for the sake of appearance only is unintelligible and repulsive.[49]

Morrison shows himself aware of several of the more horrific aspects of the treatment of females in China in the late nineteenth century. He has quite a bit to say about wife-beating, the sale of girls into slavery, foot-binding, and female infanticide. But whereas Fortune's contrasts with the West are aimed at showing its superiority, Morrison, like Bishop, is quite equal to comparisons that defend China. 'The prevalent idea with us Westerners appears to be, that the murder of their children, especially of their female children, is a kind of national pastime with the Chinese,' he writes. But this perception of the dominant Western image on female infanticide introduces his own research into quite a few scholarly sources which put forward an alternative view. He cites a former French Consul in China, G. Eugène Simon, to the effect that 'infanticide is a good deal less frequent in China than in Europe generally, and particularly in France'. His own general conclusion on this subject is to doubt 'whether the crime, excepting in seasons of famine, is, in proportion to the population, more common in China than it is in England'.[50] Morrison also reaches a general conclusion about Chinese women, like the one on infanticide comparative, though not with the West: 'speaking as an impartial observer who has been both in Japan and China, I have never been able to come to any other decision than that in every feature the Chinese woman is superior to her Japanese sister'.[51]

The impression that emerges is of Morrison as a nineteenth-century observer more than usually defensive of China. Yet the general picture he paints of the situation in those parts of China where he travelled is exceedingly grim. Moreover, despite his comments on infanticide, he most certainly did see the West as superior to China, as made clear by comments such as 'we, who live amid the advantages of Western civilisation, can hardly realise' the severity of particular hardships in China.[52] And as far as the people themselves are concerned, his enjoyment of his journey did not prevent him from caustic generalizations about their character. He quotes a French missionary as telling him: 'If you ever hear of a Chinaman who is not a thief and a liar do not believe it, Monsieur Morrison, do not believe it; they are thieves and liars every one.'[53] And this is followed by a little story which appears to show the priest right. It was symptomatic of the age that even an observer as perceptive and tolerant as Morrison could allow to go unchallenged so hostile a comment, not about the country, its conditions or its institutions, but about the character of an entire people with which he claimed to sympathize.

Encyclopaedias

The dominantly negative images of the nineteenth century were to some extent spawned but also strongly reinforced by encyclopaedias. There was of course nothing new to the nineteenth century about this source of instant knowledge, either in the West or for that matter in China. But entries on countries such as China grew enormously, both in length and in sophistication, during the nineteenth century, because of the leap in knowledge that went together with the expansionism, colonialism, and confidence of the Western countries. Correspondingly, the view that comes over from the encyclopaedias is heavily coloured by colonialist attitudes.

At no time has the weight of encyclopaedias as formulators of perceptions about China been greater in relation to the whole range of sources of Western images than in the nineteenth century.

There were numerous types of encyclopaedias: general, family, women's, technical, and others, and the tendency was for them to go through several editions. Some were illustrated, others not. Three specific entries on China or the 'Chinese Empire' can illustrate the kinds of images which emerged from this large range of encyclopaedias: those of the ninth edition of the *Encyclopædia Britannica*, published in 1876, the 1874 edition of *Chambers's Encyclopædia* and the tenth edition of the *Brockhaus Conversations-Lexicon*, which came out in 1852. These three encyclopaedias could claim as reasonably as any other to be called respectively the two most influential British encyclopaedias and the most image-formulating in Germany. All three, especially the first and third, created a strong impact in countries other than the ones in which they originated.

The *Encyclopædia Britannica* was designed as more scholarly than the other two. Brockhaus calls itself a 'conversations-lexicon' designed for the educated classes, whereas the title of *Chambers's* specifies that the work aims to provide 'universal knowledge for the people'.

Of the three entries on China, that of the *Encyclopædia Britannica* is by far the longest, but the most substantial section within it is the one dealing with language and literature, which are given a separate entry in Brockhaus. There is an enormous amount of factual information in these entries, especially in the *Encyclopædia Britannica* and Brockhaus. The tone of all three is extremely condescending, regarding China as an exotic, backward, only semi-civilized, and in some ways rather barbaric country. Of the three, Brockhaus is the most negative, and *Chambers's* the least so.

Chambers's takes its discussion of Chinese government largely from T. T. Meadows and is thus in places quite laudatory. The administrative machinery is described as 'very perfect in its organisation', and the 'normal government' as 'less a despotism than a morally supported autocracy'.[54] The emphasis in the *Encyclopædia Britannica*, on the other hand, is on despotism, corruption, and a cruel law system. The system of government is 'a patriarchal despotism'. The emperor 'holds autocratic sway over his household—the empire . . . Whom he will he slays, and whom he will he keeps alive'. Corruption in high places demoralizes the people, with the result that 'dishonesty prevails to a frightful extent, and with it, of course untruthfulness'. The fact that the Chinese 'set little or no value upon truth' offers 'some slight excuse . . . for the use of torture in the courts of justice'.

There are graphic and detailed descriptions of the torture not only of criminals, but also of witnesses, provoking the by now familiar reaction: 'The Mongolian race is confessedly obtuse-nerved and insensible to suffering, and no doubt Chinese culprits do not suffer nearly as much as members of more senstive races would under similar treatment.' However, the fact that Chinese do not feel pain to the same degree as Westerners cannot be seen as justification: 'even granting this [the Chinese insensitivity to pain], the refined cruelties perpetrated by Chinamen on Chinamen admit of no apology'.[55]

We have already come from government to national character. All three encyclopaedia entries convey generally caustic images of the Chinese and their society. Brockhaus dubs Chinese domestic life as 'in general cold and boring'.[56] For *Chambers's*, social relations are 'regulated by a tedious and elaborate etiquette'. Women are hardly better than slaves. The people are hypocritical and inscrutable. One authority is quoted, with approval, as saying that 'a Chinaman . . . has wonderful command of feature; he generally looks most pleased when he has least reason to be so'.[57]

The *Encyclopædia Britannica* concedes 'quiet, happy, domestic life' for those many lucky enough to escape 'the clutches of the mandarins and their satellites' and even 'much that might be imitated by European families' in the ordering of a Chinese household. On the other hand, the author is shocked by the prevalence of the smoking of opium, 'a drug which seems to have a greater attraction' for the Chinese 'than for any other people on the face of the earth'.[58] He also addresses the problem of female infanticide and, although like Morrison he is at pains not to exaggerate its prevalence, he does include some devastating material concerning parts of Fujian province. 'The people make no attempt to conceal the practice' of female infanticide, he claims, 'and even go to the length of defending it. What is the good of rearing daughters, they say'.[59]

For the Brockhaus encyclopaedia, the first point to make about the Chinese character is their lack of individuality: 'In their national character the Chinese form such a peculiarly marked whole that individuals disappear as members of the nation.' A discussion of the

facial and other bodily features of the Chinese leads on to more detail
about what they are like as people.

> Hard work, politeness, the love of peace and mildness are the
> hallmarks of the Chinese character. Nothing is more sacred to
> him than the love of a child or the fidelity of a subject. On the
> other hand, lust, gluttony, deceitful cunning in trade and traffic,
> cowardice and false flexibility, an intolerable national pride, rigid
> adherence to tradition, pitilessness, vindictiveness, and
> corruptibility form a strong dark side. The innate ability of the
> Chinese for manufacturing work, his knowledge and opinions
> are still the same as centuries ago.[60]

The list of virtues is quite short, of vices long, just as with S. Wells
Williams. But with the addition of the last sentence, even the virtues
tend to dwindle into weaknesses, for it seems that after all this is a
people which does not change, even over centuries.

Conclusion

On the whole, the images discussed above veer towards the centre—
not the extremes—of Western opinion in the nineteenth century. There
were still the strong enthusiasts. Victor Hugo's painting and poetry
shows Chinese influence and in 1848 he drew up a plan which called
on the French to educate themselves in Chinese culture. On the other
hand, several highly significant thinkers, including Karl Marx (1818–
83), were prepared to heap scorn on China for a range of reasons,
including its changelessness.[61] And outright racism of the sort found
in the London journal Punch was quite common.[62]

The rapid technological progress that resulted from the Industrial
Revolution made most Westerners extremely sure of themselves and
led them to look down on those they regarded as backward or inferior,
including the Chinese. The yardsticks of comparison, the criteria for
judgment, were European. Many, even among their 'friends', were
not sure whether the Chinese could rate as 'civilized'. Those with
experience in China certainly cared about it, and were desperate for
profits, converts or just excitement or exoticism. It is surely an
exaggeration to argue that in the nineteenth century 'every European,
in what he could say about the Orient, was consequently a racist, an
imperialist, and almost totally ethnocentric'.[63] Yet on the whole,

Western observers conveyed images conforming with the expansionist aims that had driven them to China in the first place. Their attitudes were entirely consistent with the imperialism of their day.

Notes

1   Dawson, *The Chinese Chameleon*, p. 132.
2   Cranmer-Byng (ed.), *An Embassy to China*, p. 226.
3   Macartney (ibid., p. 239) actually predicted the 'dislocation or dismemberment' of the Qing empire would occur before his own 'dissolution'. He died in 1806 but the Qing empire lasted until 1912.
4   Ibid., p. 219.
5   Staunton, *An Authentic Account of an Embassy from the King of Great Britain to the Emperor of China*.
6   Dawson, *The Chinese Chameleon*, p. 33.
7   Barrow, *Travels in China*, p. xii.
8   Ibid., p. 360.
9   Ibid., p. 179.
10   Ibid., p. 173.
11   Ibid., p. 77.
12   Ibid., p. 187.
13   Ibid., p. 183.
14   Dawson, *The Chinese Chameleon*, p. 134.
15   Ibid., p. 135.
16   David Abeel, 'A Missionary's View', in Grayson (ed.), *The American Image of China*, pp. 80–81.
17   Williams, *The Middle Kingdom* (1851), Vol. I, pp. 500–1.
18   Ibid., Vol. I, xiv–xv.
19   Ibid., Vol. I, p. 297.
20   Ibid., Vol. I, p. 458.
21   Ibid., Vol. II, pp. 95–99.
22   Ch'en, *China and the West*, p. 43.
23   Smith, *Chinese Characteristics*, p. 12.
24   Ibid., p. 94.
25   Ibid., pp. 206–7.
26   Ibid., p. 202.
27   Ibid., p. 213.
28   Ibid., p. 214.
29   Ibid., p. 320.
30   Ibid., p. 324.
31   Ibid., p. 330.
32   Fairbank, *The United States and China*, p. 294.
33   Dawson, *The Chinese Chameleon*, pp. 137–38.
34   Williams, *The Middle Kingdom* (1883), Vol. I, pp. ix, xiv.
35   Ibid., Vol. I, p. 578.
36   Ibid., Vol. I, p. 836.

37 de Groot, *The Religious System of China*, Vol. I, p. 1.
38 Meadows, *The Chinese and their Rebellions*, p. 64.
39 Ibid., pp. 72–73.
40 Fortune, *Three Years' Wanderings in the Northern Provinces of China*, p. 9.
41 Ibid., p. 7.
42 Ibid., pp. 10–11.
43 Morrison, *An Australian in China*, p. 2.
44 Bishop, *The Golden Chersonese and the Way Thither*, p. 64.
45 Fortune, *Three Years' Wanderings*, pp. 7–8.
46 Morrison, *An Australian in China*, p. 104.
47 Bishop, *The Golden Chersonese*, p. 87.
48 Fortune, *Three Years' Wanderings*, p. 319.
49 Bishop, *The Golden Chersonese*, p. 83.
50 Morrison, *An Australian in China*, p. 129.
51 Ibid., p. 13.
52 Ibid., p. 90.
53 Ibid., p. 105.
54 *Chambers's Encyclopædia*, Vol. II, p. 819.
55 Robert K. Douglas, 'China', *Encyclopædia Britannica*, Vol. V, p. 669. [Vol. V appeared in 1876.]
56 *Allgemeine deutsche Real-Encyklopädie für die gebildeten Stände*, Vol. IV, p. 107.
57 *Chambers's Encyclopædia*, Vol. II, p. 818.
58 Douglas, 'China', *Encyclopædia Britannica*, Vol. V, p. 670.
59 Ibid., Vol. V, p. 671.
60 *Allgemeine deutsche Real-Encyklopädie*, Vol. IV, p. 107.
61 See the first (1989) edition of the present work, especially pp. 111–15.
62 For instance, see two such cartoons from *Punch* of 10 April 1858 and 22 December 1860 reprinted in Dawson, *The Chinese Chameleon*, pp. 133 and 151. The former also carries the following stanza which includes several racist stereotypes:

John Chinaman a rogue is born,
The laws of truth he holds in scorn;
About as great a brute as can
Encumber the Earth is John Chinaman.
Sing Yeh, my cruel John Chinaman,
Sing Yeo, my stubborn John Chinaman,
Not Cobden himself can take off the ban
By humanity laid on John Chinaman.

63 Said, *Orientalism*, p. 204

5

The First Half of the Twentieth Century

> I grew up in a double world, the small white clean Presbyterian American world of my parents and the big loving merry not-too-clean Chinese world, and there was no communication between them. When I was in the Chinese world I was Chinese, I spoke Chinese and behaved as a Chinese and ate as the Chinese did, and I shared their thoughts and feelings. When I was in the American world, I shut the door between.[1]

This passage from Pearl Buck's autobiography refers to the period about the time of the Boxer uprising of 1900, when Western images of China were as negative as they had ever been. Pearl Buck obviously liked the Chinese as a child, and there is absolutely no hint here of the scathing images which most Westerners held at the time. Yet she was already dimly aware of a cardinal rule, that one ought not to encourage too much communication between the Chinese and those Westerners who lived in China.

Pearl Buck played a prominent role in formulating Western images of China in the first half of the twentieth century through her novel *The Good Earth*. In particular, she both influenced and represented a trend resulting in images that were enormously more positive by the time the Nationalist Party fell in 1949 than they had been when the Boxers besieged the foreign legations half a century earlier.

Buck is representative also both as an American and as a woman. The years 1900 to 1949 for the first time saw the rise of the Americans to a position of dominance among formulators of Western images of China. This was also the first period when women appear among the most important of those authors whose writings moulded Western views of contemporary China.

The Boxer Uprising

The years leading up to the Boxer uprising in 1900 saw an expansion of European imperialist penetration into China, including the 'scramble for the concessions' in 1898. Another event relevant to images of the Chinese was the discovery in 1895 of the 500,000-year-old *homo erectus* known as Java man. On 27 August 1897, an article appeared in the *North China Herald* on 'Darwinism and China'. It argued that the characteristics of the Chinese were as close to those of Java man as to those of modern European 'civilized' man. And when he is angry, he is even closer: 'watch him half bend himself downwards and then spring up with a jerk, his gesticulating arm and twitching fingers hardly under control: he is the very picture of an enraged anthropoid ape'. Unfortunately, the (unnamed) author of this article appears to have been writing seriously.

The Boxer uprising merely served to confirm the worst suspicions and fears of the Westerners. A flood of reports flowed back to the West describing what had happened. In terms of images, the main burden of the reports was the courage and generally fine behaviour of the Western missionaries and other residents in the face of attack by the ragged Chinese Boxer peasants.

The main images of the Chinese to emerge from the literature spawned by the Boxer uprising are cruelty, treachery, and xenophobia. 'The awful treachery and base cruelty of the Chinese high officials and the people governed by them are without a parallel,'[2] wrote the wife of an American diplomat, who nevertheless exempted the Empress Dowager Cixi, describing her as 'a great woman' with 'a strong character, such as history has seldom recorded'.[3] In particular, their cruelty against foreigners showed how low they had sunk. The well-known British traveller in and writer on Tibet and East Asia, Henry Savage-Landor, was shocked to find in the United States a widespread belief that the Boxers and Chinese officials had spared and respected Americans during the uprising. His own view was that 'the massacres of Europeans were by no means trifling nor unimportant, nor due to some personal spite against particular individuals'. He records flagrant cases of high officials determined to 'exterminate all "white devils"' and concludes that the 'attacks were directed against everybody foreign, regardless of age, sex, and condition'.[4]

Chinese cruelty in general and against foreigners in particular was so strong an image that when the *London Daily Mail* reported on 7 July 1900 that the diplomatic community in Beijing had been annihilated, everyone having been 'put to the sword in a most atrocious manner', most people believed it and responded with rage and calls for vengeance. Sarah Pike Conger, whose self-image was of sympathy for China, was among those prepared to argue that the 'Christ-spirit alone' should help the West to 'forgive and forget';[5] Mrs Conger pointed out that 'China belongs to the Chinese,' and that she 'never wanted the foreigners upon her soil'.[6] But vengeance is precisely what the powers inflicted on China through the Boxer Protocol of September 1901. This Protocol, which was imposed on China after the invading foreign powers defeated the Boxers in 1900, demanded various humiliations of China, foremost among them a gigantic indemnity to recompense the powers for the cost of the invasion.

The West did not ignore the cruelty which its own people wreaked upon the Chinese. But that was justified, or at least understandable, because the West was merely responding to savage and unprovoked attacks from the Chinese. Witness the following description in one of the many surviving diaries on the Boxer period. It refers to 10 July 1900, during the famous 'siege of the legations' (20 June to 14 August 1900).

> Last night twenty Chinese were captured at the French Legation. Three were shot; but the French corporal, saying it would not do to waste so many precious rounds, killed fifteen with his bayonet. Two were kept to be examined.
>
> The flies about the place are something ghastly, being attracted by the unburied corpses of the Chinese ... Just imagine having to keep watch in the blazing sun from 12 to 2 pm as I had to one of these days! My rifle got so hot in the sun that I could hardly hold it, and had to keep it as cool as possible in the shade that I afforded. Add to this steaming heat, a few hundred flies, and you have my picture.[7]

This extract was written by a member of the British consular service in Beijing at the time, Lancelot Giles (1878–1934), the sixth son of the well-known sinologist Professor Herbert Allen Giles. Lancelot Giles expresses no disapproval at the bayonetting of fifteen Chinese because ammunition was short. What interested him, the 'picture' or image he wished to convey, were the flies, which made his job of standing in the hot sun for two hours on one occasion that much nastier.

It would, however, be grossly unfair not to emphasize the more liberal currents. At the forefront was a married couple from a Western country which has hitherto been ignored in these pages. During the

Boxer period the ambassador to China of the Austro-Hungarian empire, Baron Czikann, was on home leave. In his absence the Austrian mission was headed by Arthur von Rosthorn (1862–1945), the *chargé d'affaires*. According to the authors of a large-scale study of Sino-Austrian relations, Rosthorn was 'probably one of the few, if not the only one among the foreigners living in Beijing at the time, who reported on the events with understanding and as a friend of China'. His wife Paula shared his sympathetic views.[8]

Rosthorn denied flatly that there was any inherent hostility to foreigners, or anti-foreignism, among the Chinese. Expanding on a point we have already seen touched on by Mrs Conger, he argued that if the Boxers were angry, and indeed hated the representatives of the great powers, these had only themselves to blame for the acts of plunder they had inflicted on China since 1842. 'We Europeans do not credit to Asians the feelings of patriotism which move us ourselves,' he concluded. 'This is a great mistake.'[9] Rosthorn saw the origins of nationalism in the Boxers, not cruelty or hatred of foreigners.

More Favourable Images

In his book on US images of China and India in the twentieth century, Harold Isaacs calls one section 'The Attractive People (1905–37)' and thus sees a transition—a few years after the Boxers' uprising—from negative to positive in how Americans perceived China. The eight-power invasion of China in 1900 and its aftermath had 'chastened the Manchu court' and stifled the anti-missionary and anti-Western violence among the rural traditionalists from whom the Boxers had sprung. On the whole, foreigners were physically much safer in China after the Boxers' uprising than before. In the US, meanwhile, 'there was a certain revulsion against the maltreatment of the Chinese', which certainly affected images of China itself.[10]

These trends doubtless also affected views in Western countries other than the United States. Arthur von Rosthorn went on to become Austria-Hungary's ambassador in China from 1911 to 1917 and then a sinologist and honorary professor at the University of Vienna. He maintained his opposition to imperialism. When Hitler's Germany invaded Austria he was summoned to join the Gestapo, but remained an outspoken opponent of the Nazi regime.[11]

In English-speaking countries a better-known representative of the pro-China diplomat turned academic was Professor H. A. Giles, who held the Chair of Chinese at Cambridge University from 1897 until 1932. While in the consular service in China he had compiled his enormous and still famous *Chinese-English Dictionary*, but though he wrote a great deal about China, and especially about its history, literature, and religion, he never revisited it. According to one writer, himself a diplomat, Professor Giles 'set out to transform current European ideas about China as a country of mystery and barbarism' to an image of a 'country with an unsurpassed record of civilization and culture'. In 1922 the Royal Asiatic Society in Britain awarded him their Gold Medal because he 'beyond all living scholars has humanised Chinese studies'.[12] He even quarrelled with his son Lancelot because the latter wrote him letters criticizing developments in China in the 1920s.[13]

In the United States there was the extraordinarily influential Henry Robinson Luce (1898–1967), who built a publishing empire based on such magazines as *Time*, *Fortune*, and *Life*. He was born in China into a Presbyterian missionary family and spent most of his childhood there. Luce was passionately convinced both of the truth and virtues of Christianity and of the greatness of American civilization. He was also deeply dedicated to the conservative cause in China and regarded Chiang Kai-shek not only as the saviour of China but as 'unquestionably the greatest man in the Far East'.[14] Luce used *Time* and the other publications of his empire to laud Chiang as a statesman and a Christian, the epitomy of American hopes for China: 'For a hundred years the Chinese have been waiting for him,' was Luce's verdict on Chiang, given at a pro-China religious service held in New York City late in 1942.[15] By 1941 *Time*, *Fortune,* and *Life* had a combined 3.8 million subscribers, a gigantic figure for the time,[16] and it used the style that Luce had devised to suit the tastes of the American public. So it is difficult to exaggerate the role the Luce empire played in spreading a positive image of China and its leader Chiang Kai-shek.

Chinese Influences on Western Images of China
One of the most important of all developments of the first half of the twentieth century was the beginnings of major attempts by the Chinese themselves to influence Western images of their own country. Two representative authors stand out as particularly important: Lin Yutang

and Madame Chiang Kai-shek or Song Meiling. Both spoke and wrote perfect English and were ideally suited to put over a basically positive view to Western readership.

Lin Yutang's best known work is *My Country and My People*, which was first published in February 1936 and had reached its seventh reprint by March 1938. In the book Lin sets out to refute the 'constant, unintelligent elaboration of the Chinaman as a strange fiction, which is as childish as it is untrue and with which the West is so familiar'.[17] One of the two authors he cites as a negative example is Rodney Gilbert, who in 1926 had included the Chinese among the world's 'inferior races' and China among the 'nations that cannot govern themselves, but must have a master'; while Gilbert blamed Western influence for the collapse of China's imperial authority, he believed that the West would be failing in its responsibility if, 'having done the damage', it were to withdraw 'when a firm hold upon the situation might right matters'.[18]

Lin Yutang's appeal is as a patriot who is not ashamed of his country. It is to people of 'that simple common sense for which ancient China was so distinguished' and those 'who have not lost their sense of ultimate human values'.[19] Like A. H. Smith before him, he notes the features of 'the Chinese character'. But his list is very different, and much more positive, than Smith's. The eight characteristics, in the order listed by Lin, are mellowness, patience, indifference, old roguery, pacifism, contentment, humour, and conservatism. The first given is the basic one, being in a sense the source of the others. 'A mellow understanding of life and of human nature is, and always has been, the Chinese ideal of character, and from that understanding other qualities are derived, such as pacifism, contentment, calm and strength of endurance which distinguish the Chinese character.'[20] Lin continues that 'strength of character is really strength of the mind, according to the Confucianists,' and thus makes clear the importance he attaches to Confucianism as the linchpin of the Chinese character and culture.

Confucianism looms large also in the image Lin Yutang conveyed to the West of the Chinese family system. Not surprisingly, he emphasizes the importance of the family in Chinese culture: 'it very nearly takes the place of religion by giving man a sense of social survival and family continuity, thus satisfying man's craving for immortality'. But he also brings out some points of Chinese society which might go against the grain of a Western reader's values, such as that 'the family system is the negation of individualism itself, and it holds a man back, as the reins of the jockey hold back the dashing Arabian horse'. He is quite clear also that the family system is the root of a great deal of corruption in China, such as 'nepotism and favouritism, robbing the nation to enrich the family', and so on.[21] He is thus quite happy to acknowledge the disadvantages the family system might bring.

Though Lin Yutang does not hesitate to criticize, the overall images which his book conveys are positive. Nowhere is this clearer than in the opening passage of the concluding 'epilogue'.

> In the general survey of Chinese art and Chinese life, the conviction must have been forced upon us that the Chinese are past masters in the art of living. There is a certain wholehearted concentration on the material life, a certain zest for living, which is mellower, perhaps deeper, anyway just as intense as in the West. In China the spiritual values have not been separated from the material values, but rather help man in a keener enjoyment of life as it falls to our lot. This accounts for our joviality and our incorrigible humour.[22]

An American writer who claimed to have learned from Lin Yutang an image of Chinese 'finesse and subtlety'[23] probably spoke for many of his generation. Lin identified with the Westernized traditional scholar. His book contains no section on the peasantry, who rate but few mentions throughout, even in the section on social classes. The image of China his book passed on to the West was a highly conservative one, in which the scholar class ruled as it had always done, and that was how things ought to be.

Of all Chinese image-makers, the most influential one in the United States, and especially during the war against Japan and after, was Chiang Kai-shek's wife Song Meiling. Not only did she publish in the West, but she made an official visit to the United States in 1943, making many public speeches and addressing both houses of the Congress, her primary aim being to appeal for greater assistance against the Japanese, then in occupation of China. She was enthusiastically supported by Henry Luce and his empire, as well as by the overwhelming majority of other media in the United States. Just after she appeared before Congress, whom one scholarly account claims she 'electrified' with her passion and personality,[24] President F. D. Roosevelt gave a joint press conference, at which he described China as having become one of the 'great democracies of the world' in the previous half-century.[25]

The images Song Meiling conveyed both to her own people and to the West were highly optimistic. Her favourite slogan was *resurgam*, a Latin word meaning 'I shall rise again'. This idea of resurgence, of rebirth, summed up for her 'the spirit that is China'.[26] It recurs throughout her articles and was given to the title of her very popular book *China Shall Rise Again*, which was published during the War. An allied image is that of patriotism, the major Chinese quality that will bring about the resurgence.

The images that Song Meiling conveyed to the West were not all positive. She balanced Lin Yutang's eight Chinese characteristics with 'seven deadly sins', which had held the country back. They were: self-seeking, 'face', cliquism, defeatism, inaccuracy, lack of self-discipline, and evasion of responsibility. 'Long ago they combined to retard our emergence as a first-class world power, and they now delay our victory in this war,' she wrote.[27] The invasion by the 'barbaric enemy' Japan brought one strong advantage, namely that it has 'shocked the suffering patriotic people into a realization of the nature of some of our national problems' and would give them the will to overcome these deadly sins, and lead on to resurgence.[28] So even a negative image ends with optimism.

Western Residents in China

Apart from scholars, Western or Chinese, another important group of image-formulators in the first half of the twentieth century was Western residents in China. These themselves fell into several categories: journalists, diplomats and their families, long-term travellers, and others.

Despite the very low opinion Lin Yutang held of them, one group of foreign residents worth noting as transmitters of images to the West was the 'old China hands'. The term was formerly applied usually to the veteran British businessman, 'the old-time treaty port resident who had never outgrown the outlooks and attitudes of the previous century'.[29] These people were attached to their comforts, their clubs, and their profits. They were mainly imperialist in their views, but were not without good will towards the Chinese in general and individual Chinese in particular.

A well-known example is Carl Crow, who wrote several books about China. At first a newspaperman he later became an advertising and merchandising agent. His style is flippant and it is often hard to tell when he is writing seriously. His book *Four Hundred Million Customers*, the writing of which he justifies through his profession,[30] reads mainly like a parody, but was certainly serious in attempting to tell Western businessmen how to cash in on China's large population. The book was first published in March 1937 and went through two more impressions in as many months. Its fourth was in November 1937, the outbreak of war in China not having diverted the publishers from yet another impression.

In another book written during the war itself and published in 1941, Crow exults over the prosperity of his life in the first seven months of 1937. 'We foreign devils were making money,' he says. 'The reformed National government had been in power for ten years,' doing good things such as building public works like railways and hospitals, 'instead of stealing the money more or less openly as had been the immemorial custom in China'.[31] But the good times of profits under Chiang Kai-shek were destroyed by the Japanese, and Crow and his cronies had to get out. 'The Shanghai which we left behind as refugees is a city which will live only in memories.' For such people, China was just a playground for the rich foreigners, and basically that was the image they passed on to the West. Crow finishes his book with the sentence: 'The era of the foreign devil is ended.'[32] Flippant as ever, the phraseology suggests also bitterness, but with resignation.

The years 1900 to 1949 saw the climax of Western missionary activity in China, especially from the United States. In 1908 the American Congress voted to dedicate the unused balance of the Boxer indemnity to education. While it would be unfair to deny generous motives in this action, the effect was to enable Americans to use money paid to them for the 1900 invasion to impart their own values to Chinese intellectuals. Foreign missionary schools, and even other sorts of social services like hospitals, mushroomed. The missionaries went as teachers and 'old-fashioned brimstone fundamentalism was still very present'.[33] But many were very impressed by Chinese culture, especially the politeness and earnestness of their students. As one prominent American missionary educator interpreted the conversion of another missionary: 'He had come to the Far East with a message that he was on fire to give, but in the process of transmission the East had spoken its message to him.'[34] Many who went to change China were themselves changed. Communication between the Western and Chinese worlds was definitely taking place, though not necessarily only in the direction intended by the Westerners.

So the image of the Chinese the missionaries presented to the West, in which courtesy and serious-mindedness held an important place, was in general incomparably more positive than that of their nineteenth-century predecessors. Henry Luce, with his missionary background, assisted in this endeavour, so that the missionaries could be assured of great support from the American media and public, and in particular *Time* and the other magazines of the Luce empire. One scholarly account suggests that it was the missionaries who 'fostered the original American sense of sentimentality and romanticism about China'. In defence of this suggestion he cites no less a person than Dean Acheson, who was US Secretary of State from 1949 to 1953. Acheson claimed that, early in the century, virtually all towns in the United States had a society which aimed 'to collect funds and clothing for Chinese missions, to worry about those who labored in distant, dangerous, and exotic vineyards of the Lord, and to hear the missionaries' inspiring reports'.[35] A positive image of China became closely bound up with the aim of spreading Christianity there.

In the 1920s, there was a major nationalist surge in China, culminating in Chiang Kai-shek's victory in 1927. Missionaries had no choice but to accept this reality, and many were quite sympathetic to its aims anyway. In 1928 the Jerusalem conference of the International Missionary Council, a body representing Protestants all over the world, accepted a statement from a Chinese Christian that missionaries in China ought to have a 'real love for China' and be 'willing to work with the Chinese'.[36] Moreover, the National Government of Chiang Kai-shek imposed regulations on missionary schools which forbade religious propaganda and aimed to promote nationalism. There was a strong move in favour of Chinese control of Christian organizations in China. Many American Protestant missionaries came to support revision of the unequal treaties which the Western powers had imposed on China in the nineteenth century, even in the teeth of opposition and resentment from their compatriots in the business and government worlds.[37] The result was that the improved images of China sent home by the missionaries tended to apply not only to the people and culture, but to the government's political aspirations as well.

A famous short-term resident was Osbert Sitwell, worth mentioning not only because of his distinction as a writer, but because he expressed images widely held at the time about China. He lived for several months in Beijing in 1934, calling it Peking, and was much influenced by several Western residents who had lived in the city for a somewhat longer time than he. His motive in going to China was escapism, as he informs the reader in the opening sentence of his preface and in the title of his book. His desire was to exult in the wonders of Peking's past, to 'see the wonderful beauty of the system of life' China incorporated 'before this should perish'. He was aware of growing communist influence among university students, but was not really interested in 'the Social Struggle'.[38] The dominant images he portrays are of a grand and to some extent surviving past, and of a witty and cheerful people, who are 'self-indulgent, fond of food and good things and gossip, kindly and deeply attached to their families', and fond of life.[39] At the same time, he was aware of a darker side of society, and of grinding poverty.

> Nowhere in the most backward European states can these crowds of blind people, beggars, cripples, lepers and afflicted of every sort, be seen: and no amount of accidental beauty can excuse their suffering, even though the national temperament of the poor creatures makes them laugh, as they do, between their bouts of professional whining and cringing, at their own misery.[40]

The benign national characteristics may not justify the poverty for Sitwell, but they do go some way towards alleviating its effects.

American Radical Journalism

In contrast to the views of missionaries and other residents in China, the United States produced in the first half of this century a radical tradition of journalism, which not only believed that the Chinese Communist Party could win, but also welcomed that possibility. The three famous names are Agnes Smedley (1892–1950), Anna Louise Strong (1885–1970) and Edgar Snow (1905–1972).[41] Much has been written about them and in September 1984 a society was set up in China in their honour. All three wrote widely in newspapers and books to bring the activities of the Communist forces to the world's attention and to promote a favourable image of the changing course of China's history.

Agnes Smedley came from a very poor background. It was her life experiences and those of her family that made her into a radical socialist and feminist. Her first major work, published in 1929, was an autobiographical novel called *Daughter of Earth*; that was how she regarded herself. In contrast to Lin Yutang, one of her major concerns was the peasantry. However, she had no time at all for the traditional peasant mentality with its oppression of the poor and especially women. 'Semi-feudal, agrarian China,' she wrote in her book on the Jiangxi Soviet and the Red Army, 'is corrupt, degenerate, ignorant, incapable of developing the country, incapable of taking one step that can possibly raise the productive or purchasing power of the Chinese masses'.[42] Even in the mid-1930s she believed that only the Communist Party was willing and able to change society; she supported it openly and strongly and predicted its victory.

Anna Louise Strong came from a much better educated and more prosperous background than Snow or especially Smedley. She had by far the longest life of the three, and was the only one who had the opportunity actually to live in the People's Republic of China for an extended length of time. She wrote numerous books and articles, not only about China, but also about the Soviet Union, Spain, and Mexico, including sixteen books published by prominent commercial American publishers between 1920 and 1946.[43] Her first visits to China were in the late 1920s and resulted in her two-volumed *China's Millions*, which, first published in 1928, later went through several versions and editions. From the middle of 1946 to February 1947, she lived in Yan'an and wrote extensively and glowingly about the society she found there, and about the Communist leaders, especially Mao. Just before the People's Republic was formally established she wrote that the Chinese, whose past century had been 'determined by every other nation,' had now 'conquered their country' so that 'China's future will be determined by the Chinese'.[44] There was no doubt in her mind that the Chinese Communist Party was responding effectively to Chinese patriotism, and would be able to transform the country to the benefit of the Chinese masses.

For Western images of China, the most influential of these three American journalists is Edgar Snow. He went to work in China in 1928 and in 1936 had what was then a unique opportunity to visit the revolutionary base area of northern Shaanxi and interview Mao Zedong. The Communist Party Chairman told Snow his life history and the reporter simply wrote it down and combined the narrative with his own impressions and experiences in the base area to form the classic *Red Star over China*. Snow himself modestly attributed its success to its being 'not only a "scoop" of perishable news but likewise of many facts of durable history',[45] but his being the first to record the early life of the eventual victor Mao ensured the continuing influence of his book. The image it transmitted to the West was of 'Chinese dedicated to national integrity and social justice'.[46] The fact that they were Communists made his book controversial but also of strong appeal to the left. In Britain it was due mainly to the Left Book Club that over 100,000 copies of Snow's book were sold within a few weeks. On the other hand, the book sold much less well in Snow's own country, the original American edition selling only some 15,000 copies.[47]

Novels

Apart from two of the three radical journalists, another female American writer on China, and born in the same year as Smedley, was Pearl Buck (1892–1973). From an American China-based missionary background she spent almost all the first four decades of her life in China. Although she wrote much about actual events and experiences in China, she is most famous as a novelist, in particular for her best-selling work *The Good Earth*, and she thus brings us to that important image-formulating branch of literature: fiction.

The Good Earth exercised a greater influence in creating Western images of China and the Chinese than any other single work in the period under discussion. The publisher—John Day of New York— and the author were both American, so the novel's main impact was in the United States, but it was read very widely in other countries and was translated into over thirty languages, including at least three in the Soviet Union. According to the John Day Company, that firm alone sold over four million copies in the United States between 1931, its year of first publication, and 1972.[48] No other book on China had ever come anywhere near such sales in the West. Moreover, in 1937 *The Good Earth* was made into a film, which its studio estimated in 1955 to have been seen by some 23 million Americans and 42 million others all over the world.[49] One writer claims that 'a safe guess' would put the number of 'Americans exposed to Buck's creation in one form or another' at no less than 40 million.[50]

The Good Earth was unusual in its day (or indeed most others) in being a Western novel set in China and entirely about Chinese people, the great majority tending strongly to take Westerners as the main characters with the 'natives' or locals confined to subsidiary roles. The hero of *The Good Earth* is the peasant Wang Lung. The novel opens on his wedding day, when he is poor, but he soon becomes quite rich and then a landlord. He is extremely traditional in outlook and behaviour and very hardworking. His last words to his two sons are 'If you sell the land, it is the end,'[51] and this shows the central theme of the novel: the peasant's love for and attachment to land, the good earth.

Pearl Buck saw the peasantry as strong and stable, and the key to China's future. She was the first to give China's peasants, both male and female, a really human face that the West could understand. For this she deserves great credit. She was all her life very critical of the intellectuals whom she believed had no understanding of or love for the peasants. The overall image she portrays of the peasantry is an extremely positive one.

However, she pulls no punches about the faults. In particular, family matters and customs naturally loom very large in *The Good Earth*. Buck portrays an utterly sexist society in which the rich male gets everything and the women are seriously downtrodden. She does not gloss over the dangers inherent in the excessive emphasis on Confucian family relationships or the sufferings they can cause.

The image that Buck portrays is an essentially conservative one. The whole thrust of the novel is Wang's ability to move up the social ladder through traditional peasant strengths and virtues. As an old man he asks his grandsons, 'Do you study the Four Books?'. And when told that since the revolution nobody studies such Confucian material he answers: 'Ah, I have heard of a revolution, but I have been too busy in my life to attend to it. There was always the land.'[52]

It comes as no surprise that though Buck for a time expressed sympathy for the Communist Party because of its attention to the peasants, she rejected its ideology totally. 'She regarded the innate conservatism of the peasant as the chief bulwark against any effort to force what Buck regarded as the natural and gradual pace of change.'[53]

Though Pearl Buck thus shared with her contemporary and compatriot Agnes Smedley a vital concern with the peasantry as the vanguard of the future, the images the two women conveyed were basically antithetical. But the Buck view has at all times been very much more acceptable to conventional wisdom than that of Smedley and much more influential in the creation of images.

For images of China during the interwar years, one other novel besides *The Good Earth* stands supreme. It is *La condition humaine* (*Man's Fate*), by André Malraux (1901–76), a man with a truly remarkable career who, in addition to writing numerous novels and other works, occupied the position of French Minister of Culture under President Charles de Gaulle from 1958 to 1969. Though *Man's Fate* is by far his most famous and influential work, it is not his first book set in China, that being *Les conquérants* (*The Conquerors*), published in 1928, which focuses attention on a major strike in Guangzhou in 1925. Malraux spent only a brief time in China itself before the first publication of *Man's Fate* in 1933, yet it is acknowledged by virtually all commentators as a very profound study, not only of humankind as a whole but of China in particular. Malraux's experience in China could not compare with Pearl Buck's and his target audience was not as vast. Malraux is concerned only with urban people and not, like Buck, with the far more numerous peasants. But, to this writer at least, the images he portrays of China in *Man's Fate* are much more powerful than those achieved by Buck.

In one sense this is ironic, because in fact the great majority of the main characters in *Man's Fate* are foreigners. Most of it is set in Shanghai and Hankou against the background of the 1927 Revolution and ends as a total disaster with the victory of Chiang Kai-shek's troops and the suppression and death of the revolutionaries. Malraux was a Marxist at the time; and his sympathies for the left and for the ultimate dignity of the revolutionaries, even in defeat, are clear. Yet there are absolutely none of the images of optimism and enthusiasm that infuse the writings of Agnes Smedley or Anna Louise Strong. Despite the political import of the novel, Malraux was concerned as much with the destiny of humanity as with the Chinese Revolution itself. He summed up his intentions in the novel in June 1933 as follows:

> No one can endure his own solitude. Whether it is through love, fantasy, gambling, power, revolt, heroism, comradeship, opium, contemplation or sex, it is against this fundamental angst that consciously or not, the characters of this novel ... are defending themselves, engaged as they are to the point of torture and suicide in the Chinese Revolution, upon which for some years the destiny of the Asian world and perhaps the West depended.[54]

The main Chinese character is Ch'en Ta Erh. The novel opens with a graphic description of the anguish he feels as he hesitates to stab a man it is his duty to kill, his baptism in terrorism. Against the wishes of the Moscow-dominated Communist headquarters in Hankou, Ch'en tries to assassinate Chiang Kai-shek. As he awaits his proposed victim and his mind ranges, his dominant feeling is solitude: 'the ultimate solitude, for it is difficult for one who lives isolated from the everday world not to seek others like himself'.[55] Ch'en's final fate is to finish himself off accidentally by shooting as he lies dying after the terrorist act, but with the dreadful irony that Chiang has escaped and Ch'en is unaware of it.

The strongest images of China to come from the novel accord with Ch'en's psychology and fate: agony and defeat for the revolutionaries, misery and grim desperation for the poor people, and the total failure

of the Chinese to control their own destiny. The concluding section of
the novel sums up these images as 'the repression that had beaten
down upon exhausted China'.[56]

The gaps between the rich and poor are devastating in this novel,
not only in terms of material wealth but in those of lifestyle. The rich,
who are foreign, are able to scoop up their profits and indulge in their
pleasures through sex or escape through opium. French financial
activities in Shanghai are hardly affected by the Revolution. Although
there are vivid pictures of poverty among foreigners, the great majority
of the poor are of course Chinese, and pictures of teeming impoverished
and diseased humanity are many and graphic. Witness the following
conclusion to the part of the novel set in Hankou:

> The peace of the night once more. Not a siren, nothing but the
> lapping of the water. Along the banks, near the street-lamps
> crackling with insects, coolies lay sleeping in postures of people
> afflicted with the plague. Here and there, little round red posters;
> on them was figured a single character: HUNGER ... But, ...
> how choose the sacrifice, here, in this city to which the West
> looked for the destiny of four hundred million men and perhaps
> its own, and which was sleeping on the edge of the river in the
> uneasy sleep of the famished— in impotence, in wretchedness, in
> hatred?[57]

The image to emerge from *Man's Fate* is that it is not Chinese
people who make the crucial decisions which decide the fate of the
Chinese Revolution. The key revolutionary characters in the novel
are foreigners. Ch'en merely set himself apart from the revolution by
his individualistic attempt against Chiang's life. It was 'Moscow and
the enemy capitals of the West' which were organizing 'their opposing
passions over there in the night' and attempting to mould them in
ways that suited their own interests. The people were supporting the
Communists. 'The Communist propaganda had reached the masses
like a flood, because it was what they wanted, because it was their
own.'[58] The disastrous collapse of the Revolution in Shanghai was
due in part to the failure of Moscow and its clients in Hankou to
provide the necessary support.

In the history of English-language literature in the first half of the
twentieth century, Pearl Buck stands below a number of other writers
with works set in or about China. One who certainly does occupy a
position at or near the peak of English literature of the time is
W. Somerset Maugham. Though the majority of his 'Asian' works are

set in Malaya, Borneo, and Singapore, there are some which concern China, including a travel book about it, and he is, among literary figures, an appropriate representative of creators of Western images of China.

About half of Somerset Maugham's novel *The Painted Veil*, first published in 1925, is set in China. It concerns a young married English woman, Kitty, who goes with her husband to a cholera-striken town in Guangdong province on the rebound from a finally unsuccessful love affair with a senior British official in Hong Kong. It is supposed to take place a few years after the 1911 Revolution. Just as in Maugham's other works, all the main characters are European, in this novel mostly English, but with some French nuns who run an orphanage in the Chinese town.

Because China is rarely more than background, the images of China are less powerful than those of the Europeans who live there. What is most striking is how kind, even saintly, are the French nuns, who work tirelessly and unselfishly for the locals against the background of a dirty, poverty- and disease-ridden country. Among the strongest images of the Chinese is gratitude for what is done for them. Notwithstanding his acknowledged cynicism, Maugham presents an immensely positive image of missionary activity in China.

Despite the epidemic, the image of China which Maugham conveys is quite positive. A French nun expresses a strong wish and an English customs official called Waddington the intention never to leave China or return home.[59] Though at first Kitty finds the Chinese orphans 'repulsive' and 'hardly human',[60] she grows very attached to them when she gets to know them; the lesson seems to be that her racism is based solely on ignorance. In an encounter with Waddington not long after arriving in China, Kitty, who 'had never heard the Chinese spoken of as anything but decadent, dirty, and unspeakable', finds to her surprise that he has adopted the Chinese view of life, namely that 'in China alone was it so led that a sensible man might discern in it a sort of reality'.[61] The image which Maugham seems to be intending to convey is that for all its faults China has a point of view worth hearing and that it grows upon Western residents to the point where they are quite happy to regard it as their home.

Maugham had travelled in China for some four months in 1919 and 1920. He had met a variety of people but had 'concentrated on the British'.[62] In 1922, he had a play premiered set in China, *East of Suez*, and in the same year published his travel notes on China, entitled *On a Chinese Screen*. In the latter work, he was himself very proud of his description of the Great Wall. Maugham makes a revealing comment on the Chinese coolies, whose faces he thought good-natured and frank. It is similar to the image of cheerfulness within suffering, which Osbert Sitwell was to convey some years later.

> It seems natural to feel admiration for their endurance and their spirit. But you will be thought somewhat absurd if you mention your admiration to the old residents of China. You will be told with a tolerant shrug of the shoulders that the coolies are animals and for two thousand years from father to son have carried burdens, so it is no wonder if they do it cheerfully.[63]

The clear message both of this passage and of Kitty's initial reaction to the Chinese orphans as 'half animals' is that Maugham himself felt no racist revulsion against the Chinese, but that he considered other Westerners to do so, at least against those of the poorer classes. 'Old residents' surely refers only to Europeans, and especially British, on whom as we saw he had concentrated his perceptive attentions, hardly to Chinese. Maugham's comments suggest that racist images of the Chinese may have been more widespread among those who did not write about China and its people, than among those who did.

Conclusion

The half-century separating the Boxer uprising from the victory of the Chinese Communist Party thus saw a very wide range of Western images of China and the Chinese, from racist and imperialist on the one hand to radically socialist and feminist on the other, with many in between. But the great weight of published opinion was, in its own terms, positive about, or sympathetic towards, China. Malraux could write with bleak pessimism about one phase of the Chinese revolution, but he still supported the revolutionary process. Most of the missionaries, and even businessmen like Eric Crow, thought they were sympathetic to the Chinese people. And the War against Japan improved China's image even more.

In the United States images became both more active and more positive with the rise of the influence of *Time* and Henry Luce in the 1930s. The Sino-US relationship from the time Japan attacked Pearl Harbour late in 1941 has been described as 'like marriage after an over-long engagement—a shotgun marriage, if you will, but still a happy union'.[64] According to Henry R. Luce, his missionary father, Henry W. Luce, died happy the very day after the Japanese attacked Pearl Harbour, because 'he lived long enough to know that now China and America are both on the same side'.[65] An American sampling in 1942, which may well have shown rather similar results in other Western countries, showed the five main 'images' of Chinese people as hardworking, honest, brave, religious, and intelligent, in that order.[66] In other words, the perceptions of Americans were very much more positive about Chinese as people than those portrayed either by Lin Yutang or Song Meiling. It is true that, even in the United States, there was a significant body of opinion from the last years of the War and down to the victory of the Communists, which became increasingly critical of Chiang and his regime and viewed the growing support of the Communists with equanimity.[67] However, they never came near to representing the dominant images of China.

The reason for the shift in opinion towards positive images of China lay not in China itself but in the West. Between 1900 and 1949 China did not improve to anything like the extent Western images of it did. The West approved of the Chinese essentially because it believed China was moving in a direction suitable to Western political, economic, and social interests, and wished to encourage the trend. This view is substantiated by the change that took place in the Western image after 1900. Having excoriated the Chinese and imposed a humiliating defeat on them, the West decided it could forge a better and more favourable relationship by generosity, or at least the appearance of it. Western images of China were still part of the 'power/knowledge' relationship of which Michel Foucault has spoken. For all her very genuine sympathy with the Chinese peasantry, Pearl Buck's view was essentially in accord with Western interests, which is why it could be so enthusiastically promoted and received. Her two worlds, with which this chapter began, the 'clean Presbyterian American' and 'merry not-too-clean Chinese' worlds, were still very much in existence in the late 1940s. Communication between them was much better than it had been in 1900, but it was still highly imperfect and selective.

Notes

1   Buck, *My Several Worlds*, p. 10.
2   Conger, *Letters from China*, p. 168.
3   Ibid., p. viii.

4   Savage-Landor, *China and the Allies*, Vol. I, p. 257.
5   Conger, *Letters from China*, p. 168.
6   Ibid., p. 188.
7   Marchant (ed.), *The Siege of the Peking Legations*, p. 148.
8   Kaminski and Unterrieder, *Von Österreichern und Chinesen*, p. 335.
9   Quoted ibid., pp. 405–6.
10   Isaacs, *Images of Asia*, pp. 142–3.
11   Kaminski and Unterrieder, *Von Österreichern*, p. 336.
12   Quoted by R. H. Scott, 'Foreword', in Marchant (ed.), *The Siege*, p. xx.
13   Ibid., pp. xxiv–xxv.
14   See Jespersen, *American Images of China*, p. 28.
15   Ibid., pp. 36–37.
16   Ibid., p. 12.
17   Lin, *My Country and My People*, p. 11.
18   Gilbert, *What's Wrong with China*, p. 14, 49.
19   Lin, *My Country and My People*, p. xiv.
20   Ibid., pp. 40–41.
21   Ibid., pp. 168–70.
22   Ibid., p. 326.
23   See Isaacs, *Images of Asia*, p. 79.
24   Jespersen, *American Images of China*, p. 95.
25   Ibid., p. 96.
26   Chiang, *China Shall Rise Again*, pp.3–7.
27   'Seven Deadly Sins', in *China Shall Rise Again*, p. 38.
28   Ibid., pp. 42–3.
29   Isaacs, *Images of Asia*, p. 150.
30   Crow, *Four Hundred Million Customers*, p. 11.
31   Crow, *Foreign Devils in the Flowery Kingdom*, p. 326.
32   Ibid., p. 340.
33   Isaacs, *Images of Asia*, p. 147.
34   Earl Herbert Cressy, 'Converting the Missionary', *Asia* (June 1919), quoted by Isaacs in *Images of Asia*, p. 148.
35   Jespersen, *American Images of China*, p. 9.
36   See Hughes, *The Invasion of China by the Western World*, p. 101.
37   See Varg, *Missionaries, Chinese, and Diplomats*, pp. 198–211.
38   Sitwell, *Escape with Me!*, p. vii.
39   Ibid. p. 204.
40   Ibid., p. 331.
41   For a full-length biography of Strong, see Strong and Keyssar, *Right in her Soul*.
42   Smedley, *China's Red Army Marches*, p. xx.
43   For a bibliography of her books and pamphlets see Strong and Keyssar, *Right in her Soul*, pp. 377–78.
44   Strong, *The Chinese Conquer China*, p. 275.
45   Snow, 'Preface to the Revised Edition', *Red Star over China*, p. 20.
46   Jerome Ch'en, *China and the West*, p. 55.
47   Ibid. and Steele, *The American People and China*, pp. 171-2.
48   See Hunt, 'Pearl Buck', p. 59.
49   Jones, *The Portrayal of China and India on the American Screen*, p. 47.

50 Hunt, 'Pearl Buck', p. 34.
51 Buck, *The Good Earth*, p. 308.
52 Ibid., p. 303.
53 Hunt, 'Pearl Buck', p. 52.
54 Quoted in Madsen, *Malraux, A Biography*, p. 128.
55 Malraux, *Man's Fate*, p. 246.
56 Ibid., p. 359.
57 Ibid., p. 167.
58 Ibid., p. 155.
59 Maugham, *The Painted Veil*, pp. 140, 149.
60 Ibid., p. 117.
61 Ibid., p. 103.
62 Morgan, *Somerset Maugham*, p. 244.
63 W. Somerset Maugham, 'On a Chinese Screen', in *The Travel Books of W. Somerset Maugham*, p. 48.
64 Steele, *The American People and China*, p. 22.
65 Jespersen, *American Images of China*, p. 59.
66 Isaacs, *Images of Asia*, p. xix.
67 For coverage of this topic see Jespersen, *American Images of China*, pp. 108–71. Probably the most important book providing the counter to the images promoted by *Time* and its supporters was White and Jacoby, *Thunder Out of China*, published in 1946, but its influence was inevitably very slight and short-lived by comparison with that of Luce's media empire. See Jespersen, *American Images of China*, pp. 130–31.

Part II

Western Images of the People's Republic of China

6
Contemporary Images of the People's Republic of China, 1949–66

The seventeen years or so separating the birth of the People's Republic of China (PRC; 1949) from the beginning of the Cultural Revolution (1966) marked the first time in history that a Chinese government had firmly, unequivocally, persistently, and successfully resisted the major interests of Western capitalism. Very early in the period, also, Chinese troops and those of several Western countries fought on opposite sides in the Korean War (1950–53). On the whole, the images of China that Western governments tried to convey to their peoples were more negative during these years than at any preceding time.

In the United States especially, and to some extent in other Western countries, there was a strong and rather widespread feeling that the West had 'lost China'. Just as before 1949, the positive image of Chiang Kai-shek, and correspondingly negative image of Mao Zedong and the Communists, was strongly promoted by Henry Luce and his media empire, in which *Time* was pre-eminent. Eric Hodgins, at one time the managing editor of *Fortune*, remarked that 'Luce stuck utterly and completely to Chiang Kai-shek until the day of his death' in 1967.[1] Not surprisingly, Luce and his media outlets supported American government policy towards China, and Western, especially American, missionary history and behaviour there. It also attacked the Communists for their hostile policies towards the United States and its representatives.

This feeling that the United States had 'lost' China was especially pronounced among missionaries, who thought of themselves as bringing to the Chinese the great gifts of their own beliefs, but was not confined to them. Harold Isaacs quotes a public opinion analyst thus: 'I would say that Americans are greatly disappointed. Their earlier idea of the Chinese as friendly, honest people was wrong. The Chinese bit the hand that fed them.'[2] The analyst's underlying assumption was apparently that refusal to be grateful for handouts from the United States was the equivalent of dishonesty.

Yet there were certain variations and gradations. The peoples of the United States and Australia accepted a more negative image of China than those of most other Western countries. One writer, noting that West Europeans began visiting China in the 1950s some two decades before the Americans did, stated that, unlike Americans, European intellectuals travelled to China without feeling the need 'to expiate the sins' their country had committed against China in the first years after liberation, and 'with less of an expectation of an impending crisis in their own society'.[3] Within each of the Western countries there were differing views. Insofar as they were concerned about China, the trade unions and the left held, not surprisingly, a far more positive view of China than conservative opinion. Communist parties saw China as a model for the rapid development of a miserably poor country.

It is important to note that the number of Westerners resident in China dropped sharply after 1949. The Americans can serve as the most spectacular example. In 1937 there were 13,300 American residents in China, but in 1957 the figure was about 100. Admittedly other countries were affected less drastically than the United States, but they, too, had far fewer residents in China after 1949 than before that date. Virtually all the missionaries went home. Perhaps even more important, the number of Western visitors to China of the kind who might contribute to creating images fell sharply after 1949. Among those who did go, most spoke to somewhat restricted audiences at home, such as peace groups, friendship societies, and other left-wing associations.

Yet although the Westerners in general had only a dim knowledge of events in China, there were in fact quite a few opportunities to find out. Some journalists and others from the West did visit or reside in China, and there was a whole army of them in Hong Kong, whose government carefully monitored what went on in China through the press, radio broadcasts, and from accounts of refugees. China became very much part of the academic political science, economics, and anthropology trades.

Negative Images 1949–66

It was a common basic assumption among those holding hostile images of China that the Communists had created a vast propaganda network, which aimed to deceive everybody, especially foreigners. To be taken in showed the observer to be naive. Guides selected excellent or exceptional sites or units to show the visitor in an effort to demonstrate how happy the Chinese were under the Chinese Communist Party (CCP). Everything ordinary was out of bounds and it was more or less impossible for a foreign visitor to establish a genuine or frank relationship with a Chinese citizen.

The image of China that separates this period, or most of it, from any other is that of Soviet domination. The origin of this important image was the American administration. On 30 July 1949, even before the formal establishment of the PRC, the US Secretary of State, Dean Acheson, made a statement on the rule of the CCP in a 'letter of transmittal' with the China White Paper entitled 'United States Relations with China', itself published on 5 August. In the letter Acheson declared, among other points, that 'the Communist leaders have foresworn their Chinese heritage and have publicly announced their subservience to a foreign power, Russia'.[4] This was Acheson's somewhat fanciful interpretation of Mao Zedong's declaration, put forward on 30 June in 'On the People's Democratic Dictatorship', that China would 'lean to one side', that of the Soviet Union.

The same image was taken up in journalistic, academic and other quarters. In a long and scholarly treatment of Sino-Soviet relations published in 1956, Richard L. Walker wrote that between 1949 and 1954 there had been no important instances 'when the Mao regime failed to extend support and allegiance to the USSR'.[5] This 'allegiance' he considered was the factor which had made it possible for 'the top leaders in Red China' to achieve 'positions of power in their own country and abroad far beyond their probable expectations'.[6] However, to his credit, Walker does go on to cast doubt on whether this allegiance would last. The 'unity, strength, and determined opposition of the world outside the iron curtain' had a chance of making the Chinese leaders change their policy.[7]

The French journalist Robert Guillain, who visited China in the mid-1950s, drew the conclusion that China was in the complete thrall of the Russians. 'China believes that the only way to go fast is blindly to copy the USSR'.[8] In contrast to Walker, he saw only 'a very remote possibility' of 'a revolt of the Chinese colossus against her Russian partner'. If it came at all, it would not be until the end of the century.[9]

Although the major split came in the late 1950s, there was one Western image of China that was related closely to that of Soviet domination but still survived, namely that of China as a threat. The

American government in the 1950s and 1960s based much of its foreign policy on the proposition that China was a threat to its neighbours and the world. The Korean War was critical in hardening the US anti-China policy and in the creation of negative Western images of China, giving the United States government the grounds it wanted to implant among its own public the verdict that China was a threat to global security. 'Aggressive China Becomes a Menace' headlined *Life* magazine on 20 November 1950, just after the intervention of Chinese troops. 'China's Red Army', it said, 'a guerrilla rabble 20 years ago, had been built into a menacingly Russianized fighting force'. On 23 January 1951 the US Senate called on the United Nations to 'declare Communist China an aggressor in Korea', which it duly did nine days later. An American army colonel predicted to a Boston audience in February 1956 that the Chinese army would grow by 1970 to be 'the world's most dynamic fighting machine' and this process would place the survival of the United States itself in doubt.[10]

The US government's image of China as a threat was widely accepted among Americans. Moreover, China's threat image worsened with the Sino-Soviet split and its acquisition of nuclear weapons in 1964. Gallup Polls were taken on the question of whether the Soviet Union or China was seen as the 'greater threat to world peace'. In 1961, 49 per cent nominated the Soviet Union, and only 32 per cent China, but by 1963 the latter figure had risen to 47 per cent and the next year to 56 per cent.[11] Not just the government, but the people too, believed that 'the sleeping dragon had awakened'.

Another important and very pervasive image in the West, exacerbated by the fact that China's government had embraced Marxism, was of China as a totalitarian society without any freedom. 'The communist regime, though it gives China strength, is a totalitarian one. It negates freedom absolutely.'[12] The US government considered as part of the 'free world' any country which supported American foreign policy objectives, no matter how it treated its own people. The way the CCP could neutralize opposition to its elimination of freedom was through 'brainwashing', a process that came to hold a quite important place in the West's hierarchy of images of China. Harold Isaacs remarks that 'for the Chinese there was a whole battery of relevant qualities to draw upon' to explain this dreadful practice, 'their inhuman cruelty, for one thing, and at its service, their inscrutability, their deviousness, their subtlety, and their devilish cleverness'.[13] On the other hand, one account from Britain explains brainwashing through the Chinese preference for trying 'to convert the intelligentsia' over the terror and killings practised by Stalin.[14]

In the period 1949–66, the CCP on a number of occasions initiated campaigns that depended on 'mobilizing the masses'. For many in the West this was part of a totalitarian system of government and conjured up an image of the 'faceless masses' with no individualism. French journalist Robert Guillain coined a famous phrase to describe the regimentation and total loss of individual freedom among the Chinese: 'An ant hill, yes, that is what they have become—ants, blue ants.'[15]

André Malraux, famous as the author of *La condition humaine* discussed in Chapter 5, visited China in the summer of 1965 as the French Minister of Culture, the year after France established diplomatic relations with the PRC. Malraux devoted most of the account he wrote of his visit to meetings with state and CCP leaders, especially Mao Zedong, but does make some general comments on China as well. He found the sending of urban people to the countryside as 'boringly rigid as was compulsory military service in Europe' and was shocked to find the Party's slogans never questioned. His comments are thus still negative, though not nearly as caustic as Guillain's a few years earlier. He adds: 'But slogans are only followed if the masses remain mobilized. Mao can only build China with volunteers. He is more anxious to make China than to make war'.[16] Even though finding the result abhorrent himself, Malraux thus seemed quite willing to give Mao the benefit of reasonably good intentions in his efforts at mass mobilization.

It is true that the CCP regarded the mass line and individualism as in mutual contradiction and favoured the former. The relative lack of Western journalists and other writers did not help attach individual personalities to the 'blue ants', or faces to the masses. In a book about China's 'red masters' that is a selection of its CCP leaders, well-known American journalist and novelist Robert Elegant praised them for being bold, but went on to argue that their 'very boldness may undo them when it strikes the bed-rock of integrity in Chinese society and the Chinese individual'.[17] He assumed that anti-individualism was not only dishonest but also un-Chinese, an image shared by many in the West.

Fiction written and wholly or partly set in the period 1949 to 1966 provides a very similar set of images. Pearl Buck, author of *The Good Earth* discussed in Chapter 5, is certainly the most famous relevant author. She had continued writing voluminously after returning to live in the United States from the mid-1930s onward and remained an image-formulator during the 1950s and 1960s. According to her own account it was the fact that she nearly lost her life at the hands of a Communist army that turned her against the Communists and made her realize she was American, despite being Chinese 'in education and feeling'.[18] In 1954, she published her autobiography and, although it does not have much to say about the Communist government, its attitudes are fiercely hostile, and show her quarrel with the Communists to have been much more deep-seated than being based on a single incident, however traumatic that may have been. In particular, she believes that China should never have overthrown the monarchy. 'The Throne should have been upheld, the system maintained, and within that framework reforms carried out.'[19] According to her, the British model is more appropriate for China than the American one. She advocated gradualist reform, not revolution. 'It is dangerous to try to save people—very dangerous indeed!' Heaven may be 'an inspiring goal, but what if on the way the soul is lost in hell?'[20]

One of Buck's later novels is *Letter from Peking*, which tells of an American woman's marriage to the son of a Chinese father and American mother. When the Communists come to power he decides to stay in China, but she returns home with their son to the United States, where her life is dominated by dreams that her husband will come to join her and their son. At first the husband is optimistic about the new order: 'I believe that a new day is coming in this old, old country of mine,' he writes in his first letter to her.[21] However, with the passage of time, the situation deteriorates for him and eventually he tries to flee from China, but is shot and killed in the process.

This story conveys the main image of the PRC. It is a government so oppressive that people eventually attempt to escape from it, so cruel that its representatives do not hesitate to shoot on sight. It is a regime that allows no freedom and censors letters, and the author goes to considerable pains to describe how the various letters were smuggled out of China. Nevertheless, a strong image in the novel is that it was patriotism that compelled the husband to stay in China in the first place, and thus expresses the initial Communist appeal to the Chinese intense love of their country. On the other hand, the virtue of patriotism comes over as negative, in the sense that it implies hostility to the West in general and the United States in particular.

A set of completely trivial adventure stories written in and referring to the period under review in this chapter is Captain W. E. Johns's *Biggles* books. Although by a man who knew virtually nothing about China, these books were powerful image-formulators, at least among boys in several Western countries. Those with sections set in China show it as an oppressed country of fear, where those 'very fine men', the missionaries, are 'brutally murdered' and require saving by courageous airmen with a legal right to fly into China to get them, no matter what the government of the day may think.[22] The country is run by sadistic and wicked Communists, utterly subservient to the Russians. The army 'will kill anybody for the pleasure of it, including their own people if they're in the mood'.[23] One of these adventure novels is set at or near the famous Dunhuang Buddhist caves. 'The first man to see this amazing shrine,' we are told, was Sir Aurel Stein, who was shown the secret library there 'by the guardian priest'.[24] (Apparently Johns does not consider the priest a man and reserves that appellation for adult male persons from such civilized continents as Europe.) Apart from its culture, this part of China is a place to avoid, because 'life is held cheaply, and death by violence a thing so commonplace that no one bothers much about it'.[25]

In economic terms, there was a tendency until the late 1950s to balance successes against the frightful human cost. Robert Guillain suggests the following formula to sum up his impressions of China: 'Material balance sheet remarkable—spiritual balance sheet terrifying.'[26] In 1956, Richard Walker was prepared to acknowledge that 'the Mao regime will accomplish further impressive feats' such as vast irrigation projects, flood control, road building, and defence works. But it is essentially brute force which makes any such achievements possible. 'Despite bureaucratic inefficiency, oppression which may increase passive resistance, and a population problem which grows more acute, it [the Mao regime] has the power to mobilize its great human resources.'[27]

In 1958 Mao Zedong instituted an unsuccessful, indeed disastrous, attempt to speed up economic and social change in China in a movement he called the Great Leap Forward, one part of which was the establishment of collective rural units called people's communes. The CCP was asking too much of the individualistic Chinese, especially the peasants, and was guilty not only of oppression, of trying to change human nature, but of incompetent planning. 'Great leap—great failure'[28] was a popular verdict among economists and ordinary people.

Its enormous population gave China an image of actual and potential economic backwardness, and made it loom large as a negative example among impoverished third world countries with serious population problems. Already the world's most populous country, China suffered from a population growth-rate that was excessive and unnecessary. The well-known and highly regarded journalist and specialist on China, Dick Wilson, wrote in 1966 that 'this "Malthusian counter-revolution" blunts the successes of China's industrial revolution by providing more mouths to feed, more hands to employ, each year'.[29] His was a sober, and typical, view.

Positive Images

Up to this point we have considered the dominant images of the PRC in the West between 1949 and 1966, most of them heavily negative. There was, however, a whole range of rather more positive images.

In the first place, there were many who did not accept the image of China as a threat to world peace. Some saw China itself as under threat from the United States or other powers and explained China's actions in those terms. Others saw China as upholding the socialist principles to which she claimed to adhere. One opinion analysed China's foreign policy actions mainly in terms of the defence of its national interests. In this view China merely wanted to wipe out the humiliations of past encroachments against itself and desired respect in the world community. There was thus no need to see its actions as a threat. Professor C. P. FitzGerald of the Australian National University was an influential exponent of this view.[30] The three particular examples of Chinese aggression most often cited to 1966 were intervention in the Korean War, the annexation of Tibet, and the Sino-Indian border war of 1962. Dick Wilson was among those who presented an alternate point of view on each of them, not so much to justify China's actions as to discredit the notion that they showed China to be bellicose, aggressive, or a threat to Asian or world peace.[31] On the basis of his own view Wilson not only favoured but also predicted detente between China and foreign countries. 'Communist China is not an impossible country, a nation condemned to perpetual mistrust and isolation,' he said. Western policies had 'fed the pain and insecurity, rather than sought to overcome them' but still he believed that 'time is on the side of reconciliation'.[32]

A very early and powerful positive image of the new communist China came from the hand of Han Suyin in her novel *A Many-Splendoured Thing*. Completed in July 1951 it was first published the following year by Jonathan Cape in London and has been through many impressions and editions, as well as being made into a film. It is primarily a story of a love affair between a Chinese-European woman and a British journalist who is eventually killed in the Korean War.

Most of it is actually set either in Hong Kong or in China *before* the final victory of the CCP. Yet the spectre of the CCP looms very large in the story and comes over as a dominantly positive force, one which might well take away individual freedoms, but would at the same time make the Chinese people once more proud to be Chinese, and save the poor and oppressed masses. Many of the best and most honest Westernized intellectuals chose to return home after the CCP's victory, suggests the author. 'They chose what might overwhelm them, not through cowardice, nor through opportunism, but because they had a social conscience, they loved their people, and they had a deep need to be whole again, unfrustrated in service to a land so much in need of them.'[33]

Among Americans it was Edgar Snow who most successfully told his countrymen that, for all its failings, China had benefitted from the revolution. The old China left behind was nothing to idealize, nothing to wish revived. As noted in Chapter 5, Snow had already worked in China as a journalist before 1949 and acquired a reputation for knowledge of the country and especially of the CCP. He revisited China in 1960 and on the basis of extensive travels and interviews, including two with Zhou Enlai, wrote *The Other Side of the River*. Because of its author's established credentials, its on-the-spot evidence, and its immense detail, it was probably not only the best but also the most influential among books depicting a basically positive set of images of contemporary China between 1949 and 1966.

Snow covers an enormous range of subjects: both foreign policy and domestic conditions, religion, education, social life, and the minority nationalities. He is critical in the sense that he does not accept data at face value, but is definitely friendly both to China and its government. It is in his chapter on Shanghai that he most warmly praises the Communists for having rid China of the scourges that had afflicted the city before 1949. 'Gone the pompous wealth beside naked starvation . . . gone the island of Western civilization flourishing in the vast slum that was Shanghai. Good-by [sic] to all that.'[34] The point his long and rhetorical list brings through with crystal clarity and unrelenting force is that, though old Shanghai may have been very comfortable for foreigners and their few rich Chinese hangers-on, it was little better than hell for the poor, who constituted the overwhelming majority of the people. For them an image of communist rule much more appropriate than 'totalitarianism', 'brainwashing', 'disappointment', or 'dishonesty' was progress and dignity; nor was it obvious to them why they should be so grateful to the West in general or the Americans in particular.

It is important to note that most of those Westerners with first-hand experience were not Americans, because their own government forbade Americans to visit China. The Africa specialist Basil Davidson, author of *Daybreak in China* (1953), was only one of a number of English writers sympathetic to the revolution. Sweden, which established full diplomatic relations with China as early as May 1950, produced several important firsthand accounts. Sven Lindqvist was a student of Chinese at Beijing University in 1961 and 1962. Journalist Jan Myrdal visited and made an intensive study of the village of Liu Ling in northern Shaanxi during the autumn of 1962. It was people such as these who helped create an image of the human face of China.

Sven Lindqvist's book details conversations with fellow Chinese students, enabling them to put forward their point of view. Lindqvist is critical of some aspects of Chinese policies, which is perhaps not surprising considering the period he was there. He criticizes the view of the outside world pushed in the Chinese media, and defends the many-sided images of China found in Sweden. However, he does convey an impression of improving conditions. 'During my time in China, Chinese society became more humane, more tolerant and more reasonable.'[35] He accepts the necessity of the revolution in China and urges the West to come to terms with it without prejudice or preconceived notions. Lindqvist stresses the need not merely to visit, but to live in China, and to know the Chinese language.

Jan Myrdal's approach was to interview as many people as possible in a single Chinese village, and find out as much as possible about their lives, what they thought about the world and about each other. The idea of such a project certainly emphasized both the importance of the peasants and their 'human faces'. Myrdal's overall impression—and the image he conveyed—was one of a puritanical rural society. He considered this both natural and reasonable, and certainly did not portray the communes as a disastrous failure, nor did he appear to favour free enterprise as a solution to their problems. He suggested that 'Western experts on contemporary China gleefully report its failings' but, while he was not prepared to predict the eventual success of the Chinese rural economy, he was quite definite that a breakdown in China would be a catastrophe not only for China but for the world at large.[36]

Myrdal comments on the popular image of economic failure in the wake of the Great Leap Forward by referring to the precarious food situation existing when he and his wife arrived in China. 'That the peasants in this book do not speak about the famine and the agricultural catastrophe after the "Great Leap Forward", does not mean that the famine did not exist.'[37] Edgar Snow's is a slightly, though not greatly, less grim picture. His experience in 1960, and research from 1959 to 1962, led him to doubt 'Western press editorials and headlines' that 'continued to refer to "mass starvation" in China'. His conclusion challenged the prevailing image in the West, which accepted the press editorials and headlines. 'Isolated instances of starvation due to neglect or failure of the rationing system were possible. Considerable malnutrition undoubtedly existed. Mass starvation? No.'[38]

As a matter of fact, it should be pointed out that even the creators of negative images tended to underestimate the scope of the calamity. In this instance it was Snow who was wrong: there certainly *was* 'mass starvation'. Figures issued in the 1980s by the economist Sun Yefang and officially by China's State Statistical Bureau suggest that this may have been twentieth-century China's most devastating famine. In 1960 the death rate reached 25.43 per thousand, as against 14.59 the previous year, while the birth rate declined somewhat and the overall population actually fell by about ten million.[39]

China's social revolution excited great praise from some in the West. Hewlett Johnson, Dean of Canterbury, was among the earlier and more fulsome admirers of China's 'new morality'. 'The moral change outweighed all other factors and lay at the root of all China's great successes; moral change which penetrated deep into the lives of the common people,' he declared.[40] Its main source he saw as 'the example of the whole-hearted self-sacrifice of the creative spirits who fashioned the new China',[41] meaning the work of the CCP members, and the similar labour of the People's Liberation Army. Johnson was naturally concerned about the fate of Christianity in China; he believed that despite the occurrence of attacks in isolated places, the government itself had countenanced no persecution of missionaries.[42]

One social issue Johnson considered was the treatment of women, and the picture he paints of 'liberated womanhood' is a very rosy one.[43] The French feminist Simone de Beauvoir (1908–86) wrote a long book on her visit to China in 1955 and includes a highly detailed and well-researched chapter on the family and the status of women.[44] She dwells at length on the sufferings of women in the past and finds enormous improvements under the current order. 'The family has been preserved and respected in such a way that it is based on free relations among individuals', she concludes. 'What has been abolished is the alienation of the individual from an oppressive and imperiously sanctified institution.' Marriage and maternity have become free, while women have won their 'human dignity'.[45] Simone de Beauvoir's account is incomparably more sophisticated than Hewlett Johnson's, her ideological assumptions very different from his, but her conclusions are actually rather similar.

Conclusion

It is true that very few Westerners went to China, let alone lived there, in the period from 1949 to 1966. Yet it appears from the above that what affected the West's images of China in those years was less ignorance than politics and ideology. Because of the severity of the Cold War split between the 'free world' and 'international communism', and the strains between left and right in politics in Western countries, attitudes towards China were a litmus test of one's ideological position on international issues.

For the United States, the leader of the 'free world' forces, a negative image of China was not only an ideological necessity but a weapon in international political rivalry. For this reason the US government worked to reinforce these negative images of China. Given the status of the United States as the dominant Western superpower, its immense wealth, and its will and influence on Western governments and communications, it is not surprising that it was so successful in maintaining the negative images of China, which were part of the Cold War climate of the 1950s and 1960s.

The response of the Chinese themselves to these developments was of course bitterly resentful and hostile. Statements and actions that to them seemed defence of their own national interests merely served to strengthen the dominance of the negative Western images over the positive. International events in Asia, such as the Korean War and the defeat of the French in Vietnam, merely proved how dangerous communism in Asia was, including or even especially that in China. The Great Leap Forward and its aftermath tarnished even the image of economic advance. The beginning of yet another war in Vietnam and the commitment of American troops against the 'Communist aggressors' early in 1965 did nothing to improve images of the northern Communist neighbour, China. And then the following year came the Cultural Revolution and with it new realities in China which, initially at least, merely served to confirm the West in its negative perceptions of Chinese communism.

Notes

1   Jespersen, *American Images of China*, p. 131.
2   Isaacs, *Images of Asia*, p. 194.
3   Hollander, *Political Pilgrims*, p. 279.
4   Quoted from MacFarquhar (ed.), *Sino-American Relations*, p. 68.
5   Walker, *China under Communism*, p. 271.
6   Ibid., p. 297.
7   Ibid., p. 300.
8   Guillain, *The Blue Ants*, p. 225.
9   Ibid., p. 66.
10   See Isaacs, *Images of Asia*, pp. 237–38.
11   See ibid., p. xvii.
12   Wint, *Common Sense about China*, p. 155.
13   Isaacs, *Images of Asia*, p. 218.
14   Wint, *Common Sense about China*, p. 156.
15   Guillain, *The Blue Ants*, p. 107.
16   Malraux, *Antimemoirs*, p.390.
17   Elegant, *China's Red Masters*, p. 254.
18   Buck, *China as I See It*, p. xi.
19   Buck, *My Several Worlds*, p. 381.
20   Ibid., p. 382.
21   Buck, *Letter from Peking*, p. 110. The novel has been through numerous paperback and other editions.
22   e.g. Johns, *Biggles in the Gobi*, p. 13.
23   Ibid., p. 50.
24   Ibid., p. 8.
25   Ibid., p. 51.
26   Guillain, *The Blue Ants*, p. 233.
27   Walker, *China under Communism*, p. 325.
28   For example, such was the heading of the relevant section in Robert F. Dernberger, 'Economic Realities', in Adams (ed.), *Contemporary China*, p. 135. Dernberger was in the Department of Economics, University of Chicago, and was one of thirty-five panelists at an important seminar on contemporary China held in Chicago in February 1966 and reflecting images just before the Cultural Revolution.
29   Dick Wilson, *A Quarter of Mankind*, p. 155.
30   See, for example, C. P. Fitzgerald, 'Chinese Foreign Policy', in Adams (ed.), *Contemporary China*, pp. 7–25.
31   Dick Wilson, *A Quarter of Mankind,*, p. 211–34.
32   Ibid., p. 275.
33   Han Suyin, *A Many-Splendoured Thing*, p. 282.
34   Snow, *The Other Side of the River*, p. 529.
35   Lindqvist, *China in Crisis*, p. 104.
36   Jan Myrdal, 'The Reshaping of Chinese Society', in Adams (ed.), *Contemporary China*, pp. 90–1.
37   Myrdal, *Report from a Chinese Village*, p. xxxiii.
38   Snow, *The Other Side of the River*, p. 620.
39   See *Zhongguo tongji nianjian 1983* (*Chinese Statistical Yearbook 1983*) (Chinese Statistical Press, Beijing, 1983), pp. 105, 103.

40   Johnson, *China's New Creative Age*, p. 175.
41   Ibid., p. 185.
42   Ibid., p. 110.
43   Ibid., pp. 32–40.
44   de Beauvoir, *La longue marche*, pp. 123–59.
45   Ibid., p. 159.

7

The Cultural Revolution, 1966–76: Images of a Present and Past Decade

In 1966 the Cultural Revolution erupted on the streets of Beijing and other Chinese cities, while the year 1976 saw the deaths of the Premier of the State Council Zhou Enlai and Communist Party Chairman Mao Zedong, as well as the fall of the Cultural Revolution's main supporters, the 'Gang of Four'. In China the decade 1966 to 1976 has, since 1977, been officially considered the period of the Cultural Revolution.

The same decade saw a change in the balance of power in the world and the East Asia region in particular. A war raged in Vietnam, which weakened the strategic position of the United States in the region. Although both China and the Soviet Union supported the victors in Vietnam they were even more hostile to each other at the end of the decade than they had been at the beginning. Meanwhile China and the United States moved closer to each other, and from 21 to 28 February 1972 US President Richard Nixon actually visited the PRC.

No sooner had Mao Zedong died in September 1976 than the main supporters of his Cultural Revolution, the 'Gang of Four', were overthrown. In the middle of the next year Deng Xiaoping, who had been one of the main victims of the Cultural Revolution, returned to the leadership. At the end of 1978 he consolidated his power and instituted the reform period that has made so enormous a difference to the Chinese people's livelihoods. In June 1981 he had the Central Committee issue an enormously long document which, among many other points, negated and condemned the Cultural Revolution in extremely strong terms. It also criticized Mao Zedong for his behaviour and policies in his last years, and especially for launching and sustaining the Cultural Revolution.

Contemporaneous Images of the Cultural Revolution

There were enormous ramifications for Western images of China in the changing balance of power and the Cultural Revolution. The

Vietnam War changed the United States deeply. Doubts about and then revulsion against the war caused Americans and other Westerners to rethink their attitudes towards and assumptions about Asia in general and Asian revolutions in particular. The Cultural Revolution also raised questions about the whole nature of the Chinese revolution.

Nixon's visit to China marked a major dividing point in Western images of that country. 'A week that changed the world' was Nixon's characterization of his own trip and his view, vain though it might have been, was shared by many Americans[1] because it symbolized that the United States no longer regarded China as a major enemy, perhaps even not as an enemy at all.

In his typically colourful language Harold Isaacs has described the direct impact of the new US diplomacy and the Nixon visit on Americans' images of China.

> When the American pendulum swings in such matters, it swings high and hard. The new medium of television lent all its enormously expanded scope and coverage to the event this time. When the president ... announced his forthcoming trip to Peking, the passage from the China-minuses to the China-pluses became a mad and even gay rush. Pearl Buck reappeared ... to remind everyone how great a time it was when Americans and Chinese were friends. The 'lo-the-wonder-of-the-wonderful-Chinese' reappeared in the country's print and on its screens.[2]

He goes on to comment on an expansion of interest in Chinese food, art, fashions, and acupuncture. The number of Americans going to China rose quickly. There was a 'mania for everything Chinese'.

To back up these generalizations Isaacs cites the results of Gallup polls taken in 1966 and March 1972 showing the qualities, positive and negative, that Americans attributed to Chinese people. The table on the following page shows the numbers that chose particular adjectives in the two years.[3]

When the Cultural Revolution began, the dominant images were hardworking, ignorant, warlike, and sly, three of them negative. But by the time Nixon had returned from China in 1972 the main images of Chinese among Americans had changed to hardworking, intelligent, progressive, practical, and artistic, all of them positive. Moreover, even though the sample was larger in 1972, the negative images such as ignorant, sly, treacherous, warlike, and cruel, had shrunk by 1972, in most cases substantially. On the other hand, the positive ones, like

QUALITIES	1966	1972
Hardworking	37	74
Honest	—	20
Brave	7	17
Religious	14	18
Intelligent	14	32
Practical	8	27
Ignorant	24	10
Artistic	13	26
Progressive	7	28
Sly	20	19
Treacherous	19	12
Warlike	23	13
Cruel	13	9

hardworking, brave, intelligent, practical, and artistic, had gone up. These represent very great changes in public opinion in the US.

The most detailed public analysis of contemporary China from 1966 to 1976 was carried out in universities and colleges. Although some China specialists moved from profession to profession, especially in the United States, most were basically academics. Correspondingly, it has long been practice in the US for government to seek advice from academics.

The Western academic world was split over China but initially mainly hostile to the Cultural Revolution. One of the best known and most outspoken purveyors of negative images was Pierre Ryckmans, and he is an appropriate representative example. A Belgian who at that time worked at the Australian National University in Canberra, Ryckmans wrote his polemical works under the pen-name Simon Leys. There is, however, no secret about his identity and the credit sheets of most of his books acknowledge both names, even though the title page still gives the author formally as Leys. He aroused very great interest among those interested in China and has written for a variety of well-known and influential journals.

His first book on the Cultural Revolution was published in 1971 in French and in 1977 in an English translation. It is a chronological account of the Cultural Revolution, but its main analytical burden comes in the first sentences: 'The "Cultural Revolution" had nothing revolutionary about it except the name, and nothing cultural about it except the initial tactical pretext. It was a power struggle waged at the top between a handful of men and behind the smokescreen of a fictitious mass movement.'[4] It was thus not irrational, as others claimed, but it certainly was cruel and orchestrated by despots, first and foremost Mao.

In later writings, Leys has expanded the scope of his condemnations, which became more intense in the early 1970s, when the general trend was in the opposite direction. China was totalitarian and its government bureaucratic with more hierarchy and less equality even than in the old days: 'In the sixth century BC . . . China's social hierarchy had only ten degrees. We have progressed since then: the Maoist bureaucracy today has thirty hierarchical classes, each with specific privileges and prerogatives.'[5] It was impossible for a foreigner to talk to a Chinese, because the latter were all too terrified. The Cultural Revolution and the Maoists destroyed a beautiful ancient and mass culture, replacing it with a narrow 'monstrous' nothingness.[6] Ryckmans has almost nothing positive to say about the period 1966–76. It is true he does concede that the 'maoist regime . . . has very nearly succeeded in feeding and housing its people,' but goes on: 'yet if we stop and think about it, this is simply the minimum that any self-respecting stockbreeder would want to provide for his cattle.'[7] Even the ability to feed and house the people becomes an object of scorn.

The Vietnam War and the inability of the US government to deal successfully with problems at home led many younger scholars to a far more sympathetic attitude towards communism in China and to the Cultural Revolution than those of the older school had. In the United States a good symbol of the new approach was the foundation of the Committee of Concerned Asian Scholars in 1968 by students and academics, and while its primary aim was opposition to American intervention in Vietnam, most of its members were directly and vitally concerned with China. It should also be emphasized that there were in all the other countries of the West academics sympathetic to the aims of the Cultural Revolution from the mid-1960s.

Members of this Committee were among the first to visit China as soon as it became possible for Americans to do so, and a group of fifteen of them stayed for a month in the summer of 1971, all students or teachers of China and all able to speak Chinese. They produced the highly laudatory book *China! Inside the People's Republic*. Their 'overwhelming impression of China' was 'vitality—the enthusiasm, the humor, and the tremendous commitment of her people to their new China'.[8] They accepted the aims of the Cultural Revolution as desirable,[9] even if they did not express them in the same terms as the

Chinese propaganda media were doing at the time.

A particularly influential American academic was the Harvard sinologist John Fairbank, possibly the foremost Western specialist of his day in the combination of China's past and present. When the Cultural Revolution first began he saw it as a movement both insane and anti-foreign, with some striking parallels to the Boxers of 1900. However, when the worst excesses of the Cultural Revolution had settled down in the early 1970s and Nixon had made his visit, Fairbank also stayed in China for six weeks in mid-1972, at the invitation of Zhou Enlai. He was very favourably impressed, especially with the improvements in the situation in the villages of North China, where he had travelled widely in the early 1930s. 'Compared with 40 years ago the change in the countryside is miraculous, a revolution probably on the largest scale of all time.'[10] While he was still not enthusiastic about the Cultural Revolution, calling it a period of 'stress and even violence', he did believe it had produced some positive results and in 1972 sensed 'relaxation and euphoria' that made the year 'a happy time to be in China'.[11]

Perhaps most important of all, he was prepared to denounce the US policies which had kept China and the United States so hostile to each other for so long. They were based on false images and a misunderstanding of history, he said.

> MacArthur's push for the Yalu [his attempt to push the Korean war into Chinese territory] in late 1950 was folly. Only Stalin, perhaps, profited from the Sino-American war in Korea. The ensuing Dullesian cold war against Peking in the 1950s was fundamentally mistaken and unnecessary, based on an utter misconception of Chinese history and the Chinese revolution. Only the Nixon visit could get us beyond this quagmire of errors, and we still have a long way to go to reach firm ground.[12]

In addition to such general works based on personal observations, Western academics read the Chinese sources voluminously; they argued and wrote endlessly on what the Cultural Revolution was about, what its results were and what had happened to the various aspects of Chinese society, education, health, industry, agriculture, communications, etc. In addition, they argued about their own and their colleagues' underlying assumptions about China and revolution. A great deal was written and, although most works were not individually image-creating in their own time, the cumulative effect did help to alter popular images of China.

Images from Journalists and Others

It was the job of journalists to gather what information they could, either from Hong Kong or China itself. A highly influential magazine based in Hong Kong but read widely both in Asia and the West is the *Far Eastern Economic Review*. One of its issues nicely summarizes two rather contradictory images, though both negative, of China at the beginning of the 1970s.

The first was of the violence of the Cultural Revolution and resultant military rule: 'Murder, arson, rape and corruption, committed at the peak of the Cultural Revolution, and in the anarchic period since, are today meeting their just rewards at the hands of China's army'.[13] One of the most vivid images of China in the late 1960s in the West was of corpses floating from the Mainland into Hong Kong harbour, their hands tied behind their backs. The violence and turmoil of the late 1960s are major themes of such books as Stanley Karnow's *Mao and China, From Revolution to Revolution*, which came out in 1972. Karnow is worth a special mention because of his status as one of the most influential American journalists writing on eastern Asia.

The other, supplementary, image comes forward from the front cover of the same issue of the *Far Eastern Economic Review* of 2 April 1970. It shows ten models of Chinese, apparently representing various groups but with the military towering over them. The headline is 'China's communists, the Maoist mould' and the image is of a passive, lifeless, long-suffering population, tired out through chaos and oppression, but too exhausted to resist further. In the minds of many in the West, a powerful image of the Cultural Revolution in its early stages was of hordes of young people waving little red books containing the thoughts of the pretended saviour Chairman Mao. But with the passage of time this enthusiasm had given way to a soulless uniformity, a mould.

One journalist and novelist to convey similarly negative images was the American Robert Elegant. Part of his popular and widely read novel *Dynasty* is set in the China of the late 1960s. The novel is about a distinguished part-Chinese, part-British family called Sekloong, one of the members of which joins the Communists and rises to be a full general in the People's Liberation Army. Called James, or in Chinese Shih Ai-Kuo, he opposes the Cultural Revolution on the grounds that it could consume the Communist Party and even lead to civil war and 'put China back a generation', a view which was, ironically, to become official policy in China only a few years after Elegant published his novel. Even Zhou Enlai, who was a friend of James, is quoted as saying 'we live in ridiculous times'. James does not dare to say too much, not even to his own wife and daughter, the latter an ardent supporter of the Cultural Revolution, because 'candor was not merely imprudent, but dangerous in a divided household'.[14]

The novelist clearly sides with James, and the image he portrays of the Cultural Revolution conforms quite well to what others were suggesting at the same time. It is an 'insane storm',[15] characterized by 'mindless violence', including even pitched battles, one of which, as it turns out, causes severe and permanent injury to James' revolutionary daughter.[16] Another image is of public humiliation of leaders, especially that of the Chinese President's wife Wang Guangmei, an actual historical event which is described in some detail.[17]

Amid the confusion a very strong image to emerge from Elegant's novel is that the Cultural Revolution was a fraud. It did not seek equality, as it pretended to do. James' wife 'knew that her fate was directly linked to his, despite the Party's cant about "perfect equality between male and female"'.[18] His daughter, for all her revolutionary ardour, does not hesitate to accept privileges, even those emphasizing her sex: 'She deliberately suppressed her awareness that the cotton fabric was finer than that worn by others, while the skilful tailoring accentuated her rounded hips and full breasts.' She 'preferred to forget the external marks of the privilege she enjoyed because of her father's rank'.[19]

In the end James admits that 'absolute loyalty to any man or system is ultimately destructive, evil'.[20] The one constant power is the family. The strongest image to come out of the novel is that in China family loyalties in the end triumph over political or even nationalist ones. Beside the family, the Cultural Revolution is but a fleeting nightmare.

One category of accounts condemning the Cultural Revolution was those by former Red Guards who had escaped the horrors of China and found help to write in a European language to relate their story to the West. A well-known case in point is a Chinese who under the pen-name Ken Ling wrote a book called *The Revenge of Heaven*. It describes his meteoric rise, even in his teenage years, from being a mere schoolboy to occupying a high-ranking official position in charge of the economic production of Amoy, a city of 700,000 people. His beloved, whom he met while working for the Cultural Revolution, is killed in a battle fought in Amoy University, and he blames himself. 'Was this fate? Was it because I offended the Lord of Heaven' through taking part in the Cultural Revolution so actively?[21]

The images of China Ken Ling presents are bleak in the extreme: children involuntarily turning against their teachers, pointless torture and cruelty, violence on a horrific scale, and public humiliations of individuals, especially Wang Guangmei. He also gives a picture of miserable backwardness and poverty. Describing the view from the window during a train journey in Anhui province, he writes: 'The trees had been stripped of their bark. From time to time we saw corpses by the tracks; once I glimpsed a child's leg. The stations were filled with ragged, starved people.'[22] Later he visits a village in the mountains west of Amoy where there are no primary school, no electricity, and no shops. He meets there a nineteen-year-old girl whose life has been so hard that she looks very much older. She is totally ignorant of anything outside her direct experience, and does not even know that the earth is spherical. She believes Mao Zedong a god 'in heaven, constantly watching over everybody', who 'would know whoever was not working hard and have him punished'.[23]

These negative images of the Cultural Revolution were most certainly the dominant ones in the first part of the decade 1966–76. While it is true that they tended to lose popularity in the early 1970s, they remained widely held in the West until after 1976. They were not, however, the only views on China put to Westerners by people working outside the educational profession. Even in the late 1960s there were those prepared to put over to the West a line supportive of the Cultural Revolution and, even more, one sympathetic to the Chinese revolution as a whole. The idea of China as a bureaucratic yet chaotic hell was very much under challenge.

Among journalists working in the West, by far the most important of the pro-China lobby was Edgar Snow, who has been mentioned in earlier chapters. Although he died on 15 February 1972, less than a week before Nixon arrived in Beijing, his 1970–1 visit to China, and in particular his 10 December 1970 interview with Mao Zedong, won widespread publicity and certainly facilitated and contributed to Nixon's visit to China. His last book, *The Long Revolution*, was published in 1971. Though still incomplete, it recorded his notes on his conversation with Mao, 'Breakfast with the Chairman', discussions with Zhou Enlai, 'A Night with the Premier', and many observations on China in 1970 and 1971.

Snow supported the aims of the Cultural Revolution and appears to have believed it successful by the time of his visit: 'Mao's Thought had by 1970 permeated the whole nation' with several aims, including the smashing of all bourgeois thought.[24] He also emphasized that one

Cultural Revolution would lead on to many more. However, what distressed him most about the Cultural Revolution was the cult of personality. He even raised it over breakfast with Mao, who told him that certain ultra-leftist officials had successfully opposed Snow's return to China in 1967 and 1968 for writing about it. Snow reported Mao as acknowledging that the personality cult had been overdone but that most of the epithets like 'great leader' and 'great helmsman' would be eliminated sooner or later.[25] The point is important because Snow was not alone among those sympathetic to the Chinese revolution in finding the Mao cult an extremely negative image.

Snow also reported on life and conditions in China as he found them. The images he puts forward are of a well fed, healthy, and adequately clothed people. The average citizen 'is free from bank mortgages, debt, and the fear of starvation and beggary which plagued his parents'.[26] On the other hand, Snow is critical of the lack of variety in the cinema and the lack of foreign news, which is 'scant and carefully screened'. His picture is generally positive and shines with enthusiasm for China and its people, although it also includes criticism. His conclusion of life in China is half joking, half serious: 'In short, China is, as some wit has remarked before me, a veritable sink of morality.'[27]

There were quite a few Western admirers of the morality and simplicity of Chinese life. The lack of obsession with material possessions, greed and sex attracted several Western authors on China. Other than Snow, these included the Italian journalist Maria Macciocchi, the American psychologist Carol Tavris, capitalist David Rockefeller and, most famous of all, actress Shirley MacLaine. Some senior Christian clergymen, like Hewlett Johnson, saw China's morality and purity as essentially religious, because it freed people from the slavery of acquisitiveness and covetousness. Many challenged Leys' view on inequality in China, claiming that while its society was in no way perfectly equal, it was much less hierarchical than before 1949.

Views from the 1980s

It did not take long after the ascendancy of Deng Xiaoping for nearly all streams of thought to move against the Cultural Revolution. At the forefront of the attack were those observers who had never had any time for the Cultural Revolution anyway. A case in point is Pierre Ryckmans, who was able, on the authority of the CCP itself, to point to the correctness of his own judgments and predictions. Others had been generally positive about the Cultural Revolution at the time, but turned not only against that movement but against China as a whole. A third group consisted of those who were sympathetic to the Cultural Revolution at the time, but who were influenced by the revelations the Chinese themselves made about it in the late 1970s and early 1980s.

A particularly important contributor to the image of the Cultural Revolution, as China correspondent of the widely read and extremely influential *Time* magazine, was Richard Bernstein. He regarded the Cultural Revolution as so extreme as to be unbelievable and 'one of the most irrational occurrences in modern history', destructive of art and education and also murderous. 'Nobody knows how many people died during the Cultural Revolution, but the Chinese now say hundreds of thousands, maybe more.'[28] Bernstein was horrified by the personality cult and was not alone in this view. 'The chairman had used his last remaining power-base ... to build up a semi-magical cult of his own personality' wrote two historians, who go on to denounce the suffering meted out to intellectuals and to others.[29]

Roger Garside, a British diplomat who lived in China from 1976 to 1979, wrote a book called *Coming Alive, China after Mao*, 'the story of how life returned to a nation that had been half-dead'. He described the Cultural Revolution years as 'an Orwellian nightmare' and suggested that China's 'coming alive' proved the relevance of that mainly Western phenomenon liberal democracy.[30] There is a certain irony in the contrast between the Committee of Concerned Asian Scholars' 'overwhelming impression' of 'vitality' in 1971, as noted in the previous section, and Garside's verdict that the Chinese were half-dead in 1976.

Television programmes and films on China invariably put forward the same images of the Cultural Revolution. Destruction, regression, and irrationality are the chief features, whether the programme concerns the arts, the minority nationalities, religion, or general conditions. The famous 1981 Academy Award winning documentary feature film *From Mao to Mozart: Isaac Stern in China*, recording the famous violinist's experiences and impressions of China, and especially its musical life, leaves suppression of artistic talent as the major image of the Cultural Revolution. Musicians were forced to clean lavatories and undertake other such demeaning tasks, but were not allowed to practise their art.

The brilliant British television series *The Heart of the Dragon*, which was shown throughout the Western world and translated into several major European languages, describes the Cultural Revolution as 'an outburst of hysterical fanaticism', which suppressed religion. It likens the utopianism of the Cultural Revolution to the 'religiously based popular uprisings of imperial times'. 'But unlike them,' the programme goes on, the Cultural Revolution 'was deliberately instigated from the capital; it was promoted, like the Nazi excesses, by mass-communications'. One of the results was that the young urban students who were the main adherents 'decided that their idealism had been manipulated. They had lost their youth for nothing; they had lost hope for the future and trust in their leaders, or in nearly all of them'.[31] The comparison with Nazi excesses is a particularly telling one in terms of the associations of cruelty and evil.

Quite a large part of the magnificent feature film *The Last Emperor*, about China's last emperor Puyi, is set in the PRC years. Directed by Bernardo Bertolucci, the clear image of this 1987 film is that the CCP did indeed save China. The governor of the prison of which the former emperor is an inmate for his collaboration with the Japanese invariably treats him humanely and kindly and thus wins his respect and even affection. The end of the film is set in 1967 at the height of the Cultural Revolution, and shows the governor with a dunce's cap accused of being a reactionary, while Puyi comes to plead unsuccessfully on his behalf. It thus suggests the late 1960s as the black period of the generally positive era of the PRC. On the other hand, no violence is shown, nor is the Cultural Revolution blamed for Puyi's death, which also occurred in 1967.

Just like the 1970s, the 1980s saw the publication of several extremely negative books about the Maoist years, and especially about the Cultural Revolution, recording the experiences of individual Chinese, but actually written in large measure by Westerners. A well-known and certainly image-formulating example is *Son of the Revolution* by Liang Heng and his American wife Judith Shapiro, first published in 1983. The 1984 Fontana paperback edition carries on its front cover an extract from a review saying that the book is 'a terrifying tale, so vividly written it almost makes you feel you were there . . . and thank God you were not'. The nature of the images conveyed by the book is summed up fairly accurately by the extract, for the major thrust of Liang Heng's experiences was of continual obeisance to political ideology, of corrupt bureaucrats interfering incessantly in his life and those of others, and of witnessing violence and cruelty on a horrific scale. Asked in an examination to write a composition on 'the words I have in my heart to tell the Party', his private reaction, which naturally he did not write at the time, was 'what I had in my heart was bitterness, my life's accumulated bitterness, the accumulated bitterness of the lives of the people around me'.[32] And the concluding lesson from the narrative is 'the danger that lies in blind obedience'.[33] Although Liang Heng's life had not been entirely without bright spots, the overall impact of the book is savage and near total condemnation of the Cultural Revolution.

Son of the Revolution reads like a novel in many ways, but is in fact a record of actual events. On the other hand, several novels have been published since 1976 which use the real happenings of the PRC, including the Cultural Revolution decade, as their background. Of these, the most important is *Till Morning Comes*, by the well-known writer Han Suyin, several of whose works have already come under discussion. *Till Morning Comes* is unquestionably image-formulating, even though her status as a commentator on China had declined because of her tendency to give full support to whatever regime happens to be in power in China.

The core of this very long novel is the love between a Chinese doctor called Jen Yong and an American, Stephanie Ryder, set against the history of China from the mid-1940s until the early 1970s. Stephanie remains in China until 1957, when both are attacked during the anti-rightist campaign, she as 'an agent of American cultural imperialism' and he as a rightist. She goes back to the US to live, while he is sent to work in a remote region. Stephanie returns to China only at the very end of the novel when the forthcoming Nixon visit enables Americans to visit China. By that time, Jen Yong has been publicly humiliated and later beaten to death by young Red Guards during the Cultural Revolution, a fate she finds out only after her return to China at the end of the novel.

Han Suyin had clearly changed her mind about the history of the People's Republic and in particular the Cultural Revolution. She had earlier declared the late 1950s as the time when the mass line and revolutionary enthusiasm would accelerate China's passage to socialism and transformation,[34] but now the anti-rightist campaign of 1957 had become an early and important stage in the rot of harmful revolutionary fanaticism. The Cultural Revolution no longer carried the image of immense progress and optimism we saw in her work in the previous chapter, but instead one of killing good people in cruel ways. She portrays the Cultural Revolution as the classic example of a movement that causes young people to carry out destructive and sadistic actions because they are misled by an excess of revolutionary enthusiasm. As had happened in the past, her thinking had changed to accord with the current official policy laid down by the CCP.

Since the Party must remain optimistic, it follows that the overall image of China and the Chinese to come from this novel is an optimistic one. The climax, or at least conclusion, is the reconciliation between China and the United States. The last sentence of the novel is 'Love had come to her, at last',[35] because as an American she was now able to go back to China. This is the 'morning' of the title, following the night of which the darkest hour was the Cultural Revolution.

For Robert Elegant in *Dynasty* the overriding Chinese phenomenon to endure against all political turmoil is the family, but for Han Suyin in *Till Morning Comes* it is China itself and patriotism. In an interview with American senators near the end of the novel, Stephanie is asked why her husband chose to remain in China. Her answer clearly reflects the view familiar from the author herself in *A Many-Splendoured Thing* and other works:

> There are millions like him in China. The non-Communist intelligentsia. Who elected to remain in Communist China. Because 'China is China is China'. Immortal, forever. Not because of communism ...
>
> They have seen the Communist Government at work. However abhorrent, authoritarian, crassly bureaucratic it is, it has also done an enormous amount of good for the ordinary people of China. For the ninety-five percent who were living in gross misery ...
>
> My husband is Chinese. He loves his country and his people. He is a patriot, as are so many like him. Should we not understand, respect that patriotism?[36]

Han Suyin can turn against the Cultural Revolution but retain faith in China and even its system. One novel set in the period beginning at the same time as *Till Morning Comes* ends is *The Chinese Assassin* by Anthony Grey, a journalist who was himself imprisoned in China for two years during the Cultural Revolution. In view of this experience it comes as no surprise that Grey does not share Han Suyin's optimism, but gives a picture of bleak pessimism. The novel is about the intrigue and counter-intrigue, both Chinese and international, of the last five years of Mao Zedong's life, that is from 1971 to 1976. The main images of China are of a country ruled by a kind of imperial court, where the imperial tyrant, Mao, has his torture chamber to keep control over his courtiers and rival claimants to his throne. Socialist ideals are totally irrelevant. Neither the revolution as a whole nor the Cultural Revolution has changed anything significant: 'The modern scientific truths of Marxism have become the same empty symbol to be hoisted aloft in the same vicious and unprincipled personal intrigues that had racked the imperial courts.' It was true that 'much had changed for the better in the lives of the ordinary people. But it was a precarious change. The great unknowing masses were still helpless prey to the caprices of the secret court of the modern Son of Heaven, Mao'.[37]

There were of course counter-images of the Cultural Revolution decade, even in the 1980s. A guidebook, which claims to be the 'world's best-selling guide to the People's Republic of China', put forward a rather positive view of the Cultural Revolution, even in its 1982–83 edition. The 'egalitarian spirit of that movement' was thwarted by 'unexpected chaos and violence', despite which 'the worst of the disruptions had ended' by the late 1960s, allowing the 'major reforms in education, factory management, economic planning, and medical care' noted earlier in the guidebook to take shape.[38]

Views from the 1990s

By the 1990s it was very difficult to find any Western defenders of the Cultural Revolution. The Beijing massacre of June 1989, to be discussed in a later chapter, had worsened Western images of China considerably. Meanwhile, the fall of the Berlin Wall later the same year had brought about the end of the Cold War and further worsened the reputation of anything associated with Marxist–Leninist parties.

By far the most famous representative of these negative images is *Wild Swans* by Jung Chang. Of all books about China published in the period of the PRC this one has sold best and exercised the profoundest influence on Western images of China. Published first in 1991, it has been through numerous reprintings. It has drawn acclaim both from China specialists and literary critics. It has won several major book awards, including the 1993 British Book of the Year Award. It is doubtful if any book of any period has influenced Western images of China more deeply than this one. Its author was among the many members of the Chinese intelligentsia who went to live in the West with the reform period, in 1982 becoming the first student from the PRC to gain a PhD degree at a British university.

The book is subtitled *Three Daughters of China*, the three being the author, her mother, and her grandmother, two of them having the character *hong*, meaning a 'wild swan', in their given name, hence the title of the book. A fourth major figure in the book is the author's father. The book is a detailed history of these four people, and hence of the writer's family, over three generations, covering virtually all of the twentieth century up to 1978. Much of the book is about China under Mao Zedong.

The dominant image to emerge from this account is of a country dominated by politics in its cruellest forms, a country where people are afraid, both of their government and of each other, a country where Mao's power was so enormous, godlike, and tyrannical that nobody dared to disobey, let alone defy him. The revolution, which dominated the period, was truly one which ate its own children, for Jung Chang portrays enormous loyalty by her parents to Mao and the revolution, only to find themselves punished and ill-treated for their trouble. And the Cultural Revolution saw the climax of these evils: Party hacks driving her father to madness and death through arrests, savage beatings, and general persecution. This is a tale featuring people who denounce each other in order to ingratiate themselves with the tyrannical Mao and his faction.

As for the author herself, she accepted the Cultural Revolution because that was what Mao had ordained.

> Like many Chinese, I was incapable of rational thinking in those days. We were so cowed and contorted by fear and indoctrination that to deviate from the path laid down by Mao would have been inconceivable. Besides, we had been overwhelmed by deceptive rhetoric, disinformation, and hypocrisy, which made it virtually impossible to see through the situation and to form an intelligent judgment.[39]

This book cannot fail to move even the stoniest of hearts. It is a story replete with human misery and emotion, beautifully told. The characterization is excellent, with the main figures coming over to the reader as dedicated and passionate, able to put up with almost anything on behalf of their beliefs and family relationships. Most moving of all is perhaps the loyalty of the author's mother to her father. Intense pressure, including being subjected to public mass humiliation herself, failed to get her to denounce him, despite the fact that he 'had always given the Party and the revolution priority over her'.[40] The images of China before 1978 are overwhelmingly negative, yet this book has something positive to say about particular Chinese people and about the human spirit.

Although the post-Mao years have very little place in *Wild Swans*, one brief comment is worth recording as a contrast with the grimness of life under Mao: 'Between 1983 and 1989, I went back to visit my mother every year, and each time I was overwhelmed by the dramatic diminution of the one thing that had most characterized life under Mao: fear.'[41] The comment identifies two dominant images of the Maoist years, especially those of the Cultural Revolution. One is the total power of the tyrant/god Mao, before whom all stood, or bowed down, in awe and dread, mingled with worship and admiration. The other is the cowed Chinese population, many of whom believed in the superhuman Mao, but virtually all of whom paid the price in the way China's progress was held back over those ten years.

One work which is very clearly focused on the person of Mao himself is *The Private Life of Chairman Mao* by his personal physician Li Zhisui. This book paints a picture of a conspiratorial tyrant who cared nothing for anybody but himself but wielded immense, even total power over a huge population. One of the most prominent, and best-known images to emerge from the book is of a sexually virulent Mao, who favoured peasant women as partners and, for a time, held dancing parties to satisfy his sexual desires. In December 1993, BBC Television had broadcast a documentary called *Chairman Mao: The Last Emperor* based largely on Li Zhisui's account, which had portrayed Mao as a sex-crazed tyrant. Attempts by the Chinese Embassy in London to prevent the screening of the documentary not only failed in their aim but fuelled interest in the film and even strengthened its credibility in the eyes of the West, despite the fact that 'its case rested mainly on the strength of one man's recollections'.[42]

Another book, of a very different kind but interesting as representative of an author who had once believed passionately in the Cultural Revolution, is Jan Wong's *Red China Blues, My Long March from Mao to Now*. Jan Wong is a Canadian Chinese who became a youthful Maoist and went to live in China in the late days of the Cultural Revolution period, but became very disillusioned about everything to do with China. 'What first attracted me to Mao's China was its absolute purity,' she writes.[43] The picture she paints of the Cultural Revolution is not altogether negative, but what finally shocked her into renouncing Maoism and confirming herself as an 'ex-Maoist' was the suddenness and ease with which friends who had previously seemed so committed could abandon revolutionary ideals. She came to the simple but stark conclusion: 'The Cultural Revolution wasn't a radical-chic game. It had wrought untold suffering.'[44] The lesson for Jan Wong was scepticism of all authority, a lesson she applied as much to Deng Xiaoping's as to Mao Zedong's regimes. 'I'm suspicious of anything that's too theoretically tidy, too black and white. If I adhere to any creed today, it's a belief in human dignity and strength.'[45]

Of all the images of the Cultural Revolution years to emerge in the 1990s, perhaps the most ghastly were based on stories of cannibalism reported from a town called Wuxuan in central Guangxi, southern China, and ascribed to mid-1968. In 1992, the writer Zheng Yi, who had gathered a great deal of material on this matter, escaped to Hong Kong and wrote a book on his findings, which was published in Taiwan the next year. Several reports based on Zheng's accounts appeared in the *New York Times* and other Western media. In October 1993 John Gittings actually visited Wuxuan in an attempt to find out the truth of the stories. His experiences there and examination of the evidence left him in no doubt that 'the picture of a wave of cannibalism over a limited period of time is substantially correct'.[46] He quotes a secret report carried out by local investigators which claimed that in the summer of 1968, at the height of the savagery of the Cultural Revolution, 526 people had been killed in Wuxuan County, and that, in 75 of these cases, 'the victims' livers were then extracted and eaten'.[47] The question of how so terrible a crime could be committed in the 1960s is one on which Gittings speculates. He has no clear answers, but we do know that this was an area of particularly savage brutality at this time. Gittings suggests a combination of political vengeance, historical experience, mob hysteria and particularly poor education and backward circumstances in the region, but makes no pretence to have a full explanation.

Conclusion

During the period of the Cultural Revolution itself, there were those in the West prepared to be tolerant of it, and even sympathetic towards it. During the 1980s and 1990s the number of its supporters dwindled in number and the strength of conviction of the remaining ones weakened. As the Chinese themselves turned against the Cultural Revolution, it became increasingly obvious that the movement had failed disastrously in its aims, causing untold misery along the way.

The world of the 1980s and 1990s is decisively more hostile towards revolutions in general than was that of the 1960s. Even in China there was far more interest in privatization than in left-wing revolutions. The fall of the Berlin Wall not only ended the Cold War but brought Marxist-Leninist parties into further disrepute. Jan Wong's comment that 'the Cultural Revolution wasn't a radical-chic game' is simple but apt, because it draws attention to the misplaced trendiness which had once led some observers to defend Mao's most destructive absurdity.

Notes

1   The influential American journalist Joseph Kraft was one of those who accompanied Nixon to China. He wrote a short book called *The Chinese Difference*, the first section of which, pp. 3–43, deals with the Nixon visit and is called 'the week that changed the world'.
2   Isaacs, *Images of Asia*, p. xv.
3   Ibid., p. xviii.
4   Leys, *The Chairman's New Clothes*, p. 13.
5   Leys, *Chinese Shadows*, p. 113. For further examples of the inequality image see Hollander, *Political Pilgrims*, pp. 303–7.
6   Leys, *Chinese Shadows*, pp. 30–1.
7   Leys, *Broken Images*, p. 107.
8   Committee of Concerned Asian Scholars, *China! Inside the People's Republic*, p. 2
9   Ibid., pp. 102–3.
10   John K. Fairbank, '1972, The New China and the American Connection', in *China Perceived*, pp. 21–2. This article first appeared in *Foreign Affairs* in October 1972.
11   Ibid., p. 31.
12   Ibid., pp. 29–30.
13   MacDougall, 'The Maoist Mould', p. 17.
14   Elegant, *Dynasty*, pp. 571–2. Although this novel came out the year after the death of Mao, the last section was written during the Cultural Revolution years and the finale is set in 1970. It certainly reflects contemporary images of the Cultural Revolution.
15   Ibid., p. 579.
16   Ibid., p. 583, 584–88.
17   Ibid., pp. 567–70, 581–82.
18   Ibid., p. 585.
19   Ibid., p. 566.
20   Ibid., p. 618
21   Ling, London, a.o., *The Revenge of Heaven*, p. 368
22   Ibid., p. 148.
23   Ibid., p. 301.
24   Snow, *China's Long Revolution*, p. 29.
25   Ibid., p. 114.
26   Ibid., p. 31.

27   Ibid., p. 32.
28   Bernstein, *From the Center of the Earth*, pp. 65–66.
29   Blunden and Elvin, *Cultural Atlas of China*, p. 169.
30   Garside, *Coming Alive, China After Mao*, p. vii.
31   Clayre, *The Heart of the Dragon*, pp. 30–31.
32   Liang and Shapiro, *Son of the Revolution*, p. 266.
33   Ibid., p. 292.
34   Han, *Asia Today, Two Outlook*, p. 54.
35   Han, *Till Morning Comes*, p. 620.
36   Ibid., pp. 598–99.
37   Grey, *The Chinese Assassin*, p. 73.
38   Kaplan and de Keijzer, *The China Guidebook*, p. 27.
39   Chang, *Wild Swans*, p. 404.
40   Ibid., p. 476.
41   Ibid., p. 675.
42   Gittings, *Real China*, p. 164.
43   Wong, *Red China Blues*, p. 319.
44   Ibid., p. 189.
45   Ibid., p. 390.
46   Gittings, *Real China*, p. 208.
47   Ibid., p. 196.

8
Images of Post-Mao China,
1976–89

The death of Mao Zedong and the fall of the 'Gang of Four' in 1976 marked a gigantic turnaround in Chinese history. One of the features of the new era was 'opening to the outside world' (*duiwai kaifang*), and as a result the range of images presented to the West expanded, especially after the formal establishment of diplomatic relations between the United States and the PRC at the beginning of 1979. There was to be another major change in images in 1989 due to the Beijing massacre of June that year, making the period 1976–89 an appropriate one to consider as a bloc. Because of the enormous scope of Western images over those years it is necessary to focus attention on a few major topics, most of them selected not only for their importance but also to give a clear idea of how Western images have changed or remained the same over time.

Foreign Relations

There was a time, not so long ago, when China's large population was seen in some influential quarters as a reason why China was about to attempt conquest of other countries. But in the period 1976–89, the nightmare image of the millions spilling over borders was very weak, certainly not dominant. In the West, China was seen by most people as peace-loving and not expansionist. 'China needs a peaceful environment to modernize' was a typical comment showing how obviously China's interests lay in supporting stability and peace. *Time* magazine wrote that 'the motto under Deng seems to be: try to get along with everyone so that the nation's energies can be concentrated on economic development'.[1] Indeed, China was seen in many quarters as being itself under threat, from the Soviet Union. A rather typical article in the 'world's most-read magazine', *Reader's Digest,* relates how 'Moscow hopes to chip away at American influence' in the Pacific through such mechanisms as 'military buildup and economic aid', with China remaining 'subject to Soviet enmity and suspicion'.[2]

At the same time, the Chinese had long been, and remained, famous in the West for their patriotism and nationalism. The well-known American political science specialist Tom Bernstein, not to be confused with namesake Richard, could ask 'what values will bind China together now that Maoism, and indeed socialism, have lost their attractiveness?' His reply: 'the answer, of course, is nationalism, but it is not an expansionist nationalism'.[3]

It was a typical view among well-informed people in the West that Chinese foreign policy reflected and was determined by 'the country's unique culture, history, its domestic politics and the geopolitical calculus'.[4] Few believed that China would do other than pursue what it saw as its own national interest, nor perceived it as different in that respect from any other country.

From much of what has been said it is clear that Westerners saw China as a country appropriately compared and contrasted with those of the Third World. There were also very many who compared and contrasted China with Western countries, usually to say how different the values of the Chinese were or how much lower the standards of living and the economic level in general. Certainly, most people in the West saw China as an emerging power that liked to compare itself with the West and found no psychological problem in dealing with the superpowers. China might still be within the Third World, but its main foreign policy concerns were its relations with the superpowers, the United States and the Soviet Union, and with two Asian neighbours, Japan, with which it was friendly, and its number one enemy, Vietnam. Leaving aside its obsession with the evils of Vietnam, a typical Western perception would see China as relatively little concerned with the developing countries, its own public statements to the contrary notwithstanding.[5]

Of the United States, the Soviet Union, and Japan, the overwhelming image in the West is that it is the US that is the most important, not only for the West itself, but also for China. David Bonavia, well-known British journalist and former correspondent of two influential image-formulators, *The Times* and *Far Eastern Economic Review*, writes that China's friendship with the United States and other capitalist countries was pursued 'doggedly' by China throughout the 1970s and into the 1980s, and 'has been perhaps the most important single factor' in the development of international relations throughout the world down to the end of the twentieth century.[6] Many in the West, especially in government circles, perceived China as 'a balance' against the Soviet Union, and thus helpful to Western interests.

Looking at the other side of the picture, the dominant Western image of why China should tend so heavily towards the United States and other capitalist countries could be summed up in one word: modernization. It was the Western nations and Japan that could supply not only 'badly needed goods and technologies', but also markets for exports, management know-how, tourism, and the 'capital necessary for industrial development'. It follows that a prevailing image of Chinese foreign policy in the Deng era was of characterization 'by the "open door" to the West' and at the same time 'a cold posture toward the Soviet Union'.[7] Very few would concede the possibility that the Soviet Union could contribute to China's modernization remotely as well as the West or Japan.

Government

Western observers remained fascinated with leadership. Generally their image of the 1976–89 leadership was extremely positive, especially in the case of Deng Xiaoping, renowned as the architect of reform. The American magazine *Success!* selected him as the 'success story of the year' for 1985. Harrison Salisbury, who wrote the feature article on him, claimed that he had 'put China on a new and successful fast track, and he has not hesitated to borrow from the West'. High praise indeed. 'The whole Chinese economy has surged forward', he continued, because Deng had 'introduced free enterprise, entrepreneurship, price competition, stock offerings, and even toyed with reopening the wild and woolly Shanghai Stock Exchange', in other words behaved rather like a capitalist.[8] In 1985, *Time* magazine selected Deng as 'man of the year' for the second time, the first being in 1978.

The British editor of the influential *Far Eastern Economic Review*, Derek Davies, was, if anything, even more enthusiastic about Deng. His view was that 'for my money Deng Xiaoping is carving out a sizable claim for the title Man of the Last Quarter of the 20th century'. Davies was impressed by the changes and progress Deng had wrought in a country 'once thought of as a giant buried inertly under its party and the bureaucracy'. But whereas Salisbury emphasized turning to the West, Davies' focus was on Chinese tradition. Deng's 'fabled pragmatism sits comfortably within the Confucian tradition of moderation'. Above all he admired the Chinese leader's optimism, his belief that problems 'can be solved as long as common sense prevails'.[9]

Davies praised Deng for his resilience in repairing a career which seemed to lie in ruins 'within a totalitarian Maoist society'. Much of the right wing in the West continued to apply the term 'totalitarian', which Davies had used for the Maoist period, to China in the 1980s. An example is Fox Butterfield's lengthy account of China's 'control apparatus', which dwells at length on restrictions placed on the people's lives, including their most private affairs. Butterfield even quotes one Chinese as complaining 'we are like caged animals'.[10]

The other extreme is perhaps represented by the view, put forward in a much used guidebook, which sees the Chinese government as 'promoting citizens' rights and democratic processes in its continuing effort to modernize by the end of this century'. PRC law, which most in the West see as deficient, this guidebook portrays as making an effective contribution towards the introduction of freedom and democracy. The guidebook takes a quite remarkably positive view of Marxism: an appropriate combination of tradition and modernity, resembling Daoism in stressing the interconnections of human experience and knowledge, and Confucianism in placing social relationships at the core of its political theory.[11]

Many observers pointed out the totalitarian and authoritarian traditions within which the present government operated and the immense problems it faced. One example was the much-used, green-covered Lonely Planet guide to China (1984 edition), so popular among travellers that many called it 'the green bible'. Its view was that 'for China to have come even as far as it has today [in the area of democracy] is extraordinary. So far the Communists have not delivered all that they promised, yet it seems unlikely that anyone else could have done a better job'.[12] A scholarly French account conveyed an image of 'supervised liberty' (*liberté surveillée*), in which Deng Xiaoping confronted the difficulty of 'granting more freedom but refusing complete freedom'. He faced dangers in such an approach because he risked 'alienating the old elites without winning new supporters'.[13] The television series *The Heart of the Dragon* drew attention to the Confucian tradition of 'rites' (*li*), signifying 'all behaviour in accordance with the requirements of the moral order'. It saw in this concept 'one of the chief reasons why the Chinese have been able to live in large family groups or modern collectives, apparently with less friction than other peoples'.[14] The image was not so much that no 'control apparatus' existed, but that the main basis of social order was not fear or compulsion but moral suasion.

A question of great importance for a socialist society is equality. Here again images varied greatly. Both Butterfield and influential *Time* correspondent Richard Bernstein painted a shockingly unequal society in which rank, power, and privileges were rampant and ubiquitous.[15] Neither, it is true, went quite as far as Pierre Ryckmans, whose views on this subject were discussed in Chapter 7. Butterfield conceded that 'in purely monetary terms . . . the Communists still maintained the appearance of their old egalitarianism' but went on to argue that money was not what mattered; 'the real differences are the hidden privileges, prerogatives, and perquisites that go with political status'.[16]

At the other extreme were those who put forward an image of a China where the ideals and reality of egalitarianism more or less corresponded. One such was Clyde Cameron, a minister in Gough Whitlam's Australian Labor Party government of 1972–75. He visited China in 1977, 1978, and 1979 and drew an extremely favourable impression of social equality in China. He saw 'no evidence of either opulence or abject poverty'. 'No-one dies of gluttony or of starvation.' 'Housing is not luxurious but it is cheap and no-one goes without shelter.' 'Privately-owned motor cars are not permitted but in China that rule applies to the leaders as well as to the led.'[17] Though Cameron made no claims to great learning on China, he spoke for a body of opinion and both represented and helped formulate images.

Numerous contacts with Westerners on the subject led this writer to the view that the dominant image on the question of equality in the 1980s lay somewhere in between these two extremes. Such an image recognized the widespread existence of privilege and corruption, and the continuation of a hierarchy among Party and government workers. The CCP was an élite in political and power terms. On the other hand, such a view gave the CCP credit for some degree of sincerity in creating a society much less unequal than that of the past. It saw China as far less unequal than other societies of a comparable level of economic development. According to a scholarly textbook on China's political system widely used in the 1980s, 'in general, contemporary Chinese society is not marked by powerful class distinctions'. The authors did indeed see 'differences in income, social status, and political influence among different strata of the population,' but considered 'they have a relatively moderate character'.[18]

It is not surprising that many saw inequalities as having widened in the years 1976–89 as a result of the new policies followed by the government. One widely used general history of the PRC, and one generally quite sympathetic to it, claimed that such growing inequalities had spawned resentment in some quarters and could 'conceivably nourish a backlash of opposition'.[19] The context of this image was of the strong economic growth and reform on which China had recently embarked.

The Economy

Over the period 1976–89, the Open Door policy became a major part of the government blueprint for China's economic development, with Western countries occupying a major section of foreign dealings with China under the policy of 'openness to the outside'. Westerners saw themselves as paramount in economic dealings with China and the new policy as in a sense designed especially for them. Western business and government circles were particularly positive about the new economic policies, because these opened the possibilities of investment and more customers. The overriding image such people held of China was as a potential source of large-scale profits.

China's large population had made it a market attractive to the West for a long time. However, it appeared to offer a better prospect than in earlier periods, because the large population was not only larger than ever but also better able to buy the sorts of goods Westerners might sell. 'For foreign investors,' wrote one reporter, 'the prospect of having access to a market of one billion consumers no longer seems like a pipedream'. The reason she gave was that 'the Chinese—in particular the rural population—are getting richer and now want visible improvements to their standard of living: they aspire to their own colour TV sets, refrigerators, trucks, washing machines and better radios, bicycles, and clothing'.[20] One popular novel of the 1980s, which its publisher presented as a 'shattering superthriller of ultimate high-finance global warfare', ends with the central character, an American, leasing an islet from the City of Shanghai for fifty years in order to live and do business there. He intended 'to build trade between China and the rest of the world' because he believed that 'in several years, maybe less, this will be the largest trading city in the world'.[21]

The prevailing image of the current state and future prospects of the Chinese economy in the mid-1980s was probably not too far from the reports of the World Bank. These are examples of works which both reflect and also formulate Western economic thinking. The first major World Bank study of the Chinese economy was completed in 1981 and published in 1983; it 'broadly endorsed China's economic reforms and was widely influential as the most comprehensive study of the Chinese economy yet undertaken'.[22] Its successor was completed in May 1985 and published in October that year by the Johns Hopkins University Press; and is worth some discussion as an economic image of China in the 1980s.

The 1985 World Bank report quotes the Chinese government's stated aim of quadrupling the gross value of industrial and agricultural output, and increasing national income per person from about US$300 to US$800 between 1980 and 2000. This aim 'seems feasible' because of, and assuming, two factors: China's 'unusually slow' population growth, about one per cent per year, and its consistently and 'unusually high' investment rate.[23] It called for more efficient use of available resources, including labour, and regarded them as the key to modernization, outweighing in importance even availability of energy or access to advanced foreign technology. The report stated that, in these terms, the 'conditions for rapid, sustained growth are at present far from fully met in China, except in agriculture, where outstanding progress has been made in recent years with the introduction of the production responsibility system'.[24] It advocated greater use of market regulation to stimulate innovation and efficiency, and expansion of the service sector, which in 1985 occupied less than 20 per cent of the gross national product, far less than in India, Indonesia, South Korea, or Japan.

The World Bank report supported China's Open Door policy and suggested that greater involvement in the world economy was necessary to introduce modern technology, 'but also—more importantly— increase the efficiency with which all resources are used'. Although this policy was essential 'to achieve rapid, sustained growth', the report acknowledged certain risks in it, such as exposing China to inflation and fluctuations in world demands for industrial products and increased regional inequalities.[25] Despite criticisms, the report was essentially optimistic about China's economic future and strongly in support of the basics of current policy. The conclusion of the section entitled 'Overview' was that 'China's long-term development objectives seem attainable in principle, and if recent experience is any guide, there is a good chance that they will be attained in practice'.[26] The thrust of the report certainly promoted a positive image of the Chinese economy in Western business communities, and encouraged them to continue investing in and trading with China.

The singling out of the agricultural sector for special praise due to the production responsibility system became a persistent feature of

Western images of the Chinese economy at this time. An American report of 1983 on China the previous year stated that 'agriculture remained a relative bright spot in the Chinese economic picture'. The new system had 'succeeded in unleashing latent productivity and quickly improving peasant incomes'. The report also expressed worry that the system would 'widen inequality in the countryside'.[27] The British Granada television series *Inside China*, first broadcast in 1983, includes a programme called 'The Newest Revolution' on Chinese agriculture in the 1980s; it portrays an image of rising prosperity in a village near Wuxi, Jiangsu Province.

To illustrate the dominant image of a good and improving standard of living some discussions of markets can be cited. The first refers to Chongqing in the autumn of 1979 and comes from the acid pen of Richard Bernstein. He describes the principal meat and vegetable market in the city as 'truly abysmal, unprosperous, empty, depressing, even shocking. There were people in large numbers but there was, almost literally, nothing for them to buy'. His only concession to an alternative point of view is an afterthought: 'Perhaps an afternoon in fall was a bad time to judge.'[28]

There could hardly be a more spectacular contrast than a description of rural markets in Guangdong by Orville Schell, published in 1984. He quotes a Western anthropological friend as saying that in one brigade in 1979, 'there was virtually nothing in the market', echoes of Bernstein and Chongqing. He goes on that in 1981, 'things had started to pick up', but in 1983 he couldn't believe what he saw. 'There were hundreds of people selling things. There were tanks of live fish, and piles of fruit and vegetables heaped up everywhere. Lots of pigs were being slaughtered for meat—something you rarely would have seen in the past. You could buy Coca-Cola, Budweiser beer, and foreign cigarettes at private shops. The prosperity was impressive.'[29] Schell visited a rural market town in Guangdong himself in January 1984, and was also much impressed by the prosperity shown in the markets. Even on normal non-market days, he writes, the main streets 'were lined with hundreds of booths and peddlers selling everything from clothing, household goods, and hardware to produce and wild animals. But at official market times—every fifth day—the number of private merchants swelled into the thousands'.[30] During extensive travelling in China's south-west—Sichuan, Yunnan, and Tibet—in the autumn of 1985, this writer found that Western tourists invariably placed great weight on visiting the free markets and were always impressed by their bustling activity, the range of goods on sale and their general air of prosperity.

In terms of images of China's economy the most obvious question to flow from these discussions seems to be 'was China going capitalist?' There was a degree of consensus that the reforms undertaken in China went beyond precedents in other socialist countries, causing some people to 'see China as giving up on socialism and copying capitalism'.[31] The dominant view was that, while China was still a socialist country, its direction was towards capitalism. This was evident in the comments of numerous Westerners in all sorts of contexts, most of whom favoured the trend, because they saw it as part and parcel of China's opening to the West.

Lifestyle, Westernization

In an image-formulating Time-Life picture book published in 1978, David Bonavia notes the transformation Beijing underwent after 1949, 'changing more rapidly and profoundly than any other capital city on earth'.[32] He praises the absence of malnutrition, poverty, brothels, opium dens, beggars, and drug pedlars. 'More extraordinary, it is a city without privately owned cars, without churches (excluding two relics, one Catholic and one Protestant), without commercial advertising, and without any night-life (even most restaurants are closed by 8.30pm).' He also notes the lack of birds and flies.[33] The prevailing image of the Chinese lifestyle, even that of the main cities, was that it was puritanical and insufferably virtuous, stark, drab, colourless, and downright boring. Clothing was far too uniform, with too many Mao suits; women tried to avoid their sexual attraction to men by wearing dull garb and no make-up. Social dancing, which to most Westerners meant that in the Western style, was banned as bourgeois.

In his visit to China in 1978, playwright Arthur Miller had been horrified by the 'nearly total ignorance of the West's culture' he found in China, even among the intelligentsia. He had assumed that, even in a totalitarian state such as China, the leaders and intellectuals would 'not be foolishly bound by the isolation imposed on the people', but had found this belief quite wrong.[34] Miller's commentary on China is frank, provocative, and insightful, but generally sympathetic to the Chinese and defensive of what they do. His comments on their ignorance of Western culture is among the more trenchant sections in its criticism.

But in the 1980s, things were vastly different in China's urban lifestyle and in its knowledge of, and influence from, the West. 'New

new China, a stunning change in lifestyle', gloated the American, Hong Kong-based *Asiaweek* (19 April 1985) on its front cover. The feature article on China's lifestyle emphasized enthusiasm for Westernized pop music and social dancing. 'In the wake of unprecedented sales of hi-fi equipment and leather shoes has sprouted a new generation of dancebugs, who have been tangoing and discoing since late 1984.'[35] The 'chart-topping British duo, Wham!' made it to China, being rapturously welcomed by young Chinese and portraying a generally positive image of China to the West. 'The quasi-bourgeoisification of everyday life in China has progressed dramatically. Big spending and the indulgence of personal tastes are not only sanctioned but in many instances encouraged by the Communist Party.'[36] But of course it was still fashionable to point out how out of date most of the pop music was: 'Back in the late 70s,' said the 'green bible', 'Saturday Night Fever (1940s style) hit Beijing'. 'Discos popped up in various hotels,' it added, 'and even attracted locals for a time, despite the high price.[37]

Luxury wedding feasts, another feature of the new prosperity, came back with a vengeance. Of course we here confront not a new but a revived phenomenon, for the image of the Chinese as lovers of banquets is as old as the culture itself. 'Whether the occasion is a business deal or a family gathering, a birthday or a New Year festival, the Chinese love to celebrate it at the table,'[38] declared the British television series *The Heart of the Dragon*, referring to all periods of Chinese history, including the 1980s.

This was representative of a more general important image that emphasized social stability as a Chinese virtue, and which tended to place a high priority on the Chineseness of lifestyle in China at all times. A good exponent of this view was David Bonavia, who saw China as 'a genuinely ancient polity which had set up social cohesion and stability as the most important goal of human life'. Life there 'is geared to make everyone feel wanted—the surest defence against personal insecurity'. His conclusion about the Chinese people was that they are 'of a fundamentally stable temperament—industrious when properly motivated, unambitious of conquest or expansion, good-humoured in the main, appreciative of all the pleasures of life, and inventive in coping with problems'.[39] He explained the exceptions as a result of misgovernment.

On the other hand, what is most striking about Western images of the new lifestyle of the 1980s is the extent to which it was seen as nearly synonymous with Westernization. *Asiaweek* called the change 'the modernisation and Westernisation of lifestyle' and saw it as a central element in an official 'effort to bring China into the ranks of the world's most advanced nations'.[40] It was the experience of the West and other advanced capitalist countries that modernization, advancement, and economic power had gone hand in hand with luxury cosmetics and beauty parlours, with ever-changing styles of social dancing, and Western or Westernized pop music, in short with that originally Western phonomenon of consumerism. So obviously the Western image was that China's experience was following this well-tried model.

Probably the great majority in the West saw this new consumerism as highly desirable, both for the West and for the Chinese themselves. Certainly it could do no harm to trade and other economic relations between China and Western countries. There was, however, another side to the picture: people worried about the short- and long-term effects of Western consumerism on China.

Coca-Cola, that almost universally favoured symbol of American capitalist consumerism, made its entry into the Chinese market, provoking amusement and delight among most Western tourists, but concern among those who had admired China's ability to resist 'Coca-Colonization'. Clyde Cameron, the former Australian Labor government minister, wrote that 'the idea of the Coca-Cola banner over China left me feeling much the same as I guess a good Catholic would feel at seeing the hammer and sickle hoisted over St Peter's Basilica'. Still, he did see 'the need to cater for foreign tourists' and ended up with the belief, and hope, 'that Coca-Cola will earn more foreign currency for the Chinese people than it does for its own shareholders'.[41]

A more broad-ranging, though less hard-hitting, attack on the excessive Westernization some perceived to have reached China came from Orville Schell. On a visit to China in the mid-1980s he was very struck by the rapid growth of large and magnificent luxury hotels, Western-style restaurants such as Maxim's, fashion parades and a thriving cosmetics industry, and other such manifestations of consumerism and Westernization. 'Once again China is looking westward.' In some ways, he states, this is well and good, since China is now 'unified and stronger' than in the past. Schell continues:

> But as Westerners flood back into China, reviving foreign enclaves
> of privilege in the old coastal cities that once comprised the
> ignominious 'treaty ports', one cannot help but wonder what
> has become of that very tender place in China's collective psyche

which in the past had felt so humiliated in the face of Western wealth, power, and technological superiority. At least in those areas through which I travelled in 1983 and 1984, the Chinese appeared to have at least temporarily lost touch with this current in their recent history.[42]

Such comments probably spring from surprise at the speed, extent, and manner of Westernization in China. Among the Vietnam War generation were many who saw good in those prepared to resist the consumerism of their own society, and China was a model. Even though the great majority could admit that they misread the nature of the anti-consumerist society they admired, they still felt let down by many of the manifestations of the 'open door'. Just as delight over Westernization was for some the expression of a hope fulfilled, so for others it was one of disappointment.

Family, Women

It was a dominant image of China to suppose that the key social unit had always been, and remained, the family. 'So Chinese . . . bred for loyalty, the family always coming first,'[43] thinks a popular 'superthriller''s main character about a Chinese male friend. Of course there was a time, in the 1950s, when some image-creators claimed that the CCP was trying to break down and destroy the family but very few indeed still believed that in the 1980s. Perhaps more important, the general revival of tradition meant that the family as an institution was seen as stronger then than at any other time since 1949. 'Since the death of Mao the family has been given an increasingly positive role, especially in the economic sphere,' said an influential television programme.[44]

One persistent image was thus of comparatively little change, especially in the countryside. 'The patrilineal family remains strong. The state, in a sense, has been pre-empted by the family both in authority over individuals and even in economic organization,' stated academic specialist Margery Wolf. 'Social and kin relationships persist to this day, retarding and sometimes deflecting ideological change.' In the cities 'changes have been greater and less superficial. Ideological education has been more persuasive and more pervasive'. Thus authority over individuals had been transferred from family to state in a much more thoroughgoing way in the cities than in the countryside.[45]

One area to show some change in the 1980s, for the first time in the People's Republic, was 'the new infatuation with romantic love'.[46] The image was hardly of anything even remotely approaching a sexual revolution, but was closer to the Hollywood era of the 1930s and 1940s, with 'tender but chaste embraces in the moonlight, and couples living happily ever after'.[47] This 'falling in love with love', as Beverley Hooper entitled her chapter on the subject, was thus seen as another example of Western influence, albeit very, even absurdly, old-fashioned.

The discovery of romantic love carried no implications about the disappearance of arranged marriages. One very well informed coffee-table book claimed that 'the choice of marriage partners still lies mainly with the parents' in the Chinese countryside, 'but the young people have a right of veto', so there was some improvement on the past. In the cities, 'choice of partners tends to be initiated by the young themselves, but is subject to a degree of veto by the parents and cadres in the unit in which they work'.[48] Hooper's research confirmed not only the image that marriages arranged with the agreement of the spouses concerned were still normal in the countryside, but also the 'considerable parental influence' in marriage in the cities.[49] This became a popular image found both in academic and journalistic literature. It suggested change from pre-1949 patterns, but not nearly as much as observers of the Vietnam war generation believed in the late 1960s and early 1970s.

So marriage remained essentially a partnership between two families, rather than two individuals. It was certainly the popular Western perception that this system worked to the disadvantage of women. British academic Elisabeth Croll was among those who cited 'the persistence of the betrothal gift' as one of the reasons why arranged marriages were still so numerous in the countryside. The betrothal gift from the groom's family made the marriage the 'thinly disguised purchase' of a bride from another family.[50]

The role and status of women in Chinese society since Mao was examined by quite a few Westerners in the 1980s, especially feminist academics, resulting in some clear images on these subjects. Possibly the leading one was Margery Wolf, whose book *Revolution Postponed: Women in Contemporary China* in some ways represented the fairly general opinion in well-informed circles in the West. Her view was that although women had always been part of the revolution, they had not benefitted from it to an extent even slightly approaching their commitment to it. Life for the average person in China 'has been raised to standards beyond the hope of the previous generation', but whenever a crisis occurred the CCP sacrificed the interests of women first. Under Deng Xiaoping 'women are being told to step aside in the interests of the nation' yet again. 'Though the revolution for women has never been repudiated, it has been postponed all too many times.'[51] It may be added that Wolf's view contrasted on this point with the even stronger one presented by Judith Stacey, who argued that the Party had not postponed the women's revolution but, despite its numerous statements to the contrary, never wanted or encouraged it in the first place. What the Party had always wanted for women was a stable family life in the traditional patriarchal style.[52] In this image, socialism was the enemy of feminism, not its friend.

The scholars researching women included many who at one time had admired what they perceived as China's leading role in the liberation of women, especially as a result of the Cultural Revolution. But whereas Western feminist women once looked to China for guidance, they no longer did so in the 1980s. One scholar, taking part in a seminar discussion on the position of women in China since 1978, was moved to ask, what do Chinese women 'have to teach us now?' What 'vision' did anyone find in China? And the answer: 'there was a collective sigh . . . neither the speakers nor anyone else in the room could cite recent lessons from the Chinese women's movement'.[53] The collective sigh was perhaps a rather patronizing way of expressing disappointment of a sort encountered before in these pages, those who saw good in the Cultural Revolution and felt let down when China denounced it as a fraud. But whatever one thinks about the feminist stand, it is very striking to find anybody expecting to draw a lesson for the West in China, not the usual converse.

The reasons for the 'postponed revolution', in the view of Western observers, were various. One writer in an influential British encyclopaedia on China selected three. One was 'the lack of sustained commitment by leaders', a view which agreed with Wolf and Stacey in attributing blame to the government. But a second, more important, reason was that structural change in rural life had not been on a scale large enough to force a greater rise in women's status. Finally, there were not enough 'social settings in which informal contacts between boys and girls occur'. So what alternative remained but to retain arranged marriages, including 'the payment of a substantial bride price to the girl's family'?[54]

Is it possible to draw any general conclusions on images of the status of women in China in the 1980s? The dominant view was that, for all the many shortcomings, they had indeed come a long way since 1949. David Bonavia wrote that 'there can be no question that women have immensely improved their social and economic position since 1949, and if they have sacrificed certain cultural and political freedoms in doing so, the men have sacrificed them too'.[55] A husband-and-wife team of journalists attached to two influential American newspapers wrote of 'an ironic aspect of how important women have become' in the fact that it was nearly always the woman who sued for divorce. They were also struck by the fact that the age-old deference and strict obedience women once had to pay their husbands had to some extent declined, even in the countryside.[56]

Elisabeth Croll retained a degree of optimism about the future when she ended her book on Chinese women since Mao by writing that 'they may yet become equal with the men of their household, their community and their society'.[57] On the other hand, Margery Wolf's concluded her 'none too cheerful book'[58] by speculating that if a revolution for women was ever to occur, 'they must be allowed to do as Mao did, to gather together like-minded people who see the shortcomings of the present social order and want to change it'. The positive reference to Mao is highly ambiguous, and could be taken as support for the policies of the Cultural Revolution as they affected women or as a call for violent overthrow of the social system. She believed a revolution was desirable and in accordance with the wishes of at least a section of Chinese women, but nevertheless unlikely in the short term. 'Everything I read and hear suggests that those people are out there, but thus far they are isolated souls only partially aware of their shared oppression. Until they join together, they are not a movement, let alone a revolution.'[59]

Population Policy

Most people in the West acknowledge that China needs to keep its population growth rate low if it is to modernize. As we saw, the 1985 World Bank report, based on already established Chinese policy, specified 1 per cent per year. However, China's one-child policy has aroused much heated controversy in the West and a number of different images and views.

In the 1980s a great many people admired China for having dared to take serious action to come to grips with an extremely serious problem. The United Nations undoubtedly expressed a view widely shared in Western countries when in September 1983 its Secretary-General Javier Pérez de Cuéllar presented one of its two first annual population awards to Qian Xinzhong, Chinese minister in charge of the State Family Planning Commission, for his outstanding contribution to family planning. In August 1984 the UN held an international population conference in Mexico City. One report states that amid the airing of many problems the conference heard some good news, including that developing countries as a whole had slowed their birth rates by 11 per cent in fifteen years. 'Much of the credit for this goes to Asian countries. The most startling example is China: the country's one-child-family programme has resulted in a thirty-three per cent drop in the population growth rate in fifteen years.' Indeed, China's achievement is so great as to cover up failures elsewhere, 'since China's statistics affect the world average so heavily'.[60]

The alternative image of China's relative failure in population control also had its supporters, especially when considering the vast countryside in the late 1980s. The 'draconian' birth-control policy 'does not work' was the flat verdict of the influential Italian journalist Tiziano Terzani.[61] Such reductions as occurred to the mid-1980s still fell short of the authorities' targets. The conclusion of one general history of the PRC that 'the whole problem proved both insistent and intractable' would certainly find enough supporters in the West to be described as an image.[62]

To attain a drop in population growth rate, it has been necessary to carry out intensive organization and surveillance. One value shared by most people in the West is that the state should not interfere directly in the private lives of the people. However, most have been prepared to concede that China's values may be different and the problem it faces is grave enough to warrant the necessity of the one-child policy. An example is a fifty-minute BBC *Horizon* television documentary of 1983 entitled *China's Child*, which focused attention on the city of Changzhou in Jiangsu Province. It explained in some detail the quota system and the women who went round keeping an eye on younger women, persuading them to sign pledges and to undergo abortions if they became pregnant by mistake. The programme concluded by supporting the policy as necessary, whatever the disadvantages for the individual person. 'It *is* harsh, but is there an alternative?' was the final rhetorical question.

An essentially similar verdict resulted from an International Workshop held in England in 1983. In particular, the discussion of the problems in the countryside found the achievements to that time remarkable but recognized the great human cost: 'A whole generation is being asked to give up the children it wants. Millions of women undergo abortions which they would prefer not to have.' But 'against all this must be balanced the potential cost of inaction', the implication being that failure of the programme would bring disasters very much greater than long-term persistence in it.[63] This image is similar to that of a Western diplomat friend of the author who commented about the 1980s that he had never met a Chinese who liked the population policy, nor one who did not concede its necessity.

The reference to abortions, partly or fully forced, was perennial in the discussion of China's population policy and aroused very negative images. Bergère refers to 'the brutality of this family planning policy'. She cites an example of 'terrorism' in one part of Guangdong province in 1981, when the official press reported that the public security had forcibly taken pregnant women to the local hospital for abortions. She does not claim such cases as necessarily representative but does conclude that coercive methods are in widespread use to procure abortions to end pregnancies not permitted by the relevant authorities.[64]

Steven Mosher lived and travelled in southern China from September 1979 to April 1980 as a graduate student of Stanford University. He had the opportunity to study intensively a commune in Shunde county near Guangzhou and reported frequent forced abortions, including in the third trimester.[65] He also photographed a woman undergoing an abortion, and published the resultant picture, both actions without her permission. For this and other breaches of anthropological and academic ethics he was expelled from Stanford University in February 1983, and following extensive internal reviews, the Stanford University President, Donald Kennedy, upheld the termination in September 1985. However, Mosher became a *cause célèbre* throughout the Western world, many supporters arguing that freedom of speech should have prevented his dismissal from Stanford's graduate programme.

Quite apart from its attitude towards China, the US administration of Ronald Reagan (January 1981–January 1989) introduced anti-abortion and other similar anti-feminist measures in the United States. Despite strenuous protests from China, the US Agency for International Development in 1985 and 1986 actually withheld significant pledged contributions to the UN Fund for Population Activities, arguing that it was not prepared to contribute money towards a programme like China's, which involved forced abortions. Such action enjoyed support from a substantial number of people in the United States and elsewhere, whose image of China's population policy was that it seriously violated human rights because it infringed the right to procreate and involved unwarranted interference by the state in the private affairs of the people, as well as forced abortions, even in the third trimester.

Not only the methods but several by-products of the population policy became widely known and were discussed in the West, even among people not normally interested in China. These include the problem of the only-child syndrome. Terzani's belief was that the population policy was producing a generation of 'lonely, pampered, overprotected, overfed' children, of 'spoiled people'.[66] But the one to arouse the greatest interest and concern was the 'tragic problem' of female infanticide,[67] which was widely discussed in academic, journalistic, and other circles. The 'green bible' probably reflected the views and images of many ordinary non-China-specialists in the West who believed that the population policy was both necessary and at least partly effective. Its commentary on the problem of infanticide reads as follows:

> If the Chinese can be convinced or cajoled or persuaded or pressured into accepting birth control, the one thing they cannot agree to accept is the sex of their only child. The desire for male children is deeply ingrained in the Chinese mentality, and the ancient custom of female infanticide continues to this day—as the Chinese government and press will freely admit.[68]

The desire for sons, as well as female infanticide, are thus seen as part of a return to tradition. Terzani is more outright in his condemnation. His account of the population policy is headed 'The Best Baby is a Dead Baby', a title giving the impression that infanticide is more or less official policy, and begins with horrific stories of female infanticide and forced abortions so late as to be hardly different from murder.[69]

It is obvious from earlier chapters that the image of China as a country with an enormous population is nothing new. But whereas in dynastic times it was usually a positive image, a feature appropriate to China's prosperity, grandeur or power, in the 1980s it was dominantly a negative one. The majority of Western observers regarded it as an obstacle to modernization. David Bonavia expressed a thoroughly typical view when he said that 'the solution of many of

China's most pressing problems has created a new monster, population growth'. What he meant is as follows: 'improved medical services, an end to protracted civil war, and reasonably stable food supplies have led the country into a demographic crisis which must be solved in the near future if past achievements are not to be wiped out'.[70] That was a view essentially similar to Chinese policy. It is true that for some people in the West, the chances of modernization did not balance out the negative features of the birth control policy. But few still saw China's large population as a reason for admiration, certainly not as a source of prosperity.

Conclusion

One of the dominant images Westerners held of China was that, while retaining its essential Chineseness, it was progressively and willingly becoming more like the West which, in general, meant that China was moving in the right direction. The overall Western image of China was thus a broadly positive one. In the United States in 1979 a Gallup poll took a survey on China that asked respondents to place China on a scale ranging from +5 to -5. Only 29 per cent put China in the plus categories, but the next year the proportion had leapt to 42 per cent. In 1980, another surveying body, Potomac Associates, found 53 per cent of people 'mildly favourable' and 17 per cent 'highly favourable' in their feelings about China.[71]

Although extremely negative images remained familiar in the 1980s, they were no longer dominant. The expressions of public opinion would suggest that another more positive image would find much more support. David Bonavia articulates it well.

> The Chinese are beginning to enjoy a richer and more satisfying cultural life, greater political freedom, and the prospect of an easier, more comfortable existence. The country's international prestige has never been higher, and the rich nations are all keen to lend China money for development.[72]

Bonavia's book has some quite trenchant criticisms to make, but the overall impression is quite positive about China. And the last words of the book call for a greater attempt to understand China: 'The other two superpowers have made gross miscalculations in their past dealings with China. To do so in the future will be dangerous for all.'[73]

The changes in the realities of China in the decade and more under discussion in this chapter were probably more substantial than in the Western images of them. The reason for this is that the major change in the policy of the United States and several other Western countries towards China came in the early 1970s, whereas the reform period in China itself did not begin until the late 1970s. By then the images of Westerners generally concerned a friendly nation, at times even nearly an ally.

Although China remained under the rule of a Communist Party which still claimed to adhere to Marxism–Leninism, there was much to be gained through friendship with the capitalist West. Most Westerners saw absolutely no reason why the West and China should not trade and hold other economic dealings with each other, deriving extensive and mutual profits. At times, China even seemed to exult in the rejection of socialist notions and in the adoption of economic and governmental patterns usually associated with capitalism. It was quite possible for Westerners to appreciate China without too much need to come to grips with unfamiliar or challenging values.

On the whole, Western images of China in the 1980s were remarkably positive. There are of course major exceptions to this suggestion. Images of Chinese society, especially its treatment of women, were in many ways decidedly critical, and the reaction of the American government to China's population policy was condemnatory. Yet prevailing views on China's foreign relations, economy and standard of living, government, and other topics, are definitely sympathetic to, and even admiring of, China's performance.

In line with Foucault's power/knowledge correlationship, Western images of China in the 1980s fitted the strategic and economic interests of Western government and ruling groups nicely. In the economic sphere, in the 1980s Western interests led towards the expectations of major profits deriving from dealings with China and thus towards more positive images. In some ways they were rather too positive, preparing the way for a major disappointment when a major crisis erupted in 1989.

Notes

1   Church, a.o., 'China', p. 17.
2   Haberman, 'Russia's Reach for the Pacific', pp. 22, 25.
3   Bernstein, 'China in 1984, The Year of Hong Kong', p. 50.

4   Lam, 'Peking Pursues Its Own Path', p. 48. Lam is reviewing and summarizing the views put forward in a book by six American sinologists: Harding (ed.), *China's Foreign Relations in the 1980s*.
5   For instance see Bonavia, 'Superpower Links are the Prime Concern', p. 92.
6   Bonavia, *The Chinese*, p. 279.
7   Dietrich, *People's China*, p. 284.
8   Salisbury, 'China's CEO', p. 72.
9   Davies, 'Traveller's Tales', p. 35.
10   Butterfield, *China, Alive in the Bitter Sea*, p. 325.
11   Kaplan and de Keijzer, *The China Guidebook*, pp. 29–31.
12   Samagalski and Buckley, *China—A Travel Survival Kit*, p. 51.
13   Bergère, *La République populaire de Chine*, p. 192.
14   Clayre, *The Heart of the Dragon*, p. 93.
15   See especially Bernstein, *From the Center of the Earth*, pp. 127–40, and Butterfield, *China, Alive in the Bitter Sea*, pp. 64–88.
16   Butterfield, *China, Alive in the Bitter Sea*, p. 88.
17   Cameron, *China, Communism and Coca-Cola*, p. 2.
18   Townsend and Womack, *Politics in China*, p. 413.
19   Dietrich, *People's China, A Brief History*, p. 278
20   Lee, 'The Curtain Goes Up', p. 50.
21   Cudlip, *Comprador*, p. 468.
22   Delfs, 'Economic Marathon', p. 50.
23   Porter, a.o., *China, Long-term Development Issues and Options*, pp. 1–2.
24   Ibid., p. 8.
25   Ibid., pp. 98–9.
26   Ibid., p. 20.
27   Bush, 'Introduction', in Bush (ed.), *China Briefing,1982*, pp. 3–4.
28   Bernstein, *From the Center of the Earth*, p. 52.
29   Schell, *To Get Rich is Glorious*, p. 50.
30   Ibid., p. 51.
31   Townsend and Womack, *Politics in China*, p. 194.
32   Bonavia, *Peking*, p. 5.
33   Ibid., p. 7.
34   Morath and Miller, *Chinese Encounters*, p. 14.
35   'Enjoying Life', p. 30.
36   Ibid., p. 29.
37   Samagalski and Buckley, *China—A Travel Survival Kit*, p. 568.
38   Clayre, *The Heart of the Dragon*, p. 122.
39   Bonavia, *The Chinese*, pp. 300–1.
40   'Enjoying Life', p. 30.
41   Cameron, *China, Communism and Coca-Cola*, p. 253.
42   Schell, *To Get Rich is Glorious*, pp. 209–10.
43   Cudlip, *Comprador*, p. 335.
44   Clayre, *The Heart of the Dragon*, p. 81.
45   Wolf, 'Marriage, Family, and the State in Contemporary China', p. 235.
46   Hooper, *Youth in China*, p. 176.
47   Ibid., p. 177.
48   Blunden and Elvin, *Cultural Atlas of China*, p. 217.

49   Hooper, *Youth in China*, pp. 190–92.
50   Croll, *Chinese Women Since Mao*, p. 79.
51   Wolf, *Revolution Postponed*, p. 26.
52   Stacey, *Patriarchy and Socialist Revolution in China*, pp. 155–57.
53   Young, 'Introduction', p. 209.
54   Gilbert Rozman, 'The Status of Women', in Hook (ed.), *The Cambridge Encyclopaedia of China*, p. 116.
55   Bonavia, *The Chinese*, p. 80.
56   Mathews and Mathews, *One Billion, A China Chronicle*. Jay Mathews was attached to the *Washington Post*, his wife Linda to the *Los Angeles Times*.
57   Croll, *Chinese Women*, p. 129.
58   Wolf, *Revolution Postponed*, p. 261.
59   Ibid., pp. 272–73.
60   *Far Eastern Economic Review Asia 1985 Yearbook*, pp. 38, 40.
61   Terzani, *Behind the Forbidden Door*, p. 189.
62   Dietrich, *People's China*, p. 291.
63   Davin, 'The Single-child Family Policy in the Countryside', in Croll, Davin and Kane (eds.), *China's One-Child Family Policy*, p. 74.
64   Bergère, *La République populaire de Chine*, p. 187.
65   See Mosher, *Broken Earth*, pp. 256–61.
66   Terzani, *Behind the Forbidden Door*, p. 196.
67   Davin, 'The Single-child Family Policy', p. 62.
68   Samagalski and Buckley, *China*, p. 56.
69   Terzani, *Behind the Forbidden Door*, p. 189.
70   Bonavia, *The Chinese*, p. 91.
71   'A Romance Turns Sour', p. 44.
72   Bonavia, *The Chinese*, pp. 292–93.
73   Ibid., p. 305.

9
Western Images since 1989: Politics and International Relations

There have been two basically contradictory images of China in the period from 1989 to the middle of 1998. On the one hand, China has had the image of a burgeoning economy and a rising standard of living. On the other hand, it has had the reputation of a country with a poor human rights records where, despite the increasing prosperity, individuals are not well treated and dissidents, both political and religious, are persecuted.

The Beijing massacre of early June 1989 produced a catastrophic effect on Western images of China. Whereas before that event the West viewed China as a country advancing towards democracy and capitalism, it saw itself as deceived and its illusions shattered by the massacre. The period since 1989 has seen changes, with a notable improvement from mid-1997 thanks to China's handling of the Asian currency crisis. But if the comparison is with the years before, then the 1990s form a more or less coherent period.

Images of the Student Demonstrations of 1989

The West, and in particular the Western media, were more or less fully on side with the students' rights from the beginning of the student movement of April to June 1989. There were several reasons for this. One was that the students were shouting slogans that were seen as in conformity with Western values, especially 'freedom and democracy'. The students' values were in large measure influenced by the West. The period of reform had put a premium on copying the West for its wealth and freedom, and many students had studied either in, or about, the West, or both. Perhaps the best example of the debt which the students owed the West was the statue of the *Goddess of Democracy* (*Minzhu nüshen*), erected in Tiananmen Square on 30 May 1989, which in its structure and style was quite clearly modelled on the Statue of Liberty. As one Western journalist commented: 'Smack in the political centre of a communist state, students had planted freedom's most powerful beacon.'[1]

A second, and rather more important, reason why the West and Western media supported the students was that the confluence of events brought numerous Western journalists into the thick of the movement, and the students were more than willing to use them to further their own cause. Soviet leader Mikhail Gorbachev visited China from 15 to 18 May 1989, bringing numerous Western journalists to China. In the event, the Gorbachev visit was totally overshadowed by the student demonstrations in the centre of Beijing, and the occupation of Tiananmen Square by the students on 13 May. The American television companies CBS and CNN transmitted the student demonstrations more or less around the clock, as they were happening. This was the first time such intensive on-the-spot Western reporting had occurred in China. The demonstrations were dramatic enough as they were, but they also had another effect: they 'thrust the journalists themselves onto center stage'.[2] It is hardly surprising that the journalist community reacted to this situation with exultation.

The third reason why the Western media, and consequently the West, supported the students was because of the nature of the media in the contemporary developed world. Numerous thousands of people demonstrating along the vast Chang'an Boulevard in central Beijing towards the magnificent and enormous Tiananmen Square make good television. Students able and willing to give interviews in English cannot fail to impress. 'Democracy or death' and 'Liberty or death', favourite slogans of the demonstrators, inevitably stir the emotions. In television terms the contrast with statesmen, even Gorbachev, is highly dramatic. Who wants to see politicians banqueting on television? The only memorable shot that the Gorbachev visit produced lasted hardly more than a minute. It was that of Deng Xiaoping dropping his food, with the reporter's comment that he could not even control his own chopsticks any longer, let alone the situation in China. A press conference about a joint communiqué on the normalization of relations is lacklustre, almost by its very nature. But the students were exciting and new. There was always a story to come from the hunger-strikers, and there was the occasional romance among the occupiers of the Square. The combination of politics and romantic love can be relied on for a highly reportable story. The students could command attention more or less indefinitely. The main interest in the government side was its power struggle, showing the government in a bad light. Of course there was a power struggle among the students too, but that was not nearly so clear at the time, and not nearly as vicious or important as the one in the government between Premier Li Peng and Party General Secretary Zhao Ziyang.

Although the last of these three reasons applies much more powerfully to television than to other media, students and demonstrations can capture the imagination in print. The following little episode carries its own powerful image of sympathy for the students and their cause.

> In the centre of the crowd at Tiananmen Square—right at the foot of the monument to revolutionary heroes—are 3000 students who have been on a hunger strike for five days. Some take shelter from the broiling sun under umbrellas. Others, near exhaustion, are lying on the hot concrete. A cheer goes up and an elderly woman hobbles forward, holding aloft a rough placard that reads: 'The students are right in their actions.' Her lined face is tense, and tears stream down her cheeks.[3]

What is so moving here is the human image of the suffering students and the supportive old woman. Everybody was against the pig-headed government, with its old men. Even Deng Xiaoping, who had actually enjoyed a very positive image in the West until not long before, had lost popular support. A story reported in one of the most widely read of American weeklies crystallized the image of his fallen reputation. He is said to have argued against Zhao Ziyang—who favoured conciliation with the students—in favour of imposing martial law on 20 May. Said Deng in defence of martial law: 'I have 3 million troops behind me,' to which Zhao replied, 'I have all the people of China'. Deng dismissed him, 'you have nothing'.[4]

The image of the cruel old men, caring naught for the people, or apparently for anything but their own power, comes over very clearly in a summary of the whole crisis from April to June 1989 in *Reader's Digest*. The passage introduces a series of journalists' extracts on the period from British and American newspapers and magazines. The intention of the writer is to express reality, but since the readership is so large, the passage is also an excellent articulation of Western images of China during those months. The images are strengthened by the fact that the written text is set against a picture of Tiananmen Square filled with peaceful demonstrators.

For a few heady weeks in the Beijing spring, Tiananmen Square pulsated to the intoxicating rhythm of students and workers speaking out for freedom and democracy. As the movement spread to other cities, people throughout the free world prayed for a successful outcome. However, locked in the fortress-like Great Hall of the People, China's ageing leaders—in a great leap backwards—were preparing a purge as potent as any inflicted by the ancient Chinese warlords.[5]

The Beijing Massacre and the Human Rights Issue

Obviously the potent purge is a reference to the incident of the night of 3–4 June 1989. This frightful event, with tanks and troops violently crushing opposition moving into Tiananmen Square, signalled the defeat of the student movement. The government declared that the troops had quelled a 'counterrevolutionary rebellion' aimed at overthrowing the CCP, and that their success had saved the PRC. English-speaking Western countries usually know this incident as 'the Tiananmen massacre' or 'the Beijing massacre'.

In the West, the issue of human rights overnight became a crucial one, both in popular images and in the policy of governments towards China. The previous support for the students and opposition to the government strengthened. Whereas before the incident China as a whole enjoyed a reasonably positive image, it changed overnight to a very bleak one.

Given the horror of what had happened, this change requires no explanation beyond the event itself. However, there were several factors which exacerbated the negative image. One was that this event occurred right in the middle of a national capital, with numerous journalists, diplomats, and others there to record what had happened and to relay it instantly to the world. This was not the case with several other massacres of significant proportions, in particular that in Kwangju, Republic of Korea, in May 1980.

A second reason applies much more to the United States than to any other Western country, and it is a feeling found in the aftermath of the revolution in 1949 as well (see Chapter 6): the sense that China's leaders had turned against them. An American writer exclaims that 'on 4 June 1989 China's leaders violently rejected America's tutelage', which apparently they had been accepting before that. 'Once again the peaceful and courageous Chinese people were being oppressed by the cruel hordes of an alien ideology. The old image of the People's Republic as an evil empire came unbidden to the American mind.'[6]

A third, and related, point is that most people in the West were genuinely surprised and disappointed that the government reacted in this brutal way. Despite the decline in Deng Xiaoping's reputation, very few in the United States or any other Western country believed he would actually authorize a massacre.

One exception to this pattern was Simon Leys, encountered previously. On the morning of 3 June 1989, an interview with him was published in which he denounced the CCP regime for its brutality but emphasized that the demonstrations would go down in history as a landmark in the Long March of humankind towards democracy and away from totalitarianism.[7] Ryckmans gained and deserved a great deal of creditable publicity for his prescience. On the other hand, an important flaw in his view was his observation on 'the heart of the crisis', which was 'that the Chinese communist regime is actually dead—and has been dead for several years already'. While he did concede that 'it might still take a while before it is finally buried', the implication was fairly clear that he expected the imminent overthrow of the CCP.

Several particular images from the incident and its aftermath may be specified as of unusual interest. The most important is that of a nineteen-year-old man, carrying a jacket and a book-bag, standing defiantly in front of a line of tanks. One source has him as 'the hero of that day, perhaps of the whole nightmarish week'.[8] Several different pictures of him were taken at slightly different stages of his confrontation with the tank. A version of the picture found its way onto the front cover of *Time* magazine[9] and on at least two well-known books published shortly afterwards, one of them being a diary of *New York Times* foreign correspondent Harrison Salisbury whom the back of the book describes as 'the West's best-known China commentator'.[10] The following is a detailed account explaining the picture of the man and the tanks.

> Walking casually, a man stepped into the street, and stood stock-still before a column of tanks.
> The lead tank slowed to a crawl and stopped. Those behind halted, too, their huge engines roaring.
> The lead tank turned to its right; the man dodged to his left.
> The tank shifted to its left; the man shuffled to his right.

An incredible dance of death ensued between a man and a mechanical monster. The tank, like a befuddled robot, halted, and the man clambered onto its massive front. He climbed atop its turret and, for a glorious moment, stood there, the conqueror of the tanks.

People lining the side of the road burst into cheers. The man came down and stood at the tank's front.

There seemed little doubt this time that the driver would crush him. But other men dragged him away. The tanks moved on.

For a few minutes, the indomitable spirit of one man had triumphed over the war machine of China's rulers.[11]

A second powerful image was of a serious crackdown on dissent following the massacre, and large-scale arrests of dissidents, running into thousands. The first executions relating to the crisis took place in Shanghai on 21 June 1989. Three men were executed for setting fire to a train, which on 6 June had run into a human barricade trying to prevent soldiers from entering the city. John Chancellor on *NBC Nightly News* (21 June 1989) described how a crowd of several thousand had been assembled to watch the three men die by having bullets fired into their skulls. He expressed a commonly held image when he added: 'the word for that is barbaric'. 'It wasn't students who were executed today. It was three ordinary workers, murdered because a cynical government wants other workers to stay in line.' Chancellor's view was that the executions say 'more about China today than all the lies told by its government'.[12] In brief, the image of China as a cruel country where the government attempts to deceive the people revived strongly as a result of the incident.

In the aftermath of the massacre, Western governments reacted quickly in downgrading their relations with China and on the whole the people followed their governments. Tourism declined sharply. The Chinese found themselves relatively shunned by Western businessmen. Occupancy rates in the hotels in China's main cities fell drastically. Press comments continued to stress the crackdown and poor human rights records of the Chinese, presenting very negative images of China.

Because of the Gulf Crisis of 1990 and the Gulf War of early 1991, Iraq and its leader Saddam Hussein became the world's main international pariah, with the result that much Western odium moved away from China and towards Iraq. Yet the Beijing massacre continued to loom very large, with the lesson that this was a country with a poor human rights record. The 1990s saw a voluminous literature on the

1989 crisis in China by journalists, academics, and others, the great bulk of it severely critical of China and its regime. The massacre continued to be seen as the event that made Westerners wake up to themselves about the evils of communist rule in China. One American writer summed this perception up for the US itself as a progression 'from American illusions to Chinese reality'.[13]

Many of the student leaders left China for the United States and other Western countries after the defeat of their movement, and exerted considerable influence in their new homes concerning images of China. Western opinion remained positive about their role in 1989. Yet divisions emerged among the student leaders, which tended to lessen their impact and individuals came under criticism. Most notably a long documentary film entitled *The Gate of Heavenly Peace* appeared in 1996 about the 1989 crisis. While still hostile to the government and sympathetic to the student cause, the film was distinctly critical of several individual student leaders. In particular, it portrayed the main female leader Chai Ling as ambitious and selfish. It released an interview with her in which she said that she expected, and implied even wanted, blood to flow in Tiananmen Square, because this would expose the authorities as evil monsters and arouse the masses to resistance.

The Beijing massacre began to lose its immediacy as the 1990s progressed. Tibet (considered in Chapter 10) more and more joined the massacre as an example of the brutality of China's leaders and their lack of concern for human rights. Yet, the massacre remained a blot on China's record and the prime example of the suppression of individual liberties and abuse of human rights.

A powerful, though not generally dominant, American lobby argued that trading privileges should be subject to improvements in China's human rights performance, and both sides of the debate gained enough support to qualify as images of China. On several occasions, China released imprisoned dissidents on the eve of a major American decision over trade with China, giving rise to the image of a cunning China out to exploit American goodwill and naivety for its own material benefit.

A related and powerful image was the savage treatment, arrest, and imprisonment of dissidents, with Western opinion seeking to compensate through condemning the Chinese authorities and defending the right of peaceful disagreement and protest. By far the most important example was the case of Wei Jingsheng, China's most famous dissident. Sentenced to fifteen years' imprisonment in 1979 and released in 1993, Wei had again been imprisoned late in 1995. In theory his crime was to attempt the overthrow of the Chinese state, but in practice what riled the Chinese authorities was Wei's strong disagreement with Deng Xiaoping and opposition to the Chinese Communist Party. Western popular opinion was always supportive of Wei Jingsheng and condemnatory of China for its abuse of Wei's human rights.

Just after President Jiang Zemin's 1997 visit to the United States, the Chinese authorities released Wei Jingsheng. In the West most people regarded China's decision to release Wei as a goodwill gesture on which Presidents Clinton and Jiang had agreed during the latter's American visit. When Wei actually arrived in the United States, Clinton gave him a personal interview and the American media went out of its way to lionize him as a hero for his opposition to the current Chinese political system. Wei himself did what he could to influence popular opinion and governments against China. It is true that, after the initial gloss of Wei's release wore off, he suffered some criticism for arrogance and one-sidedness. Yet the overall result was that Western images of China regarding human rights did not improve nearly as much as the Chinese government had hoped.

Politics, Corruption

As China's economy recovered and grew with extraordinary rapidity from the early 1990s onwards, Western businesspeople and tourists returned to China. While the economy was quick to receive a favourable image, as discussed in Chapter 10, China continued to be regarded as an oppressive political system in which political reform was failing to keep up with economic reform. Even the opposite side of the coin is not particularly flattering to Chinese politics. Cheng Li, who was brought up in China but then emigrated to the United States, wrote a scholarly/journalistic book on his return to China in the mid-1990s called *Rediscovering China*. With a relatively positive view of China in general, the book characterized China as having progressed 'from a totalitarian regime to an authoritarian one'.[14] Meanwhile, governments tended to argue that the processes of democratization in many parts of the world, including East Asia, and the development of China's economy would inevitably lead to greater freedoms and eventually democratic elections in China as well. However, this was not universally accepted and in the meantime the Chinese government and party continued to receive bad press.

An image of China's politics to command enormous coverage was that of corruption. It came from all sides of the political spectrum and loomed large in popular, journalistic, and academic accounts of China in the 1990s. A major example, coming from the influential and image-making magazine *Time*, is from a series that in general is actually extremely positive about China.

> There has been a significant rise in corruption within the government, particularly in the south. Some officials in Shenzhen, for example, have become instant millionaires by using inside information on stock market coups. So extensive is corruption that party propagandists have called for people of 'noble spirit' to come forward and combat such decadent capitalist trends.[15]

A review of four books[16] describing '"real" Chinas' in the 1990s places corruption as the most important downside of rapid growth and the shift towards the market economy in China: 'First and foremost is the pervasiveness of corruption in China, ranging from mega-corruption involving high officials to rake-offs by village officials when collecting fines for excess births.'[17]

John Gittings sees corruption in the countryside not only as extremely serious but also as associated with a whole change in the way the Party regards the peasantry. Whereas it used to place a high priority on the peasants and take measures genuinely designed to raise their status and standard of living, this is no longer the case in the 1990s. In his view, on the contrary, millions of peasants believe that the Party's control has become more oppressive than it ever was. 'Local cadres and their families no longer feel inhibited by "revolutionary morality" from engaging in blatant corruption.' He argues that the cadres ripped off the assets of the former people's communes instead of allowing them into the market. His conclusion is stark and to the point. 'Peasants in the disadvantaged areas of Middle China get the worst of both worlds: the rural reforms have stopped half way between socialism and capitalism.'[18]

James Miles devotes a whole chapter in his book to 'the virus of corruption', of all kinds and at all levels. And the image he portrays is that it is not only all-encompassing, even essential to the system, but getting worse. While not denying that it is part of China's traditional way of life and exists elsewhere besides China, he regards it as worse there because of the tight connection between money-making business and bureaucracy in China in the 1990s.

What makes official corruption so destabilizing in China now, however, is that officials already have grossly disproportionate advantages in the race to set up a market economy. China may have given the go-ahead to engage in capitalism, but with land, property, and funds already concentrated in the hands of the state, the winners are bound to be those with bureaucratic connections. Japan and the 'little tigers' of Asia began with somewhat more level playing fields. In China, officials can often take virtually whatever risks they like with the money at their disposal, knowing they would nearly always be protected by their positions and the party. They and not legal codes usually determine what is sound business practice.[19]

In 1997 Hollywood issued several films showing China in an extremely bad light. Tibet was the main focus, and will be discussed in the next chapter. One that was set entirely in Beijing and presented very powerful negative images of China's law system and corrupt politics was *Red Corner*, in which the hero was the American attorney Jack Moore, played by the famous anti-China film star Richard Gere.

Moore is accused of murdering a Chinese woman, found dead after he had slept with her. He is defended by a Chinese female lawyer, Shen Yuelin, who becomes convinced that he is innocent. At the end, the two overcome the iniquities of the Chinese law system to prove that the whole murder was set up by corrupt officials.

The images presented in this film are of cruel police serving corrupt officials and a vicious law system in which it is appropriate to plead guilty, even if one is actually innocent, because of the slogan 'leniency to those who confess, severity for those who resist'. The police are shown as cruel and indifferent to justice or to human life. The female judge is portrayed as being without feeling, although to her and the film's credit she does hand down a not-guilty verdict at the end when confronted by the evidence. Several scenes show unimaginable cruelty and filth in the prison system.

Although she does not leave China, Shen Yuelin's conversion to the American point of view is central to the film's plot. At first she defends Chinese justice, by pointing out that the crime rate in China is far lower than in the United States, and that China has too many people to allow it to emphasize the individual rather than the community. However, she later regrets the silence of the people, herself included, which had permitted so much corrupt power to amass in so few hands. American liberal democratic thought is shown to triumph over Chinese communism, symbolized in the title of the film.

In short, the image of China that emerges is of a cruel country, where an outdated ideology reigns supreme, and where the law carries out the wishes of corrupt officials. The human rights of individuals are totally irrelevant to power-holders. The only bright spot is that justice prevails in the end. However, that is because of the superiority of the American way of life, which teaches individuals to stand up for themselves, and because the American hero has succeeded in influencing a Chinese lawyer to support him against her own system, despite the dangers this poses to her.

An image relating to China's polity that has aroused quite a bit of discussion in academic circles, though considerably less outside them, is whether the civil society exists in China, even in nascent form. 'Civil society' is understood as one that includes an emphasis on non-state, autonomous centres or groups of influence. The beginnings of such a society were seen in China because of the relaxations that emerged in the 1980s, and especially the large-scale student movement of 1989. Although the Beijing massacre implied a strong reversal, the money-making capitalist trends of the 1990s appeared to suggest at least some autonomy in some parts of society. And of course the use of the term 'civil society' raised the age-old debate about the appropriateness of applying an essentially Western term to a non-Western environment such as China. Although an academic book on 'civil society' published in 1997 canvasses various views,[20] it appears as though the notion of civil society as applied to China lessened in influence as the 1990s progressed and it became increasingly clear that China would not quickly adopt liberal democracy.

Leadership Images

Among Chinese leaders of the 1990s one, Deng Xiaoping, dominates Western images, with a small amount of space allocated to others, especially Jiang Zemin. There is some irony in Deng's almost exclusive domination, because, although he was certainly influential for much of the 1990s, he held no major official position after his retirement from the chairmanship of the State Military Commission in March 1990.

The images of Deng in the last years of his life were primarily two-fold. On the one hand, he was chiefly responsible for the Beijing massacre and for keeping in place the rule of the CCP, with all its attendant human rights abuses. On the other, he had brought about an extraordinary growth in the Chinese economy, far greater than most people had expected. David Goodman, who has written possibly the most successful biography of Deng Xiaoping published in the 1990s, sums him up as follows: 'Undoubtedly for some time to come in the public consciousness world-wide Deng Xiaoping will be associated not only with China's rapid economic growth and transformation but also with the events in Beijing during June 1989. The images associated with first the demonstrations, and then the use of military force in Tiananmen Square and its surroundings, were extremely powerful.'[21] A similar view, but with a somewhat different slant, is given by Jim Rohwer, who compares Deng's reform policies and his role in the Beijing events as follows: 'I suspect that it is for these reforms and their beneficent effects on the fate of hundreds of millions of people, rather than for the blood of thousands of people undoubtedly on his hands from Tiananmen and earlier atrocities, that Deng will in the end be mostly remembered'[22]

These images were approximately the same when Deng died in February 1997, but the balance appears to have shifted towards the overall view of him as the architect of modern China, whose rule had brought enormous benefits to the Chinese people. Patrick Tyler, of the *New York Times* (20 February 1997, p. 1), led his report on Deng's death with the comment that, as a kind of modern-day emperor, the leader had indeed enjoyed the 'mandate of heaven'. His formal obituary gave some space to 'the dark shadow of Tiananmen', but the major thrust of the obituary was positive. The headline ran 'Deng Xiaoping: a political wizard who put China on the capitalist road'. And one of the major verdicts on the man was that 'in the 18 years since he became China's undisputed leader, Mr Deng nourished an economic boom that radically improved the lives of China's 1.2 billion citizens'.[23]

A particularly laudatory obituary headlined that Deng Xiaoping was the 'man of the century', the following passage showing its flavour:

> When Deng Xiaoping died in Beijing last week at the age of 92, his place in Chinese and world history was assured. Arguably, the scale and scope of his achievements entitle him to be called the century's greatest political leader, certainly Asia's.
> Foremost among them was the restoration of hope—and a burgeoning self-confidence—to a proud civilization that had known little but war, famine and turmoil for the better part of the past two centuries. The great expectations ushered in with the founding of the People's Republic in 1949 proved cruelly ephemeral as China was soon brought to its knees again by the

excesses of Chairman Mao Zedong's rule. It was only 18 years ago that Deng grasped a demoralized, sulking nation of a billion people and yanked it to life. Since then, his reforms have not only given the Chinese their highest-ever living standards but also transformed the country into a global economic power. ...

In the number of lives he affected positively, Deng far outdistanced any other leader—anytime, anywhere.[24]

As a general statement of achievement for a national leader it is very difficult to imagine anything stronger than the last sentence of the quotation, which is highlighted as a subtitle to the whole obituary. The article does mention the 1989 crisis and Deng's role in it, but the impression left is that in the long haul of history this was no more than a minor hiccup in China's upward rise masterminded by Deng.

Among other leaders, Premier Li Peng generally has an unfavourable image, an unlovable bureaucrat whose enthusiastic support for the crackdown on the students in June 1989 disastrously sullied his reputation. On the other hand, Zhu Rongji, who succeeded him as Premier in March 1998, enjoys a very favourable image in the West. Free from any taint of involvement in the massacre, the most important images attached to Zhu are those of good economic sense and management skills, and hatred of bureaucracy. One commentator describes him as a 'dynamic financial reform wizard'.[25] A dictionary of Chinese politics has it that he has earned 'the name "one-chop" Zhu because of his brisk, no-nonsense approach and his keenness to cut through bureaucratic processes to achieve quick decisions'.[26]

Jiang Zemin, who became CCP General Secretary in June 1989 and State President in 1993, has mostly been portrayed as well-intentioned but lacking in charisma. Although thus occupying the top Party and State positions for most or all of the 1990s, he remained a rather nebulous figure for most of the decade. It was only after Deng's death in 1997 that he was able to establish himself as China's leader in most Western minds.

Jiang's official visit to the United States in late October and early November 1997 certainly did his image some good, if only in the sense that he had, by that time, moved out of the shadow of Deng Xiaoping. The Western media gave him reasonably good marks for his attempts to court the American corporate world and his fairly obvious attempts to show his knowledge and appreciation of American culture. Yet noted journalist Matt Forney commented that he still had to 'combat the impression that he is light-weight'. There was a much publicized public disagreement with Clinton over the Beijing massacre, and there were many anti-China demonstrations over the issues concerning Beijing, Taiwan, and Tibet. Certainly his efforts to explain China's position on these three issues failed to overcome negative American images on Chinese behaviour concerning them, and Forney goes on that 'he dashed his chance to win over the American people, as patriarch Deng Xiaoping had done so easily during his 1979 voyage to America'.[27]

In Chapter 7 the dominating and tyrannical leadership of Mao Zedong was identified as a major image of China at that time. To a far lesser extent the image of Deng Xiaoping was of a leader dominating the Chinese stage like a colossus. But in the mid-1990s some saw 'the power structure in China' as 'more collective and balanced than at any time since the heady days of Yanan', the CCP's wartime capital. In particular, some viewed the relationship between Jiang Zemin and Zhu Rongji as very good for China. Jiang himself 'does not stand out as having a distinctive character', but 'he has managed to surround himself with a number of brilliant leaders, such as Zhu Rongji'.[28] Thus, leadership images in the 1990s are a long way from those that were prevalent in the 1950s and 1960s.

China as a Threat?

One of the most striking Western images of China in the 1990s is the revival of the fear of China. There are two separate but closely related aspects to this image. The first is the perception of a growth in nationalism, the second that this nationalism will make China wish to spread outwards, constituting a threat both to its neighbours and to Western interests, especially those of the United States.

The perception of an increase in nationalism began with the Beijing massacre. The idea is that the incident showed the total disintegration of Marxism-Leninism as a viable ideology, with the result that the Chinese leadership was forced back on nationalism to provide some kind of credible alternative, with a view to maintaining its own rule. The feeling of nationalism intensified greatly with the decision taken in September 1993 that Sydney would host the 2000 Olympic Games, Sydney defeating Beijing by only a handful of votes. Although it was the International Olympic Committee that had taken the decision, the United States had gone out of its way to influence the vote against Beijing, on the grounds of its poor human rights. To China, this was an enormous humiliation, since it had been very confident of success, even feeling it had the right as a strengthening Asian nation to host the Games. The Beijing lawyer Lu Zhifang is quoted as commenting on the decision: 'That was the moment when the Chinese started believing that the US wanted to contain China. It really hurt China's feelings.'[29]

Lu's use of the word 'contain' brings us to the other part of the image, namely the perception that China is a growing, modernizing power, which will eventually become aggressive and a threat to regional and world stability, and therefore requires to be checked in some way, or 'contained'. Of course images are strongly divided in the West over this matter, but what is not in doubt is that the issue of China as a threat has again come onto the agenda of issues for debate concerning China. In the 1950s and 1960s this was one of the dominant images of China, but it began to wane in the late 1960s and early 1970s, disappearing more or less altogether by the 1980s. It is thus both important and striking to find the image reemerge in the 1990s.

Nowhere is the image of China as a threat more obvious than in the publication of two books in 1997, one from the United States, the other from Great Britain. They are *The Coming Conflict with China* by Richard Bernstein and Ross Munro, published by Knopf in New York, and *Dragon Strike: The Millennium War* by Humphrey Hawksley and Simon Holberton, published by Sidgwick & Jackson in London. Three of the four authors are well known for their knowledge of China and are influential in the formulation of images of the country. In particular, Richard Bernstein and Humphrey Hawksley were noted reporters on China, the former for the *New York Times*, the latter as the BBC's correspondent in Beijing. When his book with Bernstein came out, Ross Munro, though a Canadian, was head of the Foreign Policy Institute in Philadelphia, but had worked with the American human rights organization Asiawatch, being in Beijing at the time of the 1989 crisis.

Bernstein and Munro argue that China is an emerging hegemony, which is becoming increasingly assertive and aggressive as its modernization process proceeds. The United States is adopting a naive policy towards it, which in effect gives it what it wants without calling it to account for its aggressive policies. The book argues that China and the United States are on a collision course which will likely result in a war over Taiwan early in the twenty-first century. It argues further that the ones largely responsible for this coming conflict are corporate America, which fattens on economic dealings with this emerging threat, and other 'friends of China' who make up the 'New China Lobby' prepared to play by China's rules. *Dragon Strike*, a novel-like work which calls itself a 'future history', also posits a war fought mainly between China on the one side and the United States on the other. But this time the *casus belli* is not Taiwan but an oil-rich area in the Spratly and Paracel Islands and Vietnam.

A much more positive view is exemplified by a special report in *Time* magazine. Entitled 'The World's Next Superpower' the article sees China as 'stepping forth decisively from its intermittent isolation to claim an important place in the sun'.[30] Although the article does attribute this bright future of power largely to China's ability to learn from the West, it takes strong issue with American lecturer, poet, and essayist Ralph Waldo Emerson (1803–82) for his derision of China as a 'mummy' and relic, which had made only one contribution to civilization: tea. The final sentences of the article put the emphasis on China's great civilization, and is reminiscent of a Chinese nationalist attitude. 'The relic is showing world-shaking signs of vitality. It is helping make East Asia less a westward-looking exporter and more a seamless civilization that can stand and thrive on its own. Some monument. Some mummy. Tea, anyone?'[31]

Perhaps even more striking is James Walsh's contribution to the special report. His part of the report deals with the military and is remarkably positive about its growth and efforts to professionalize. Although charging China with being 'confident, even cocky enough to swagger a bit', Walsh does not seem to think this is anything to worry about. Indeed, his concluding sentence definitely has China's army in the role of the good guy: 'To the degree that it now has an important stake in professionalism, a freer economy and the open door, neighbors may one day have cause to be grateful for the Middle Kingdom's thoroughly modern military.'[32]

Admittedly this *Time* special report predated the decision to reject Beijing's bid for the 2000 Olympic Games. Yet already the notion of the rising China was very evident. Another, and somewhat later, view with a similar thrust was that put forward by Dr Stephen FitzGerald, one of Australia's most eminent Asia and China specialists. He agrees that China is nationalist and thinks it likely that China will become the dominant power of its region. But he sees nationalism as generally positive, a factor that holds the Chinese together, and especially against the outside world, and refuses to see a dominant China as necessarily an aggressive military power. FitzGerald advances several reasons why China is likely to 'make it', meaning apparently play a successful role as a modern power in the 2020s. 'Between now and 2020, China's influence will begin to permeate the region and Australian society in ways which we have only known previously with Britain and the United States.' This is not necessarily a bad thing. He sees East Asia coming together into a formal 'East Asia Community' dominated by China, but with reasonably distributed influence if the other participants are far-sighted enough to push effectively in that direction.[33] In short, although FitzGerald shares with Bernstein, Munro, Hawksley, and Holberton the notion of a rising China, he remains quite optimistic about what this country might be like if handled properly. There is no hint in these perceptions of the gloomy doomsday predictions so evident in the two books noted above.

Chinese emigrant to the United States Cheng Li argues strongly against the notion that an aggressive and nationalist China could pose a military threat to the West in general or the United States in particular. He believes that a radical and xenophobic foreign policy requires a radical and charismatic leader, and he sees no sign of the emergence of such a leader 'now or in the foreseeable future'. He is also very critical of any policy of 'containment'. He believes that human rights issues should be confronted by dialogue, not containment, which 'cannot change any of the tensions in the region'. 'Nothing could be more counterproductive than to establish an American alliance against China,' he suggests. American interests lie in ensuring 'a secure and cohesive China, rather than an unstable and fragmented China'.[34]

A poll conducted late in September 1997 by the Pew Research Centre, shortly before Jiang Zemin's state visit to the United States, found that 46 per cent of 2,000 people questioned said they believed China was 'a serious problem' for the United States, 14 per cent saw China as an 'adversary' and 32 per cent did not consider it much of a problem. What these figures suggest is that Americans in general take a rather pessimistic view of their own country's relationship with China. [35] This is not to say that they are expecting war. But when Jiang Zemin made his much-touted visit to the United States, the images of that population towards his own country veered somewhat more towards the negative than the positive.

Conclusion

In political terms the Beijing massacre is the main event that has caused a fundamental change of Western images, from the dominantly positive existing before 1989, to the mainly negative which have prevailed since. The incident placed human rights high on the agenda for Western governments and their people, especially in the United States, and they have remained there. The burgeoning economy, to be discussed in the next chapter, and the rising power of China mean that the West knows it must deal with China. But there is a certain sense that some do so reluctantly and with the suspicion that this is a power with the potential to pose a challenge to their own dominating place in the world.

Certainly the new nationalism has meant that many people in China are convinced that the preoccupation with human rights in the West represents a demonization of their country and is merely an excuse for the United States to try and prevent the rise of China. Such people believe that the United States would like to see China follow the Soviet Union into dissolution, with the overthrow of its communist party, so that the Americans could remain the only superpower and continue to dominate the world indefinitely. The new nationalism makes many people in China feel it is not only their right but their duty to resist any such demonization.

Notes

1   Claudia Rosett, in *The Wall Street Journal*, 31 May 1989.
2   Zuckerman, 'Thrust onto Center Stage', p. 54.
3   *Financial Times* (London), 18 May 1989.
4   Manegold with Magida, 'Upheaval in China', p. 62.
5   'China—The Hope and the Horror', p. 54.
6   Mosher, *China Misperceived*, p. 20.
7   Ryckmans' interview with Greg Sheridan was published in *The Australian*, 3 June 1989, pp. 29 and 33. It was later republished, in abridged and edited form, as Leys, 'When the "Dummies" Talk Back', pp. 14 and 19.
8   Fathers and Higgins, *Tiananmen, The Rape of Peking*, p. 130.
9   *Time Australia* 4 (25) (19 June 1989), front cover and also pp. 12–13.
10 Salisbury, *Tiananmen Diary*. The other was Goodman and Segal (eds.), *China at Forty, Mid-Life Crisis?*. Unlike Harrison Salisbury's, this is an academic book.
11 NZPA-Reuter, Knight-Ridder, 5 June 1989, quoted in 'China—The Hope and the Horror', p. 61.
12 Quoted in 'China—The Hope and the Horror', pp. 62–64.
13 The title of the concluding chapter of Mosher's *China Misperceived*, pp. 202–16.
14 Li, *Rediscovering China*, p. 12.
15 Elson, a.o., 'The Party Isn't Over—Yet', p. 43.
16 The four are Gittings, *Real China*; Miles, *The Legacy of Tiananmen, China in Disarray*; Wong, *Red China Blues*; and Li, *Rediscovering China*; all of them mentioned in these pages.

17 Hooper, '"Real" Chinas in the 1990s', pp. 85–86.
18 Gittings, *Real China*, pp. 267–68.
19 Miles, *The Legacy of Tiananmen, China in Disarray*, p. 167.
20 See Brook and Frolic (eds.), *Civil Society in China*.
21 Goodman, *Deng Xiaoping and the Chinese Revolution*, p. 115.
22 Rohwer, *Asia Rising*, p. 121.
23 *New York Times*, 20 February 1997, p. A12.
24 Polin and Healy, 'Man of the Century', pp. 31–32.
25 Brahm, *China as No 1*, p. 35.
26 Andrew Watson, 'Zhu Rongji', in Mackerras, with McMillen and Watson (eds.), *Dictionary of the Politics of the People's Republic of China*, p. 248.
27 Forney, 'Hoist with his Own Petard', pp. 20, 16.
28 Brahm, *China as No 1*, p. 35.
29 Quoted in Chanda and Huus, 'The New Nationalism', p. 20.
30 Aikman, a.o., 'China, The World's Next Superpower', p. 30.
31 Ibid., p. 35.
32 Walsh, a.o., 'A Leaner, Meaner Fighting Machine', p. 41.
33 FitzGerald, *Is Australia an Asian Country?*, p. 152.
34 Li, *Rediscovering China*, pp. 314–16.
35 See *South China Morning Post*, 29 October 1997.

10
Western Images since 1989: Economics and Society, the Future

This chapter discusses images of some aspects of the economy and society of China since 1989. On the whole, the economy is viewed rather favourably, because of China's success in its quest for modernization, but other images are dominantly and sharply negative. In addition, this chapter attempts some summation of how the West views the prospects for China's future as the twentieth century draws to its close.

Images of the Chinese Economy

The economy is the brightest spot in Western images of China in the 1990s. Yet there is complexity and change even in this area. On the whole there were several dominant themes in Western images of the Chinese economy in the 1990s. Perhaps the most important one is positive: that the Chinese economy is growing with remarkable rapidity with a consequent and highly impressive improvement in the standard of living. There are also some less favourable images of the Chinese economy. For instance, many observers believe that growth has taken place in dangerous fits and starts, involving serious bouts of inflation. Although China's energy and infrastructure have improved, they are still a major bottleneck for sustained economic growth. Quite a lot of attention has been paid to the 'behemoths' or 'dinosaurs' still existing in certain sectors of the economy, notably the state-owned enterprises, and these are still in need of serious reform. Finally, a strong image is that economic growth has entailed serious despoliation of the environment.

William Overholt is foremost in declaring a bright present and future for the Chinese economy, naming the country to be the world's next economic superpower and its takeoff as 'unique in world history'. He states that China was the fastest-growing economy in the world during the 1980s and, after a brief period of disinflation in the late 1980s, rebounded to that status in 1992. He comments that 'before China accomplished this feat, few would have judged such rapid growth possible for a nation comprising one-fifth of the world's population and an exceedingly diverse economy'.[1]

Just as strong are the views of Jim Rohwer, whose basic notion is that Asia as a whole is rising due to the strength of its emerging middle classes. His views on China are perhaps best summed up as follows:

> The Dengist reforms of 1979–94 brought about probably the biggest single improvement in human welfare anywhere at any time. During this decade and a half China's real economic growth averaged nine per cent a year, a rate that doubles the size of the economy in less than eight years. By 2000, barring disaster, China's economy should be eight times bigger than it was when Deng began his reforms in 1979: a record that would equal the performance of Japan, South Korea, and Taiwan during their fastest quarter-centuries of economic growth.[2]

Cheng Li's book has a great deal to say about the problems of reform. He is not sure that Deng Xiaoping deserves as much of the credit as most Western commentators have argued, or at least implied. He says the people who 'really created China's economic miracle' are the 'peasants-turned-industrialists'. These people mostly came 'from the poor, less educated, and unprivileged part of society'. This did not prevent them from contributing to China's rural industrial revolution, which Li characterizes as 'one of the greatest industrial revolutions in human history'.[3] This view shows clearly that, despite the problems of economic growth, he, too, is bowled over by its scale and overall effects: 'Never in history have so many people made so much economic progress in a single generation as residents of coastal China.'[4]

Inflation was perennially a source of comment in the first half of the 1990s. A commentary in *Time* typically notes the strength of China's economy in 1993, but warns of the inflationary spiral coming, the headline reading 'Red Hot: Flush with Optimism, the Emerging Economic Titan Looks to be Growing Too Far, Too Fast Yet Again'.[5] A similar, but more negative comment condemns the whole Chinese economic experience due to the tendency towards inflation, dubbing China 'the muddle kingdom?' and passing its economy off as a bubble economy. It predicts that 'China's rulers will keep rolling the presses, printing an increasingly worthless currency to fuel a dangerously inflated bubble economy'.[6] As it happened, these words, published in 1994, coincided approximately with the appointment of Zhu Rongji as vice-premier, who did succeed in bringing China's economy under control, reducing inflation drastically.

The failure of the infrastructure and the social welfare and banking systems to keep pace with economic development and the issue of the central plan have long been major issues for Western commentators on the Chinese economy. The argument runs that reform depends on things such as decent roads and professionally run banks. Overall economic reform must also entail radical change in the state-owned enterprises. As one generally positive view of China's economy in 1993 has it:

> A prime villain in the piece, as usual, is the legacy of Communist central planning. Those economic sectors in which the state retains a heavy hand have been unable to keep up with the free market's appetite. Shortfalls in energy, raw materials and transportation are choking manufacturers and raising costs. Worse, the big government-controlled enterprises are still bleeding the nation of resources that could be put to better use. Aside from direct subsidies, Beijing props up these largely insolvent dinosaurs of heavy industry by ordering banks to advance them 'policy loans', many of which go unpaid.[7]

Given comments such as these, it comes as no surprise that the Western media were generally positive in their reaction to the decision Party General Secretary Jiang Zemin announced at the Fifteenth Party Congress in September 1997, to reform the state-owned enterprises. A series of Western economists came out with the view that the measure would lead to privatization, which was rated a positive development. On the other hand, some doubted that it could be undertaken without strong opposition and warned that it could lead to serious unemployment. Agence France Press quoted economist Phillip Smyth as giving an apparently fairly typical view, representing Western images on this matter: 'Too fast a pace of reform will exacerbate the unemployment problem, undermining social stability; but too slow a pace will exacerbate the problem of SOE (state-owned enterprises) debt which is crippling the entire financial sector.'[8]

By mid-1998, the impact on China of the Asian currency crisis, which began in Thailand the preceding year, had been comparatively slight. The very positive image of Zhu Rongji, Premier from March 1998, certainly contributed towards a positive view of the Chinese economy, despite the crisis enveloping other parts of East and South-East Asia. The Group of Eight Summit meeting in Birmingham, UK, in May 1998, composed of the leaders of the main eight world economies, all Western except Japan and Russia, was extremely positive about China's handling of the crisis to that point. French President Jacques Chirac even suggested that China be invited to join the group and commented: 'If China had not decided to keep its currency value and to accept the considerable social and economic restraints that this entailed, the crisis would have been catastrophic for the whole world.'[9]

On the whole, the West views environmental despoliation as the most serious disadvantage of rapid economic growth in China. One generally optimistic view of China in the late 1990s and its future sees 'severe environmental problems' as among a fairly short list of 'daunting' problems, warning that water and air pollution, soil erosion and poor water supply north of the Yangtze River 'are beginning to pose serious health problems and to constrain growth rates'.[10] Virtually all commentators are shocked by the damage that industry has already done to the environment. 'China's environment is already a mess,' declares Kristof, the causes being largely the burning of coal for heat and industry. This is especially the case in the north, but he adds that when his wife Sheryl WuDunn went to Chongqing the smog was so bad that her aeroplane could not take off. In many cities, especially in the north, air pollution exceeds World Health Organization standards by up to six times, a grim picture indeed.[11]

Images of Chinese Society

Because the notion of society is so all-encompassing, two specific aspects of society are treated here: the place of women and children, and the population question.

There are some positive factors in the images of women: principally they have derived some benefit from the increasing prosperity which China has enjoyed in the 1990s. One generally rather negative book by two well-known journalists mentioned earlier, offers a detailed picture of a woman who fought a battle against a corrupt superior who demanded an affair with her, and actually won in the sense that she retained her position despite being able to refuse his advances. This assertion of rights is presented as something that would have been impossible in the old system. 'She would have had no way of fighting back, for if she had resisted he could have destroyed her career.'[12] The story betokens significant advance in the way in which men treat women in China.

One of the changes to which reference is particularly frequent is the acceleration in the rise in prostitution in the 1990s, especially in South China. Under the headline 'Pleasure industry booms in China's new power-house', Times reporter James Pringle reports that Shanghai was still an 'austere place' at the end of the 1980s, but in the 1990s became 'a burgeoning power-house, not only of industry but also of entertainment, with its 5,000 bars, nightclubs, dancehalls, discos and karaoke bars, all with their array of smiling hostesses'. He adds that the police still try to prevent the revival and occasionally take girls off for 'education', but his emphasis is that prostitution has staged a real comeback.[13] Another case in point is a popular book by reporter John Gittings, Asia specialist for the Guardian and a man with a long and distinguished career of reporting on China. In it we read that prostitution in the new and southernmost province of Hainan 'is widespread and unchecked' with the 'chickens' joining their clients and spectators in the Haikou Hotel as a tourist attraction. Unlike in Guangzhou or, as just noted, Shanghai, 'the police never enter hotel rooms here', according to a resident.[14]

On the other hand, the dominant Western images of the treatment and role of women in China are bleak. This was made clearest in September 1995, when Beijing hosted the Fourth United Nations World Conference on Women and the small nearby town of Huairou the related non-governmental World Meeting on Women. One of the major focuses of the Western media was the excessive security and general insensitivity of Chinese officials. While this matter had nothing to do with women specifically, it did show a generally poor image of how things are in China. The person to gain most publicity in the West was Hillary Clinton, the wife of the US president. Her speech expressed women's rights forcefully and generally, above all in her declaration that 'if there is one message that echoes forth from this conference, let it be that human rights are women's rights and women's rights are human rights, once and for all'.[15] Hillary Clinton did not attack China specifically during her speech, but she did make veiled criticisms, notably of its lack of the freedom to dissent.

What was more notable was that the Conference elicited several reports gaining coverage widespread enough to rank as images of the shocking treatment of certain women in China. One of these was the buying and selling of women, which the Chinese government had acknowledged and condemned among 'six evils' in 1989. Under the headline 'Women as chattel: in China, slavery rises', one reporter described a market in Xi'an, which for many young women from the countryside 'may be the first stop on a journey that begins with the promise of a job, sees rape and violent beatings along the way and ends in a life of domestic slavery'. The condemnation of the government is acknowledged but 'when it comes to the selling of women, the authorities show a tragic indifference'.[16]

Time took the cue to issue a long report entitled 'Born to be second class' which, among others, again took up the theme of 'a booming new slave trade: the abduction and sale of teenage girls'. The main thrust of the report was that the gains women and girls had won under Mao were now rapidly evaporating: 'In a country where female liberation posted one of the speediest, most far-reaching success stories of our time, a recrudescence of age-old prejudices is eating away the gains like acid rain at a monument's base.' Among the bleakest of all images to emerge was a picture of a naked female baby lying on the footpath, with a cup for money beside her and prosperous people walking past taking no notice. The place is Shenzhen, which is noted not as a poor backwater but among the richest places in all China. Nothing could reinforce the image of desperation better than this.[17]

At about the same time as the Fourth World Conference on Women, China became embroiled in yet another controversy featuring extremely poor images of the treatment of children, especially girls. This time the issue was orphanages, with television pictures of miserable conditions broadcast around the world. Reports were issued of 'dying rooms' in Chinese orphanages, where disabled or unwanted babies were left to die of starvation. Such reports gained widespread credence in the West, despite strong denials by the Chinese authorities, who claimed it as their policy to nourish, look after, and educate orphans.

Early in January 1996, the New York-based Human Rights Watch/Asia issued a report from a large orphanage in Shanghai claiming to be based on testimony, records, and photographs of a Chinese female doctor, Zhang Shuyun, who had worked there before fleeing China in 1995. The Human Rights Watch report reached the shocking conclusion:

> The brutal treatment of orphans in Shanghai, which included deliberate starvation, torture and sexual assault, continued over a period of many years and led to the unnatural deaths of well over 1,000 children between 1986 and 1992 alone.[18]

The report thus accused the Chinese authorities of following a deliberate policy of starving and severely abusing orphans, especially girls and mentally and physically handicapped children. Naturally enough, these accusations brought a swift response from China itself. The authorities opened the relevant Shanghai orphanage for foreign inspection, just as the Human Rights Watch report had demanded, and Western reporters and diplomats went to have a look. The Chinese leadership issued statements of total denial of the Human Rights Watch report, let alone that any policy of starvation had ever existed in orphanages. One of the former directors of the orphanages, Han Weicheng, lashed out at Zhang Shuyun for spreading lies about the orphanage because she had been denied a post as director. He called her 'crazy' and 'a woman of low morals', who 'had never done anything for orphans'.[19] Han himself had been cleared by the Shanghai Supervision Bureau of accusations from Zhang Shuyun of cruelty and sexual assault towards an orphan, and had then been reinstated. While some Western newspapers such as the *New York Times* did indeed report the Chinese denials, the damage had already been done, with the image of horrible Chinese orphanages and of cruelty towards orphans remaining in many Western minds.

As usual, there is a counter-image. An article in the 'Viewpoint' column of *Time* acknowledged that the Western press had largely accepted the blanket characterization of China's orphanages as 'a secret world of starvation, disease and unnatural death', but went on to disagree with that generalization very strongly as outrageous. The writer and her husband had adopted a little girl from China, and claimed that the orphanage where they had met her 'resembled neither the "showcase" facility that Beijing opened to foreign journalists last week nor the horror institute described by Human Rights Watch/ Asia'. Moreover, she quoted several American adoption agents to the effect that 'this description matches the conditions they routinely encounter'.[20]

As far as the population question is concerned: the one-child policy continues to be controversial, but there is still acknowledgement that it is necessary. Moreover, in world-wide terms, China's image for its attempts to overcome its population problems is still quite good, although its success in the matter is much less clear-cut.

The World Bank's 1990 *World Development Report*, which undoubtedly both reflects and influences Western images in such matters, held up China, along with Thailand, as examples to the rest of the world in reducing population growth. It also praised China for having achieved social conditions well above the norm for its income level through effective and sustained public action in the social sectors.[21]

An expression in the popular media of the image that the population policy is necessary, was repeated in a Dutch documentary television film entitled *1,2 Miljard* (*1.2 Billion*). Produced at the end of 1989, it focuses on the Chinese government's policy of restricting the population to 1.2 billion by the end of the century. It portrays the policy itself as generally successful, and the Chinese bureaucracy in charge of the programme as efficient, reasonably humane, and highly competent. The main image to emerge of Chinese society is of control over the lives of the people, because they need a permit to have a child and can expect no escape or mercy if they flout the policy. The function of the bureaucracy is to give information, advice, and supervision, but 'if all else fails, sanctions' are imposed.

A strong point is made that it is women whom the Chinese regard as responsible for birth control. All officials, police, or members of a birth control committee interviewed are female. On the other hand, the men in the family interviewed for the programme do more talking than the women. However, there is no disagreement among them. All accept the need for the birth control programme and do not either wish or dare to disobey the law that prescribes it. They are very critical of people who have a child without a permit.

This programme focuses entirely on the city of Chongqing, at that time in Sichuan. The impression of successful and necessary control is partly due to the fact that there is no mention of the countryside. The images it creates are actually rather similar to those of the 1983 BBC *Horizon* programme, *China's Child*, mentioned in Chapter 8.

A coffee-table book produced in association with a television series on the Chinese army highlights the policy's success in the cities, but points out that the peasants' traditional and still strong desire for sons makes it much more problematical in the countryside. In the villages 'very few couples will cease child-bearing until they have at least one son'. The 'precious sons . . . are the focus of all their parents' hopes' and are known as 'Little Emperors'.[22]

Unfortunately, the countryside remains far more populous than the cities. Despite the success of the population policy in the urban areas, there was a widespread belief that China had virtually no hope of attaining its target of keeping the population within 1.2 billion by the end of the century. Elizabeth Wright from the BBC, while expressing sympathy with the government in its attempt to limit the population, nevertheless claimed that the target of 1.2 billion by the end of the century had officially been discarded with an admission that it would be at least 1.3 billion. The crucial reason was the obvious one: while pointing to success for the policy in the cities, she argued that even the government admitted failure in the countryside.[23]

It is worth adding that, since Wright made this claim in 1989, events have proved her right. As the Chinese government itself admitted, China's population reached 1.2 billion early in 1995. In September 1995, Premier Li Peng announced new targets: that China's population by the year 2000 would be not 1.2 billion but 1.3 billion, and no more than 1.4 billion by 2010.[24]

According to one academic, 'Failure of national population control policies is . . . the greatest dilemma which China faces'. Extremely pessimistic about everything in China, especially in the wake of the Beijing massacre, she states simply that 'China stagnates beneath the weight of too many people'.[25] This image of China's over-population problem includes some extremely bleak comments about the implications for China's international relations and place in the world. These are worth quoting at some length:

> Constraints on funds available for foreign purchases and joint ventures, the flight of intellectuals abroad to escape poverty and in search of opportunity, increased fears in neighbouring countries of Chinese aggressiveness, decisions to engage in controversial but lucrative economic practices such as arms sales to warring countries, all are related to overpopulation. As the population continues to increase, the twenty-first century could see large-scale emigration from China, movements of population which could dwarf the nineteenth-century exodus from South China to the New World and the post-1975 flight of the Vietnamese boat refugees. Where will these Chinese economic/political emigrants go? Although the greatest impact would be on neighbouring countries, the effect of large-scale emigration on China's international relations in general would be profound.[26]

This view acknowledges, indeed emphasizes, the necessity of China's birth-control programme and in that sense agrees with the position of the Chinese government. Any problems the programme might cause pale in inconsideration beside the disasters that follow over-population. The negative images result not from the existence of the one-child policy, but from its perceived failure. While it is true that by changing its targets in 1995 the Chinese government acknowledged only partial success for its programme, it was still a long way from the near-total failure the quoted passage assumes. The fear of China's excessively large population, the image of the Chinese hordes spilling over into neighbouring countries, is certainly nothing new, but it is not a prominent feature of the period of reform. Even in the generally more pessimistic atmosphere that followed the Beijing massacre, such images are far from dominant. But it is very striking to find them re-emerging at all.

Tibet

One issue on which Western images of China have been strongly, and almost universally, negative has been its treatment of Tibet and the Tibetans. Although the Chinese have for some time regarded Tibet as part of China, there was hardly any Chinese control in the period just before the PRC was established. Tibet was reincorporated into China in 1951 but in 1959 there was a major rebellion against Chinese rule, which was suppressed quickly but bloodily and with lasting bitterness on the part of the Tibetans. Although there was criticism of China in the West in the 1960s and 1970s, the fact that almost no Westerner was able to travel there ensured that the negative images were never very powerful.

Since the 1990s, four main images of Chinese behaviour in Tibet have prevailed. The first, that over a million Tibetans have died as a result of Chinese occupation. The second, that China is destroying Tibetan culture in a process leading towards cultural genocide. A third view is that the Tibetan areas are becoming 'swamped' by Han Chinese in a process making Tibetans a minority in their own country. Finally, there is a widespread view in the West, which argues that China is suppressing religion in Tibet and practising ghastly human rights abuses in the process.

The Tibet issue was very much alive in the 1980s, especially from 1985, when Western backpackers—most of whom favoured Tibetan independence—were allowed to go there in significant numbers. In 1987 Tibet became a major focus for accusations over human rights, when major demonstrations by monks on behalf of independence were suppressed by the Chinese authorities. These demonstrations followed a visit to Washington by the Dalai Lama and provoked sharp response from the West, especially the United States.

Possibly the most famous image in the West relevant to modern Tibet, one shown repeatedly in Western countries and certainly impressive enough to be image-formulating, was a short piece of footage smuggled out of China showing a scene during a big demonstration on 5 March 1988 in Lhasa. It depicted troops chasing monks with sticks and a crowd of them standing over a monk, beating him up savagely. In March 1989 martial law was declared in Lhasa for the first time in the history of the PRC, when further demonstrations broke out in commemoration of the thirtieth anniversary of the rebellion against Chinese rule, which had seen the Dalai Lama flee Tibet for India. Later in 1989, the Dalai Lama was awarded the Nobel Peace Prize, to China's consternation and anger.

In the 1990s the Tibet issue came to occupy a much higher profile in Western images of China. The fifth edition of the Lonely Planet guide to China, published in 1996, is among those many image-formulating books to repeat the claims about destruction of culture, the 'massive influx of Han settlers', making 'Tibetans a minority in their own "autonomous region"', and the deaths of over one million Tibetans as a result of Chinese occupation. While it acknowledges some improvement in the economy, its tone is harshly critical of China and scornful of the Chinese claim to have carried out 'a mission of mercy' against the former Tibetan system.[27]

As the 1990s progressed, the image of the Dalai Lama himself rose to new heights. Early in 1998 the magazine *Asiaweek* listed him among the top twenty-five 'trend makers' in Asia, a select group of those with 'a special ability to inspire and fascinate'. It described him as 'the Patron Saint of the "Tibet Chic" phenomenon that is sweeping the planet'. In the West he has become a key figure in Asia who influences those with influence: 'By agreeing to lend out bits of his civilization, he has brought to his side many of those—especially in the West—who define the present.'[28]

The Dalai Lama's visits to Western and other countries multiplied significantly, and he visited Western presidents and prime ministers frequently. This was despite strong opposition from China, which charged the foreign nations with interfering in China's internal affairs and aiding and abetting the Dalai Lama's separatist activities. He was welcomed by the peoples of the Western countries, however, becoming a symbol of peace and progressive ideas, an icon exempt from the kind of criticism that cynical journalists reserved for the great majority of other leaders. Tibetan Buddhism became a part of the 'new spirituality' that played so important a role in the West in the 1990s. In the United States it became one of the most rapidly growing religions, gaining numerous converts from all walks of life. Although the focus was on Tibetan Buddhism as a peaceful exemplification of a great spiritual civilization, China inevitably came under strong condemnation as the ogre that had invaded this independent country and was destroying its civilization.

In July 1996 the Dalai Lama made a much publicized speech in London before the British Parliament in the Palace of Westminster. In terms of Western images of China, a particularly condemnatory passage ran as follows:

> In Tibet our people are being marginalized and discriminated against in the face of creeping Sinicization. The destruction of cultural artefacts and traditions coupled with the mass influx of Chinese into Tibet amounts to cultural genocide. The very survival of the Tibetans as a distinct people is under constant threat.

What an Asian religious leader says might not normally be considered a Western image of China. However, this speech was made in the West and under the most formal of circumstances. Moreover, the Dalai Lama's personal influence has already been noted. He is always widely reported in the West for what he says and his reputation is such that his words are accepted as valid in a way which applies to no other Asian, and hardly any other world leader.

In 1997 Tibet was the focus of the new push for negative images of China in Hollywood and the American cinema. 'With an impressive array of American stars embracing Tibetan Buddhism, from Richard Gere to Harrison Ford, Uma Thurman, and Goldie Hawn, the liberation of Tibet and the demonization of China has been a hot topic in Tinseltown.'[29] Probably the most important of these films were Jean-Jacques Annaud's *Seven Years in Tibet* and Martin Scorsese's *Kundun*.

Naturally the Chinese reacted against the Hollywood trend, issuing threats against major film companies that their business and profits in China itself may come under threat through their sponsorship of these films. And their efforts were not without some success. Ben Loeterman's documentary *Dreams of Tibet* about Hollywood's move into the anti-China and pro-Dalai Lama lobby, showed Michael Eisner, the Chair of the Walt Disney Company, which had been responsible for the production of *Kundun*, praising China as 'intelligent' for its reaction.

Eisner made it quite clear that his company would be more careful in the future about jeopardizing its fortunes in the China market. Annaud even went so far as to say: 'I don't see a studio putting any money on a movie that will vaguely be against China any more.' While conceding the Chinese success, the documentary also strengthened the image of a wonderful spiritual culture in the late stages of decline under the impact of Chinese occupation and suppression. It repeated the footage showing the 5 March 1988 demonstration and showed a prominent Tibetan exile, with the words that the destruction of Tibet as a nation was 'only a matter of time'.

Among the Hollywood 1997 films there is one, namely *Seven Years in Tibet*, which deals with the time Austrian Heinrich Harrer spent in Tibet and the friendship he there developed with the still youthful fourteenth Dalai Lama.

Actually, China does not loom particularly large in the film until the end. Most of the coverage is given to Harrer himself, played by Brad Pitt, and the effect on him of the magnificent spiritual civilization of Tibet. Although not filmed in Tibet itself, but in Argentina, Canada, and the Himalayas, the cinematography is first-rate and shows scenes that could readily be in Tibet.

Where China does impinge, the images are very negative. For a start the assumption all through, especially at the end, is that Tibet should be independent and that China's absorption of it is wicked and unjustifiable aggression. The Chinese general of the army which enters Lhasa is strikingly similar to Mao Zedong and behaves like a barbarian, passing off Tibetan religion as poison and showing no respect to Tibetan culture. Harrer excoriates Ngapei Ngawang Jigme as a traitor to his face, he being the man who signed the May 1951 agreement with China under which Tibet became acknowledged as part of the PRC. Harrer, a committed Nazi at the beginning of the film, states his rejection of countries that invade others, in particular Germany and China. The image of China is as an evil, murderous ogre similar to Nazi Germany. Above all, the film's final written statement repeats the popular image that about a million Tibetans have died as a result of Chinese occupation.

There is an alternative view to that portrayed in films like *Seven Years in Tibet*. It focuses on the historical justification for Tibet as part of China, the economic and social benefits which China has wrought in Tibet, and the very evident survival of Tibetan culture, including the practice of Tibetan Buddhism. It also disputes the notion that Tibetans are being 'swamped' by Chinese in their own country by noting the relatively small Han population in Tibet outside Lhasa. However, this image does not get much of a hearing in the West. It is associated with Chinese propaganda and hence not to be believed.

The best image on Tibet depicted in the dominant images of China is that it is not that important in the overall trend of Chinese development. Rohwer makes a reference to the Tibetan case as 'heartrending but insignificant'. It may have been a case of Chinese aggression, but it happened a long time ago and does not show that China is an expansionist power.[30] It has benefitted, along with the rest of China, from remarkable economic development, and after all, the society that went under when the Chinese troops marched in was not a particularly humane one. Films like *Seven Years in Tibet* may depict the old Tibet as a paradise, but there was, nonetheless, plenty of poverty and misery there, including a vicious system of serfdom.

Images of China's Future

Analyses of the present and very recent past generally contain implicit or explicit expectations of what the future may hold. There are certainly expectations in Western images of China on the future of that country. Yet, just like the past, the future is divisible. There is the very near-term future, thousands of years in the future, and a range in between. Because the future is unknowable, most of those who make predictions fail to distinguish near and long-term futures. This is an important failing, because it is not only likely, but probable, that China's future will contain periods of comparative prosperity and peace, as well as much less positive phenomena. Even if China manages its transition to the twenty-first century as a reasonably stable, peaceful, united, and prosperous country, who would dare predict that there would *never* be another war, or that the country would *never* again fall apart, as it has done quite a few times in the past? Because most of the forecasts for China either concern its near future or are vague about time, the images discussed here ignore this issue.

In 1994 the American Department of Defense commissioned a study on possible scenarios for the future of China over the next seven years, seventeen business analysts and academics taking part. The weight of participants took an extremely bleak view, about half expecting that the transition following Deng Xiaoping's death would result in some form of 'break-up' of China, from unresolved factionalism at the mild end of the spectrum to total collapse at the other end. Only about one in three of the participants predicted that the broad status quo of 1994 would persist, while the 'liberal reform scenario' for which Western governments were hoping did not attract many subscribers at all.

In June 1995, the Joint Military Intelligence College/National War College Workshop on the Future of China, held in Washington, heard a paper from noted China academic Richard Baum, in which he put forward ten possible scenarios on the future of China after Deng Xiaoping. These ranged from the status quo, and 'muddling through', to chaos and catastrophic implosion of the system, varying from democratic reform to a revival of Maoism. The favourite Baum selected was 'neo-conservatism' with 'early betting odds' of three to one against, the least likely scenario being a neo-Maoist revival, rated at only fifty to one against. The neo-conservative scenario is characterized by a strong bureaucratic capitalist quasi-private entrepreneurial class in the ascendancy, Jiang Zemin remaining at the head of the ruling Party. The strong traditional sense of national pride reasserts itself, while neo-conservatives play the 'Motherland card'.[31]

Yet another forum on China's likely future was organized by the Pacific Council on International Policy and RAND's Center for Asia-Pacific Policy, for which senior academic China specialist Michel Oksenberg and others wrote a brief but extremely perceptive and wide-ranging report entitled *The Chinese Future*. This group explicitly steers a median course between the doomsday scenario that sees China as 'headed for a collapse similar to that of the former Soviet Union' and the 'optimistic forecast' that sees China as being propelled 'towards political liberalization and ultimately democratization'. Instead the group 'stressed the uncertainties, openness, and complexities of the Chinese future'.[32]

The group suggests that 'the leaders of China cannot take the unity of their country for granted',[33] but recognize the importance of unity for the leadership, and appear to think that the weight of probability is that the country will remain unified. Indeed, it is quite clear that, because of the fear that the independence of Taiwan or Tibet would be disruptive to national unity, 'the United States should harbor no illusion: the Taiwan issue is potentially explosive and involves risks of war'.[34] The group accepts that Jiang Zemin is determined to preserve the supremacy of the Chinese Communist Party and the assumption is that it will remain in power, at least for a while. On the other hand, there are strong limitations on the degree of control that the centre exercises over the regions of China and even over the national-level ministries.

One very important point put forward by the group is that it is China that will determine its own future, which means that the United States, and other foreign powers, should be very careful about trying to push China around. The concluding summative paragraph is reasonably positive about China's future, but repeats that point.

> On balance, China's neighbors and the international community should welcome China into their midst, and work with China to strengthen and support the features of the international system. Then not only will Beijing's range of choice be constrained, but it will also gradually develop an active interest and a greater stake in upholding the stability of the system. It bears repeating, however, that how the outside world treats China is not the only factor of importance. Probably most important will be the perceptions of China's leaders, which are rooted deep in a troubled history and not easily influenced by outside parties.[35]

One popular author to put forward a very bleak view of China's future is James Miles, Hong Kong correspondent for the BBC World Service. His book *The Legacy of Tiananmen, China in Disarray* argues that cracks will eventually appear in China's political structure, as a result of which 'the Pandora's box of rivalry, hatred, vengefulness, and a myriad other destructive emotions will spill open', with nobody holding the authority to control the situation. This would bring about chaos of a kind which 'would be felt all over the world',[36] in short it would be 'China in disarray'. Miles sees political corruption on a large and growing scale, with dissidents only needing to 'wait for something or someone to light the fuse' to unleash an explosion with the potential to bring down the Party and the whole system.[37]

The final paragraphs of Miles's book are worth quoting extensively.

> My own prediction is that China in the early twenty-first century will be a country increasingly preoccupied with the uphill battle to maintain order and control. To achieve this, its leaders might well exaggerate external threats, making Chinese foreign policy increasingly unpredictable and threatening to the country's neighbors. I believe China will be a better place materially to live in for many millions of people, but it will also be a more dangerous one as crime rates continue to soar, riots erupt among the growing number of have-nots, and political uncertainties continue to hang over the nation. Foreign investors will find themselves in an ever more hazardous and unpredictable environment as central

authority declines, corruption spreads, and each locality makes its own rules. But the temptations of the world's largest market will remain irresistible.

This book has focused on some of the fundamental problems the country faces in an era of economic and political transition. It will, I believe, take enormous political skill on the part of the post-Deng generation of leaders to prevent these problems from plunging the country into the turmoil that so many fear.[38]

There are bright spots, however, even in this gloomy forecast. For one thing, Miles believes that millions will have a good material standard of living and that foreigners will continue to invest in China. Although there may be turmoil, he does not predict the total break-up of the country. In fact, despite ethnic unrest and repression in Tibet and Xinjiang, he states that, 'it is hard to imagine that ethnic unrest either in Tibet or Xinjiang will ever result in independence for those areas'.[39] For a supporter of independence that may not be good news, and the use of the word 'ever', with its long-term implications, puts a very different spin on things than most of the book, which is geared to the more immediate future. But the overall expectations that Miles enunciates in the above quotation are pretty grim all the same.

The series of articles in *Time* in May 1993 announced the erosion of the CCP's 'influence on people and events out the capital'. It pointed to the decline of Party authority in the villages, where clans are as likely to hold sway. But at the same time, it declared that 'China simply has no substitute for the party' and made no forecast that the Party itself would be overthrown in the near term. It quoted Robert Scalapino, an emeritus professor of government at the University of California, as predicting that politics would continue to be authoritarian, 'with substantial restrictions on freedoms and a dominant single party in power, but in the social and economic spheres, pluralism will rise'. And *Time* concludes: 'In short, the party isn't over— at least until it ceases to deliver the goods.'[40]

John Gittings' account of 'real China' in the 1990s concludes by asking several questions about the future of China. Two of these questions are 'Will China break up?' and 'Can the Party survive?'. Neither question is answered unequivocally. However, the answer to the first one seems to be probably not, because, despite widening gaps between rich and poor, the economic and communication links throughout the country are much stronger than they used to be. As for the second question, Gittings appears to think that the Party will remain in control for a while, because the 'economic reforms have actually increased the opportunities for bureaucratic control and enrichment' as well as creating a need for more modern institutions staffed by competent managers, financial experts and others, most of whom see it as advantageous to belong to the Party.[41] While not exactly contradicting it, this view is somewhat different in emphasis from the one Gittings had expressed some years before on the CCP: 'The repression which followed the events of June 1989, and the nature of the regime which conducted it, were the clearest possible illustration that 40 years after the revolution China had lost its way and the Chinese Communist Party had lost its mandate.'[42]

Perhaps not surprisingly, William Overholt takes a somewhat more optimistic view about China's future. He sees it as quite possible that China would enjoy a relatively peaceful evolution towards a more democratic society. His main comparison for China is with Taiwan or South Korea, which means that 'in this Asian context the legacy of a Bolshevik-type party can be stabilizing and helpful in the transition to democracy'. On the question of whether China will follow the Soviet Union into disintegration, he is quite forthright that 'so long as the leadership follows the policies required for rapid growth, such fragmentation is extremely unlikely'. His main reason is China's experience: 'A strong sense of history, a firm sense of national identity, and a growing economic pie do wonders for unity.'[43]

Conclusion

Western images of China in the 1990s were thus highly ambivalent. There were differences among various groups of power-holders. At one end of the spectrum were the business communities, which aimed to profit from China's rapid economic growth. At the other end were those in power who responded to human rights activists. These power-holders saw the activists, in particular those favouring independence for Tibet, as being able to influence enough voters to impact on electoral chances.

Nowhere were these contrary influences sharper than in the United States, where Taiwan remained, unlike China, 'an easy sell'. The business community continued to lobby for China. However, according to some observers, 'the lobbying opens the business community to charges of being apologists for China, and that rankles'. Richard Bredor of the US-China Business Council in Washington was quoted as saying: 'We would never want to be in the position of defending China.'[44] In other words, even those who stood to profit from China, and create jobs for Americans, were hesitant and coy about pushing China, because they knew its image was rather poor and that such action left them open to criticism.

Notes

1   Overholt, *China: The Next Economic Superpower*, p. 2. Compare the slightly later but very similar verdict of Laurence Brahm in *China as No 1, The New Superpower Takes Centre Stage*, p. 166: 'China has made probably greater progress than any other country in reforming its economy and raising the standard of living of most of its people.'
2   Rohwer, *Asia Rising*, p. 121.
3   Li, *Rediscovering China*, p. 94.
4   Ibid., p. 23.
5   James Walsh in *Time*, 15 February 1993, p. 31.
6   Hornik, 'The Muddle Kingdom? Bursting China's Bubble', p. 29.
7   Walsh, 'Red Hot, Flush with Optimism, the Emerging Economic Titan Looks to be Growing Too Far, Too Fast Yet Again', pp. 30–1. See also Rohwer, *Asia Rising*, pp. 141–2, section entitled 'Dances with Dinosaurs'.
8   See, for instance, *China News Digest, Global News*, No. GL97–128, 15 September 1997, item 150 (3).
9   *China News Digest, Global News*, No. GL98–069, 20 May 1998, item 200 (6).
10   Oksenberg, Swaine and Lynch, *The Chinese Future*, p. 7.
11   Kristof and WuDunn, *China Wakes*, pp. 388–89.
12   Ibid., p. 454.
13   James Pringle, in *The Times*, 3 February 1996, p. 15.
14   John Gittings, *Real China*, p. 223.
15   See, for example, Patrick E. Tyler, in the *New York Times*, 6 September 1995, p. A10.
16   Seth Faison, in the *New York Times*, 6 September 1995, p. 1. The issue of trafficking in women is also discussed at some length by Wong in her *Red China Blues*, pp. 326–32. The back cover of this book describes it as 'one of *Time* Magazine's ten best books of 1996'.
17   See Walsh a.o., 'Born to Be Second Class', p. 54.
18   See Patrick E. Tyler, in the *New York Times*, 6 January 1996, p. 1.
19   Patrick E. Tyler, in the *New York Times*, 9 January 1996, p. 3.
20   Smolowe, 'Saving the Orphans', p. 35.
21   See 'Population' in *Far Eastern Economic Review Asia 1991 Yearbook*, p. 20.
22   Penny Kane, 'One-child Families', in Thomson and Atkin, *The Chinese Army*, p. 157.
23   Wright, *The Chinese People Stand Up*, p. 121.

24   See Colin Mackerras, 'Population Policy', in Mackerras, with McMillen and Watson (eds.), *Dictionary of the Politics of the People's Republic of China*, p. 176.
25   Lillian Craig Harris, 'Directions of Change', in Segal (ed.), *Chinese Politics and Foreign Policy Reform*, p. 257.
26   Ibid., pp. 258–9.
27   See Taylor, a.o., *China*, especially pp. 948–51.
28   Seno and Morgan, 'The Trend Makers', pp. 33, 42.
29   Neumann, 'The New Bad Guys, US Movie Trio Depicts Chinese as Harbingers of Evil', p. 108.
30   Rohwer, *Asia Rising*, pp. 156, 316.
31   Baum, 'China After Deng', pp. 174, 159–60.
32   Oksenberg, Swaine and Lynch, *The Chinese Future*, p. 5.
33   Ibid., pp. 6, 7.
34   Ibid., p. 26.
35   Ibid. p. 29.
36   Miles, *The Legacy of Tiananmen, China in Disarray*, pp. 10–11
37   Ibid., p. 237.
38   Ibid., pp. 314–15.
39   Ibid., p. 310.
40   Elson, a.o., 'The Party Isn't Over—Yet', pp. 42–43.
41   Gittings, *Real China*, pp. 278–80.
42   Gittings, *China Changes Face*, pp. 284–85.
43   Overholt, *China: The Next Economic Superpower*, pp. 59–60.
44   Forney, a.o., 'Chinese Images, Taiwan is an easy sell in Washington; China Isn't', pp. 24–25.

11
Conclusion

Despite their variety, Western images of China have tended to follow fashions and it is legitimate to see certain types of views as dominant at any particular time. Over the centuries a pendulum can be seen of positive and negative images, though it is not one which swings regularly or smoothly.

At times China has been seen as a 'model'. In the eighteenth century Voltaire was prepared to hold up China's marvels as a way of criticizing the politics, customs, and ideas of his own times, and quite a few of his contemporary countrymen shared his views. During the 1970s, China represented one 'model' of development which found favour in some circles, though certainly not among anything like a majority of Westerners. On the other hand, China's image has at times been extremely negative. One only needs to think of the nineteenth and early twentieth centuries and the 'heathen Chinese', the 'yellow peril', hideously cruel tortures, and the murder of infant girls, or of the period since mid-1989 and the preoccupation with human rights abuses.

It is important to note that the 'pendulum' metaphor does not demand that every Western country be equally affected at all times. For instance, one study has challenged the whole metaphor on the grounds that it does not sit at all comfortably with Australian experience in part of the twentieth century.[1] The present book has very little about Australia and does not concede that a metaphor applying to centuries of time and many countries should be discarded because of one country's experience over a few decades.

Another feature of the metaphor is that it does not require each swing to be equal in size. Moreover, it takes account of alternative views. There has not for centuries been a time when a dominant positive or negative image has not been at least partly balanced by dissenting opinion. Montesquieu, who was very negative about China, was roughly contemporary with Quesnay and Voltaire, who praised it so highly. And the 1950s produced some quite important works highly sceptical of the condemnatory view the US government was pushing, while in the late 1960s the hostility of many Westerners to American intervention in Vietnam caused appreciation of Asian revolutions in general to gather momentum. In the 1980s, academic and journalistic opinion was more critical than popular opinion in general. The images of China put forward by specialists in the 1980s tended to be more restrained and sceptical than those by people discovering China for the first time. In the 1990s the emphasis on human rights abuses was to some extent, balanced by an image of great improvements in the standard of living of ordinary people.

The Introduction discussed two theories and posed the question whether they could appropriately be applied to Western images of China. The first of these is Michel Foucault's 'power/knowledge' concept. Can one validly argue that it is power, rather than any number of the myriad realities, which is the main determinant of Western images of China at any particular time?

It appears to this writer that the dominant images of most periods have tended to accord with, rather than oppose, the interests of the main Western authorities or governments of the day. There has indeed been a 'régime of truth' concerning China, which has affected and raised 'the status of those who are charged with saying what counts as true' about that country.

We may perhaps exempt the first period of Sino-European contact in the thirteenth and fourteenth centuries because it is unlikely that China loomed large enough in the European mind to warrant anything approaching a meaningful 'régime of truth'. However, from the sixteenth century onwards, the wish of the Catholic Church in general and the Jesuits in particular to convert the Chinese to Christianity influenced the images that spread to Europe about China. Mendoza's great work was written at the command of the Pope and with the aim of beginning the conversion of the Chinese to Catholicism. When the Jesuits thought they could convert China to Christianity by praising it, they were for well over two centuries active in disseminating extremely positive images about it. But as this hope dwindled and then vanished, so the perceptions became tarnished. Moreover, it was the Jesuits' defeat in the power struggle, climaxing in their suppression by Pope Clement XIV in 1773, that spelled the end of Jesuit activity in China and of the favourable images they sent back to Europe.

Although the Western images in these centuries did suit Europe's Christian interests, it is necessary to point out that secular governments were only marginally involved. In fact, quite a few of them were bitterly hostile to the Jesuits, and it was pressure from the governments of Catholic Portugal, France, and Spain that eventually resulted in their suppression by the Pope. Even within the Catholic Church there was bitter division over how to interpret and Christianize China. The 'régime of truth' was primarily a Jesuit phenomenon.

It was in the nineteenth century that Europe 'colonized' images of China. The three main types of European activity in China from about the middle of the nineteenth century until after the fall of the Qing dynasty were imperialism, including profit, and conversion to Christianity, all of them connected with a power relationship. The prevailing Western images, decisively more negative than in the preceding period, made these activities easier, not more difficult.

It suited American, and later other Western interests, to regard China as a friend during the first half of the twentieth century, and as an ally during World War II. For the first time, Chinese authors, able to write in a European language, became major conveyors of images to the West. The most famous and important examples are Chiang Kai-shek's wife, Song Meiling, and Lin Yutang, a strong supporter of the modernized traditional system of Chinese government represented by Chiang Kai-shek. Through her novels, in particular the moving and best-selling *The Good Earth*, Pearl Buck promoted essentially conservative and positive images about China and its countryside, which accorded well with the power relationship emerging between the West and China in the 1930s. The dominant Western images of China improved dramatically, especially during World War II.

The 1950s and 1960s saw a China strongly opposed to Western interests, and in particular most Western governments. It consciously strove to change the unequal power relationship which it believed had existed between China and the West in the preceding century. The United States denounced the PRC as aggressive and a 'threat' to itself and the world. US opposition to the PRC spawned many authorities eager to create and foster a public opinion that would back up the American government's policy. At least in the United States, and to some extent also elsewhere, it became possible for educational authorities to teach a little bit about China that was actually in accordance with the American government policy of the day. The dominant Western images of China meshed nicely with the most powerful Western interests.

But the most spectacular example supporting the point about the 'régime of truth' is the Nixon visit of 1972. The American government changed its policy at a time when China was still in the throes of the Cultural Revolution. It is true that the seeds of a change in public opinion had been sown beforehand, but the strength of enthusiasm for Nixon's action suggests most strongly that popular images sat beautifully with American interests as they were being perceived by the government of the day. It was the American government that changed the images much more than the other way round. It was a calculation of interests that counted much more than a perception of right and wrong.

The period following the Beijing massacre, down to the end of the 1990s, was perhaps the most complicated period of all in terms of Western images of China. What is striking about this period is that the preoccupation of Western images with matters concerned with human rights and dissidents gained an added emphasis at just the same time that the general standard of livelihood of the Chinese people rose to an extent unprecedented in China's history. This is not to deny the existence or importance of human rights issues, but the focus they received in the Western media was both ironic and unwarranted by comparison with the improvements. In Western countries, and especially the United States, the business sector was at the forefront of wishing to cash in on China's growing economy, largely because it saw extensive profits in doing so. Though governments were on the whole willing to go along with economic ties, they were to some extent restrained by those both inside and outside government circles who wished to push the human rights angle or presented China as a coming challenge and even a threat to Western dominance. The issues which loomed largest in the minds of human rights activists were the Beijing massacre and Tibet, and among those two the balance shifted away from the former and towards the latter as the 1990s progressed.

Is power influencing knowledge in such a case? Is it sensible to speak of a 'régime of truth'? To some extent such a régime exists, but it is quite different in nature from that found at other times. Its source is only partly within the government and rests mainly with vocal groups within society that are preoccupied with particular issues and have the ways and means to project their views and exert an influence on society out of proportion to their size. Power relations in Western countries became incomparably more complex as the twentieth century progressed, indicating a growing power of democratic institutions.

However, there is one other point, which is that the rapid economic rise of China's economy in the 1980s and 1990s gave many influential people in the United States grounds for fearing that China may eventually surpass them in terms of world influence. In other words, while the United States and other Western countries may wish for good general relations with China, in particular in economic terms, they may not be too keen to assist in China's rise. In this sense it is hardly in the interests of the West to present a very favourable set of images about China.

The suggestion that Foucault's 'power/knowledge' theory is indeed largely applicable to a study of Western images of China does not imply either bad motives or incompetence on the part of any but a small minority of image-formulators. Even less does it imply that alternatives to the dominant opinions or images cannot exist. Foucault's idea can be supported irrespective of any conspiracy theory. Particular power relations do not necessarily exercise a decisive impact on individuals, but they certainly do so on groups, on societies in general. The operation of power is often invisible, but in some cases quite overt. The American authorities of the 1950s and 1960s did not reveal all they were doing to influence public opinion in the West and elsewhere against China, but it was no secret that they were indeed expending an enormous amount of money and effort to achieve precisely that objective.

The second and related theory raised in the Introduction is Edward Said's 'Orientalism'. Have Western images of China been distorted by ethnocentric biases, by a failure to judge China on its own terms?

The answer depends on the period. There is very little of the 'Orientalist' in Marco Polo, despite the threat the Mongols had appeared to present to Europe not long before his time. What is striking is how fair he was, the extent to which he was prepared to see and judge China in its own terms, especially as far as its emperor and political system were concerned.

Moving into the sixteenth to eighteenth centuries, it is necessary to remember the aim of most observers, which was a frankly ethnocentric one, namely to replace Chinese religions with a European one on the grounds that only the latter was true. On the other hand, most observers saw their own Christianity not as exclusively European but as universal, or catholic. They tried to be fair according to their own criteria and they were not prejudiced against China. One can hardly charge a man like Du Halde with 'Orientalism' when his work on China was so defensive about it. While Montesquieu's views on despotism in China were both hostile and 'Orientalist', Voltaire and Quesnay praised China in order to criticize their own country, the precise antithesis of 'Orientalism'.

By the nineteenth century Europe had begun its Industrial Revolution and its confidence of its own superiority was at a peak, just at the time when China's civilization was in sharp decline. So it is not surprising that the overwhelming majority of images presented reflect that feeling of superiority in a sharply 'Orientalist' way. Even those who believed they were sympathetic to China assumed their superiority explicitly or implicitly. An example is Thomas Meadows, who was prepared to defend the Chinese as highly intelligent and to attack racism, but was still a strong and active supporter of British imperialism in China.

'Orientalism' remained very strong, indeed dominant, in the first half of the twentieth century. Yet there was arising a quite clear trend willing to analyse China in its own terms, to challenge unarticulated assumptions of Western superiority. Social science notions of cultural diversity were applied to China more frequently. The fact that Pearl Buck could write a popular novel about China in which *all* the main characters were Chinese was a clear sign of the times. China was itself undergoing a revolutionary process, climaxing in the growth and development of the Chinese Communist Party (CCP). A few Westerners, such as Edgar Snow, reported on it in a manner at odds with the prevailing 'régime of truth', making a successful attempt to judge it in its own terms despite the opposition of their own society.

The rise of the CCP to power in 1949 brought a new wave of 'Orientalism' to the West's images of contemporary China. Few commentators were really prepared to judge China on its own terms. A serious challenge was mounted to this Orientalism because of the opposition to US intervention in Vietnam, which brought with it calls to reassess socialist revolutions in Asia. With the Nixon visit in 1972 it was once again fashionable to see good in, and even admire, China, including its political system. As a result more people tried to use criteria set by the Chinese themselves, including both the government and apparently the people, to comment on China.

The 'opening up' of China from the late 1970s onwards resulted in more Westerners visiting the country, more serious and better study of it in the West, and more attempts by more Western people to learn the Chinese language. The result was a gradual decline in 'Orientalism' as more people were forced to confront Chinese values and aims. It would be difficult to impute 'Orientalism' to a film such as *The Last Emperor,* which brims with appreciation for China's problems in the twentieth century, or to a book like *Wild Swans* when its author is herself Chinese.

The controversy over human rights in the 1990s was based at least in part on whether it is appropriate to give priority to the rights of the individual or the community, with critical images of China based largely on an emphasis on the universality of individual rights. A staunch supporter of official Chinese government policy might charge such critics with failure to see the problem in Chinese terms and hence with 'Orientalism'. But what is very striking is that much of the criticism of Chinese conditions and policies is based on ideas which come from the Orient itself. A cardinal example is the praise of traditional Tibetan civilization found in a film like *Seven Years in Tibet*. Funding for such films and the influence they exert against China may well come from a Western source, but it would be difficult to charge such a film with 'Orientalism'.

Yet commentaries and statements laden with Western values and regarding China as an inferior civilization, which should expect only to learn from the West, are still very easy to find, especially in items aimed at reaching mass audiences, such as the film *Red Corner*. The assumption that China exists largely to show the superior moral virtue of the West, or for the triumphs, profits, and amusement or pleasure of Westerners, is still widespread. 'Orientalism' is certainly in decline in the West, but it is far from dead.

Even today, despite the changes that have occurred since the early 1970s, there is more than a grain of truth in Said's statement that a European or American studying the Orient 'comes up against the Orient as a European or American first, as an individual second'. His warning against 'Orientalism', against refusing to judge the peoples of other cultures in their own terms, may need refinement, but it remains a valid and worthwhile one.

⟨⟨⟨⟩⟩⟩

What is it that makes images as they are? The main determinant of Western images of China is the West itself. In this book the subject has been the West, China but the object. The conclusion that follows from the material presented here is that the major power-concentrations have usually exercised a significant, and often determining, influence over Western images of China at any particular time. An application of Foucault's 'power/knowledge' theory yields the same conclusion.

A good illustrative example comes from the United States. Public opinion no doubt affects American foreign policy to some extent, but this author's suggestion is that the impact on Western images of China as a whole is not decisive. The American government has only to feed information into a giant international mass media machine to put its own views over to the Western world. On occasion, such as during the Korean War of 1950–53, or at the time of the Nixon visit to China in 1972, it has also had the wish to influence the images people hold. On the other hand, if American government policies were the only determinant, we should be unable to explain the series of famous and bitterly anti-China books, including Fox Butterfield's *China, Alive in the Bitter Sea* and Richard Bernstein's *From the Center of the Earth,* published in the United States in the early 1980s, just after the United States and the People's Republic of China established full diplomatic relations at the ambassadorial level. In this case it was Carter who made the break in China's favour. Reagan was explicitly unwilling to retain Carter's China policy but did so for pragmatic reasons. By the time the main image-formulating anti-China material appeared, Reagan was in power. In this case it is not suggested that Reagan or any in his government orchestrated the publication of the material, but rather that the same conservative trend in American public opinion that brought Reagan to power also resulted in a backlash against positive images about China. This fashion enabled books like Fox Butterfield's *China, Alive in the Bitter Sea,* with its one-sided and black-and-white negative approach to China, to gain widespread and continuing popularity in the United States.

If the application of Foucault's theory suggests one determinant of Western images of China, that of Said's yields another: simple prejudice. Ethnocentrism usually results in negative images, because anyone who judges China with the standards and value systems of the West will find it deficient and backward. As noted above, biases that judge China and the Chinese harshly are more characteristic of some periods than others, but they are found at all times to some degree or another.

A third determinant of Western views of China is how well the Chinese treat the potential image-formulator, how effectively they project images to the West. The good treatment Marco Polo and the early Jesuits received in China was one factor encouraging them to transmit favourable images to the West. The Open Door policy in operation since the late 1970s is more likely to result in positive images than the tight restrictions on the entry, movements, and activities of Western foreigners that characterized the late 1960s.

A variant on the same theme lies in the degree to which the Chinese themselves accept the West and its influence. Ever since the sixteenth century, but especially since the nineteenth, the West has tended strongly to assume a right to influence China. On the whole, Chinese receptiveness to this influence has resulted in favourable images in the West, and resistance to it in negative ones. After China signalled in unmistakable terms in the eighteenth century that it had no intention of accepting Christianity, the positive images the Jesuits had been pushing began to wear off. China's initial resistance to the Western impact strengthened the harsh images prevalent in the nineteenth century. On the other hand, the Republican period saw a somewhat greater receptiveness to Western ways in China and a corresponding improvement in images. Perhaps the best example of all is the 1980s, which saw, in Chinese terms, a high degree of receptiveness to Western influence, in some sectors of society even great enthusiasm for it. At the same time, Western images were dominantly positive. In the 1990s China's treatment of journalists cooled, and, although it remained strong, so did the enthusiasm for things Western, with a negative effect on images.

And naturally an important determinant of Western images of China is the realities of China itself. Clearly much of what Western image-formulators say, write, or depict of China reflects some of the many realities accurately. This is especially so at times when the Chinese themselves present Westerners with the opportunities to research on or find out about Chinese realities. For instance, the obstacles in the way of a researcher doing field work in China in the 1980s or 1990s were minimal by comparison with what they were in the late 1960s and early 1970s, when it was virtually impossible to undertake any serious field research in China. And the horror of the Beijing massacre was real enough to explain the deterioration of images in 1989.

But, as noted in the Introduction, the relationship between images and realities is an enormously complex and problematic one. In fact, China has been over the centuries, and remains, a country so diverse that misery and joy, poverty and prosperity have been and are all completely real. Moreover, different observers of China attach distinct scales of importance to the same phenomena because each may differ sharply from the others in knowledge, experience, skills and assumptions. And so even for specialists the fit between images and realities is highly imperfect. How much more is this so for the great majority who make no pretence to knowledge about China and who, if interested, seek guidance in the formulation of their own images.

The China about which the West has devised images is large and the period covered here extensive. Both the West and China have changed greatly over the centuries and not always in the same direction. Is there any conceivable unity between a Mendoza who looks at the China of the sixteenth century and an Edgar Snow who observes the same country in the twentieth? Are there any observable patterns in the images created which may be worth commenting on?

A persistent issue in Western images of China has been that China was a despotism or was/is totalitarian. Early observers to focus attention on Chinese despotism were the eighteenth-century French thinkers Quesnay and Montesquieu, the first seeing this political system as benign, the second as oppressive because based on fear. Montesquieu held that China's climate and terrain were the main factors shaping its society and political order. Nineteenth-century image-makers were deeply struck by the autocracy and lack of freedom in China.

The People's Republic of China was initially for some a new, but essentially unchanged, version of oriental despotism. Western governments charged the CCP with eliminating freedom in China, and popular opinion agreed. During the Cultural Revolution, more observers than ever castigated China as totalitarian. Supporters admired the attempts to overthrow a regressive and feudal tradition, to force desirable change even on a reluctant people. Opponents saw only repression, and total disappearance of freedom.

With the fall of the Gang of Four and the development of an emphasis on modernization and openness to the outside world, Westerners again began to see their own influence grow, with a consequent growth of the image that China was moving in the right direction, favouring freedoms of various kinds. This image suffered a major reversal with the crisis of 1989, which appeared to see the reinstatement of that totalitarian impulse which punishes dissidence. The high priority that Western images place on human rights abuses in China signals the revival of the notion that China lacks freedom, and in particular by comparison with the 1980s.

Another of the main subjects of Western images has been the family. Despite some extremely negative views, including those of such diverse people as Robert Fortune and Agnes Smedley, the West's view of the traditional Chinese family system has in general been remarkably positive. Marco Polo made no mention of one of its more horrible features, foot-binding, while Mendoza was not at all shocked by that practice. Montesquieu was impressed by the Confucian family system, despite his generally critical view of China. In *The Good Earth*, Pearl Buck could remain extremely positive about Chinese society, despite the suffering she knew the Confucian family system caused the poor, especially women. It was probably consistent with such an attitude that many in the West took the CCP's onslaught on the Confucian family system in the 1950s as an attack on family life altogether and hence cause for a negative image. Robert Elegant's novel *Dynasty* could put over the image that during the Cultural Revolution the family was almost the main surviving bastion of sanity in Chinese society. Western images of the revival of family power in the 1980s, though not of the sexism of the traditional family system, have on the whole tended to be enthusiastic. In the controversy over orphanages in the mid-1990s the problem in the negative image of China was the weakness of the family system, not the converse.

Various other subjects have recurred throughout this book. For Mendoza, China's large population was a source of wonderment. Du Halde regarded it as a cause of poverty, while in the nineteenth century many saw it as a source of oppressive social relations. Since 1949 it has most often held the image of an obstacle to economic progress or modernization. The one-child policy since the 1980s may have aroused great controversy and various images in the West, but very few people anywhere would welcome another population explosion in China.

On the whole, the West has viewed China as peace-loving. In the seventeenth century, Ricci remarked on its lack of ambition for conquest, which he contrasted with the peoples of Europe. Fairbank in the twentieth century has promoted a similar image of traditional China. During and since the mid-1970s, the prevailing Western view has been that China wants peace and constitutes no threat to the world. Yet the 'yellow peril' image has also had its day. The German Kaiser Wilhelm II coined this phrase at the same time Europe indeed posed a threat to China. And the US policy of the 1950s and 1960s revived the image as part of its anti-communism. It castigated China as a threat to world peace, bent on the conquest of neighbouring countries.

⁓

Finally, what significance can we find in the study of Western images of China? One can answer this question on both a practical and theoretical level.

One of the points raised in this book has been that a general correlation exists between the images one country holds of another and state-to-state relations between the two at any given time. This author has argued that government influence on popular images is usually more important than the converse, but both play a role. It follows that well-informed images can contribute to an intelligent policy one country adopts towards another. Thus for any government to formulate policies for dealing with the people or government of another state, it should not only understand that nation but also the various levels of popular images about it. Relations between China and Western nations would have been smoother if each had held a clearer idea of precisely what the people of the other country thought. It may be comfortable to be shielded from hostile images but it serves no useful purpose.

The study of one civilization's images of another raises the whole issue of how to handle relations between peoples of totally different cultures. To understand another people's culture one should immerse oneself in it, but that does not mean that it is either possible or desirable to become part of it or abandon one's own culture. Perhaps the core of the problem lies in attitudes and mindsets. In other words, to understand another people one should know so clearly what their attitudes, views, and practices are and why, that one will not only be able to see the world from their point of view, but also to relate to them on their own terms, and to make judgements based on their criteria. This means that understanding another culture involves overcoming all prejudices. This is not as easy as it sounds. All cultures bring up their members with a whole series of unarticulated assumptions, of which the people who hold them are often unaware. To remain ignorant of them often leads to prejudices against others, untested attitudes of superiority towards others based on criteria and priorities which may be quite different in other cultures.

It does not follow from this that a fair interaction between Westerners and Chinese necessarily means agreement between them, though this will often occur. Even less does it mean that a Western individual or government should necessarily support any particular Chinese government or set of policies. New and critical interpretations by Westerners both of China's past and its present are highly desirable, whether they find agreement from Chinese counterparts or not. Western observers who denounced the Cultural Revolution at the time are not thereby 'Orientalist' just because they disagreed with the Chinese official policy of the day. It is perfectly possible for a Western observer to understand China's population problem in the 1980s or 1990s to the extent of seeing it in Chinese terms and according to Chinese criteria, and still disagree with the particular solutions adopted by the Chinese government to solve it.

Ethnocentrism and prejudice are not exclusive to the West, and have never been so. It is not only the study of Western images of China that offers the potentiality of moving against these twin evils. An equally valid and useful, but entirely different, topic of research from the one attacked in this book would be 'Chinese images of the

West'. While this is a subject which has already attracted some attention,[2] it certainly deserves more.

Notes

1   Strahan, Lachlan, *Australia's China*, pp. 2–3.
2   For example, Shambaugh, *Beautiful Imperialist*, but although a fine book this covers only a very limited period and only the views of a very limited selection of official United States specialists in such élite bodies as the Chinese Academy of Social Scientists.

Afterword

In the middle of 1998, United States' president Bill Clinton made a visit to China, the first by an American president since the crisis of 1989. Although it was not as historically significant for China's relations with the West, and especially the United States, as Nixon's in 1972, it did create an impact on Western images of China. The visit is worth mentioning briefly in an afterword, coming as it did after the typescript for this second edition was completed, but before the book actually went to press.

Clinton made a very favourable impression in China. On the whole American journalists probably exaggerated the extent of long-term differences he made to Chinese society. Totally ignoring the trend towards greater freedom, which had been operating since early 1992, many American reporters claimed that Clinton had single-handedly 'opened up' Chinese society, initiating a kind of 'Beijing spring'. Yet his live joint press conference with his Chinese counterpart Jiang Zemin, and the fact that his address to the students of Beijing University was broadcast in full, did have its effect on China.

But what is more interesting from the point of view of this book is the impression Clinton's visit made on his own country and its media, and thus on Western images of China. It appears to this writer that the overall effect of the visit on these images was both important and positive. It wrought changes in the major emphases of the treatment of China in the Western media.

Clinton appeared to get on very well with his Chinese counterpart Jiang Zemin. He spoke of partnership with China into the next century. He wished China well, and that it would become a prosperous and strong country. He made statements siding with China on some crucial international issues, notably expressing outright opposition to Taiwan's independence, a matter on which China feels extremely strongly. Such high-profile pictures of their president behaving in this way in China could not fail to make a positive impression of China itself in the minds of Americans, and even of other Westerners.

Although human rights still loom very large as a negative image, with references to the 'police state' common in the reports, Clinton's visit occasioned much more coverage of everyday life than had been the case before. Examples include images of people playing soccer or pool on the streets, of young people exulting in Western-style pop music or discos, and of relaxing and changing sexual mores among youth. Some newspapers acknowledged the growth in religious freedom and tolerance. The effect was to make China seem freer and less repressed, less like a totalitarian country where what matters most is the fact that human rights are abused, and more like a 'normal' country where people do normal things.

It would, however, be a mistake to exaggerate these impacts. For example, images of Tibet remain as negative as ever. It is true that the subject was mentioned during Clinton's China visit. At Clinton's and Jiang's joint press conference, Clinton said he thought that, were they to meet, Jiang Zemin and the Dalai Lama would like each other very much, while Jiang said he respected religious freedom in Tibet despite being an atheist. But Tibet did not bulk large as a positive feature of China. What remained uppermost in the Western mind were the negative images of China expressed in films like *Seven Years in Tibet* and *Kundun*.

Clinton's visit to China does not mark a swing of the pendulum as did Nixon's in 1972. Images in the 1990s were much more complicated and diverse than they were in the 1960s and early 1970s. After Clinton's visit, China appeared to the West as a place than it had beforehand. On the other hand, the change was only temporary, unlike that of 1972. The 'Beijing Spring' American journalists had noted proved short-lived, while Clinton's political enemies wasted little time in strengthening their attacks on his China policy and the view of China he represented.

In May 1999 aircraft of the North Atlantic Treaty Organization (NATO) bombed the Chinese Embassy in Belgrade during the war over Kosovo. The bombing was apparently an accident, but it killed three people and sparked a furious backlash against the United States and other NATO countries in China itself, where many people believed the bombing deliberate. Later the same month an American congressional report, which had been brewing for nearly a year, came out alleging that the Chinese had been stealing American nuclear secrets since the 1970s. Although Clinton continued to push his policy of engagement, the end of the twentieth century appeared to herald a new low point in Western images of China in general, and American in particular.

Works Cited

Primary Sources*

Printed Works

Adams, Ruth (ed.), *Contemporary China* (Peter Owen, London, 1969).

Aikman, David and FlorCruz, Jaime A., and others, 'China, The World's Next Superpower', *Time* No. 19 (10 May 1993), pp. 30–35.

Allgemeine deutsche Real-Encyklopädie für die gebildeten Stände. Conversations-Lexicon, 10th edition (15 vols.; Brockhaus, Leipzig, 1852).

Australian, The, Sydney.

Barrow, John, *Travels in China, Containing Descriptions, Observations, and Comparisons, Made and Collected in the Course of a Short Residence at the Imperial Palace of Yuen-min-yuen, and on a Subsequent Journey through the Country from Peking to Canton* (T. Cadell and W. Davies, London, 2nd edition 1806).

Baum, Richard, 'China After Deng: Ten Scenarios in Search of Reality', *The China Quarterly* No. 145 (March 1996), pp. 153–75.

Bergère, Marie-Claire, *La République populaire de Chine de 1949 à nos jours* (Armand Colin, Paris, 1987).

Bernstein, Richard and Munro, Ross, *The Coming Conflict with China* (Knopf, New York, 1997).

Bernstein, Richard, *From the Center of the Earth, The Search for the Truth about China* (Little, Brown and Company, Boston, 1982).

Bernstein, Thomas P., 'China in 1984, The Year of Hong Kong', *Asian Survey* 25(1) (January 1985), pp. 33–50.

Bishop, Isabella L. Bird, *The Golden Chersonese and the Way Thither* (G. P. Putnam's Sons, New York, 1883).

Blunden, Caroline and Elvin, Mark, *Cultural Atlas of China* (Phaidon, Oxford, 1983).

Bonavia, David, *Peking* (Time-Life Books, Amsterdam, 1978).

—— *The Chinese* (Penguin, Harmondsworth, 1982 ed.).

—— 'Superpower Links are the Prime Concern', *Far Eastern Economic Review* 127 (11) (21 March 1985), pp. 92–94.

Boxer, C. R. (ed.), *South China in the Sixteenth Century* (The Hakluyt Society, London, 1953).

Brahm, Laurence J., *China as No 1, The New Superpower Takes Centre Stage* (Butterworth-Heinemann Asia, Singapore, 1996).

Brook, Timothy, and Frolic, B. Michael, *Civil Society in China* (M. E. Sharpe, Armonk and London, 1997).

---

* Primary sources are all those works used to illustrate or exemplify the images discussed, including those which contain in addition cited commentaries on such works.

WORKS CITED

WORKS CITED 193

Buck, Pearl S., *China as I See It*, comp. and ed. Theodore F. Harris (Methuen, London, 1971).

—— *The Good Earth* (John Day, New York, 1931; edition of April 1965).

—— *Letter from Peking* (Methuen, London, 1957; 1984).

—— *My Several Worlds, A Personal Record* (John Day, New York, 1954).

Bush, Richard C. (ed.), *China Briefing, 1982* (Westview, Boulder, 1983).

Butterfield, Fox, *China, Alive in the Bitter Sea* (Hodder and Stoughton, London, 1982).

Cameron, Clyde, *China, Communism and Coca-Cola* (Hill of Content, Melbourne, 1980).

Chambers's Encyclopædia, A Dictionary of Universal Knowledge for the People, Illustrated with Maps and Numerous Wood Engravings (10 vols.; W. and R. Chambers, London, Edinburgh, 1874).

Chanda, Nayan and Huus, Kari, 'The New Nationalism', *Far Eastern Economic Review* 158 (45) (9 November 1995), pp. 20–26.

Chang, Jung, *Wild Swans, Three Daughters of China* (HarperCollins, London, 1991, Flamingo, London, 1993).

Chiang, May-ling Soong, *China Shall Rise Again* (Harper, New York and London, 1940).

China News Digest, Global News. This is available several times a week on the Internet.

'China—The Hope and the Horror, A Compilation', *Reader's Digest* 132 (809) (September 1989), pp. 54–64.

Church, George J., and others, 'China, Deng Xiaoping Leads a Far-Reaching, Audacious but Risky Second Revolution', *Time* 127 (1) (6 January 1986), pp. 6–21.

Clayre, Alasdair, *The Heart of the Dragon* (Collins/Harvill, London, 1984).

Coleridge, H.J. (ed.), *The Life and Letters of St. Francis Xavier* (2 vols.; Burns and Oates, London, 1872, 1902).

Committee of Concerned Asian Scholars, *China! Inside the People's Republic* (Bantam Books, New York, 1972).

Conger, Sarah Pike, *Letters from China, with Particular Reference to the Empress Dowager and the Women of China* (A. C. McClurg & Co., Chicago, 1909).

Cranmer-Byng, J. L. (ed.), *An Embassy to China, Being the Journal Kept by Lord Macartney During his Embassy to the Emperor Ch'ien-lung 1793–1794* (Longmans, London, 1962).

Croll, Elisabeth, *Chinese Women Since Mao* (Zed Books, London, 1983).

—— Davin, Delia, and Kane, Penny (eds.), *China's One-Child Family Policy* (Macmillan, London, 1985).

Crow, Carl, *Foreign Devils in the Flowery Kingdom* (Hamish Hamilton, London, 1941).

——*Four Hundred Million Customers* (Hamish Hamilton, London, 1937).

Cudlip, David R., *Comprador* (Secker & Warburg, London, 1984; Grafton Books, London, 1987).

Davidson, Basil, *Daybreak in China* (Jonathan Cape, London, 1953).

Davies, Derek, 'Traveller's Tales', *Far Eastern Economic Review* 130 (40) (10 October 1985), p. 35.

de Beauvoir, Simone, *La longue marche, essai sur la Chine* (Gallimard, Paris, 1957).

de Groot, J.J.M., *The Religious System of China, Its Ancient Forms, Evolution, History and Present Aspect, Manners, Custom and Social Institutions Connected Therewith* (6 vols.; Brill, Leyden, 1892–1910).

Dietrich, Craig, *People's China, A Brief History* (Oxford University Press, New York, Oxford, 1986).

Du Halde, J. B., *Description géographique, historique, chronologique, politique, et physique de l'empire de la Chine et de la Tartarie chinoise* (4 vols.; Henri Scheuleer, La Haye, 1736).
—— *The General History of China*, trans. R. Brookes (4 vols.; J. Watts, London, 1741).
Elegant, Robert, *China's Red Masters, Political Biographies of Chinese Communist Leaders* (Twayne, New York, 1951).
——*Dynasty, A Novel* (McGraw-Hill, New York, 1977).
Elson, John, Aikman, David and FlorCruz, Jaime A., 'The Party Isn't Over—Yet', *Time* No. 19 (10 May 1993), pp. 42–43.
Encyclopædia Britannica, 9th ed. (25 vols.; Adam and Charles Black, Edinburgh, 1875–89).
'Enjoying Life', *Asiaweek* 9 (16) (19 April 1985), pp. 28–37.
Fairbank, John King, *China Perceived: Images and Policies in Chinese-American Relations* (Random House, New York, 1976 ed.).
—— *The United States and China* (Harvard University Press, Cambridge, Mass., 1948; 3rd ed. 1971).
Far Eastern Economic Review Asia Yearbook (Far Eastern Economic Review, Hong Kong, various years).
Fathers, Michael and Higgins, Andrew, edited by Robert Cottrell, *Tiananmen, The Rape of Peking* (The Independent in association with Doubleday, London, New York, 1989).
Financial Times (London).
FitzGerald, Stephen, *Is Australia an Asian Country? Can Australia Survive in an East Asian Future?* (Allen & Unwin, Sydney, 1997).
Forney, Matt, 'Hoist with his Own Petard', *Far Eastern Economic Review* 160 (46) (13 November 1997), pp. 16–20.
Fortune, Robert, *Three Years' Wanderings in the Northern Provinces of China* (John Murray, London, 1847).
Garside, Roger, *Coming Alive, China After Mao* (McGraw-Hill, New York, 1981).
Gilbert, Rodney, *What's Wrong with China* (John Murray, London, 1926).
Gittings, John, *China Changes Face, The Road from Revolution 1949-1989* (Oxford University Press, Oxford, New York, 1990).
—— *Real China, From Cannibalism to Karaoke* (Simon & Schuster, London, 1996; Pocket Books, London, Sydney, New York, Tokyo, Singapore, Toronto, 1997).
Goodman, David S. G., *Deng Xiaoping and the Chinese Revolution, A Political Biography*, Routledge, London and New York, 1994, p. 115.
—— and Segal, Gerald (eds.), *China at Forty, Mid-Life Crisis?* (Clarendon Press, Oxford, 1989).
Grey, Anthony, *The Chinese Assassin* (Michael Joseph, London, 1978; Futura, London, 1979).
Guillain, Robert, *600 Millions de Chinois* (René Julliard, Paris, 1956); *The Blue Ants, 600 Million Chinese under the Red Flag*, trans. Mervin Savill (Secker and Warburg, London, 1957).
Haberman, Clyde, 'Russia's Reach for the Pacific', *Reader's Digest* 130 (786) (October 1987), pp. 22–26.
Han Suyin, *A Many-Splendoured Thing* (Jonathan Cape, London, 1953; Little, Brown and Co., Boston, 1952).
—— *Asia Today, Two Outlooks, Beatty Memorial Lectures* (McGill Queen's University Press, Montreal, London, 1969).

—— *Till Morning Comes* (Bantam Books, New York, 1982).

Harding, Harry (ed.), *China's Foreign Relations in the 1980s* (Yale University Press, New Haven, 1984).

Hawksley, Humphrey and Holberton, Simon, *Dragon Strike: The Millennium War* (Sidgwick & Jackson, London, 1997).

Hook, Brian (ed.), *The Cambridge Encyclopedia of China* (Cambridge University Press, Cambridge, 1982).

Hooper, Beverley, *Youth in China* (Penguin, Ringwood, Harmondsworth, 1985).

Hornik, Richard, 'The Muddle Kingdom? Bursting China's Bubble', *Foreign Affairs* 73 (3) (May/June 1994), pp. 28–42.

International Herald Tribune, Paris.

Johns, Captain W.E., *Biggles in the Gobi* (Hodder & Stoughton, London, 1953).

Johnson, Hewlett, *China's New Creative Age* (Lawrence and Wishart, London, 1953).

Kaplan, Fredric M., and de Keijzer, Arne J., *The China Guidebook* (Eurasia Press, New York, 3rd ed. 1982).

Karnow, Stanley, *Mao and China, From Revolution to Revolution* (The Viking Press, New York, 1972).

Kraft, Joseph, *The Chinese Difference* (Saturday Review Press, New York, 1973).

Kristof, Nicholas D. and WuDunn, Sheryl, *China Wakes, The Struggle for the Soul of a Rising Power* (Vintage Books, Random House, New York, 1995).

Lach, Donald F., *Asia in the Making of Europe Volume I, The Century of Discovery* (2 Books; University of Chicago Press, Chicago and London, 1965).

Lam, Wo-Lap, 'Peking Pursues Its Own Path', *Asiaweek* 11 (7) (15 February 1985), p. 48.

Le Comte, Louis, *Nouveaux mémoires sur l'état présent de la Chine* (2 vols.; Desbordes & Schelte, Amsterdam, 1698).

Lee, Mary, 'The Curtain Goes Up', *Far Eastern Economic Review* 127 (4) (31 January 1985), pp. 50–51.

Leys, Simon, *Broken Images, Essays on Chinese Culture and Politics*, trans. Steve Cox (St. Martin's Press, New York, 1979).

—— *Chinese Shadows* (The Viking Press, New York, 1977).

—— *Les habits neufs du président Mao* (Éditions Champs Libres, Paris, 1971); *The Chairman's New Clothes*, trans. Carol Appleyard and Patrick Goode (Allison and Busby, London, 1981 ed.).

—— 'When the "Dummies" Talk Back', *Far Eastern Economic Review* 144 (24) (15 June 1989), pp. 14 and 19.

Li, Cheng, *Rediscovering China: Dynamics and Dilemmas of Reform* (Rowman & Littlefield, Lanham, Maryland, 1997).

Li Zhisui, *The Private Life of Chairman Mao : the Memoirs of Mao's Personal Physician*, trans. Tai Hung-chao, editorial assistance Anne F. Thurston, foreword Andrew J. Nathan (Random House, New York; Chatto & Windus, London, 1994).

Liang Heng, and Shapiro, Judith, *Son of the Revolution* (Chatto and Windus, Great Britain, 1983, Fontana Paperbacks, 1984).

Lin Yutang, *My Country and My People* (Heinemann, London, Toronto, 1936).

Lindqvist, Sven, *China in Crisis* (Faber and Faber, London, 1963).

Ling, Ken, London, Miriam, and others, *The Revenge of Heaven: Journal of a Young Chinese* (G. P. Putnam's Sons, New York, 1972).

MacDougall, Colina, 'The Maoist Mould', *Far Eastern Economic Review* 68 (14) (2 April 1970), pp. 17–21.

MacFarquhar, Roderick (ed.), *Sino-American Relations,1949–71* (Wren, Melbourne, 1972).

Mackerras, Colin, with McMillen, Donald H. and Watson, Andrew (eds.), *Dictionary of the Politics of the People's Republic of China* (Routledge, London, 1998).

Malraux, André, *La condition humaine* (Gallimard, Paris, 1933); *Man's Fate (La condition humaine)*, trans. Haakon M. Chevalier (Random House, New York, 1961).

—— *Les conquérants* (Grasset, Paris, 1928).

—— *Le miroir des limbes. Tome I, Antimémoires* (Gallimard, Paris, 1967); *Antimemoirs*, trans. Terence Kilmartin (Hamish Hamilton, London, 1968).

Manegold, C. S., with Magida, Lenore, 'Upheaval in China', *The Bulletin with Newsweek* (30 May 1989), pp. 62–66.

Marchant, L. R. (ed.), *The Siege of the Peking Legations, A Diary Lancelot Giles* (University of Western Australia Press, Nedlands, WA,1970).

Mathews, Jay, and Linda, *One Billion, A China Chronicle* (Random House, New York, 1983).

Maugham, W. Somerset, *The Painted Veil* (William Heinemann, London, 1925; Pan Books, London, 1978).

——*The Travel Books of W. Somerset Maugham* (Heinemann, London, 1955),

Maverick, Lewis A., *China, A Model for Europe* (Paul Anderson, San Antonio, Texas, 1946). This work was originally published in two volumes, of which the second is a translation of François Quesnay's *Le despotisme de la Chine*, originally published in Paris in 1767.

Meadows, Thomas Taylor, *The Chinese and their Rebellions, Viewed in Connection with their National Philosophy, Ethics, Legislation, and Administration to which is Added, An Essay on Civilization and its Present State in the East and West* (Smith, Elder & Co., London, 1856).

Mendoza, Juan Gonzales de, *The History of the Great and Mighty Kingdom of China and the Situation Thereof*, trans. R. Parke, ed. George T. Staunton (2 vols.; The Hakluyt Society, London, 1853–54). The original was published under the title *Historia de la cosas mas notables, ritos y costumbres del gran Reyno de la China* in Spanish in Rome in 1585.

Miles, James A. R., *The Legacy of Tiananmen, China in Disarray* (The University of Michigan Press, Ann Arbor, 1996, 1997).

Montesquieu, Charles Louis de Secondat, *The Spirit of the Laws*, trans. Thomas Nugent (Hafner, New York, 1949).

Morath, Inge, and Miller, Arthur, *Chinese Encounters* (Secker & Warburg, London, 1979).

Morrison, George Ernest, *An Australian in China, Being the Narrative of a Quiet Journey across China to Burma* (Horace Cox, London, 2nd ed. 1895).

Mosher, Steven, *Broken Earth: The Rural Chinese* (The Free Press, New York, 1983).

—— *China Misperceived, American Illusions and Chinese Reality* (Harper Collins, USA, 1990).

Myrdal, Jan, *Report from a Chinese Village*, trans. Maurice Michael (William Heinemann, London, 1965; Pan Books, London, 1975 ed.).

Neumann, A. Lin, 'The New Bad Guys, U. S. Movie Trio Depicts Chinese as Harbingers of Evil', *Far Eastern Economic Review* 161 (1) (25 December 1997 and 1 January 1998), pp. 106–8.

New York Times (New York).

Oksenberg, Michel C., Swaine, Michael D., and Lynch, Daniel C., *The Chinese Future* (Pacific Council on International Policy, Los Angeles, and Rand Center for Asia-Pacific Policy, Santa Monica, California, 1997).

Overholt, William H., *China: The Next Economic Superpower* (Weidenfeld & Nicolson, London, 1993), published in the United States as *The Rise of China: How Economic Reform Is Creating a New Superpower* (W. W. Norton, New York, 1993).

Polin, Thomas Hon Wing and Healy, Tim, 'Man of the Century', *Asiaweek* 23 (9) (7 March 1997), pp. 31–37.

Polo, Marco, *The Travels of Marco Polo*, trans. and introduced Ronald Latham (Penguin, Harmondsworth, 1958).

Porter, Ian, and others, *China, Long-term Development Issues and Options* (The Johns Hopkins University Press, Baltimore and London, 1985).

Ricci, Matteo, *China in the Sixteenth Century: The Journals of Matthew Ricci: 1583–1610*, trans. and ed. Louis J. Gallagher S.J. (Random House, New York, 1942; 1953). This is a translation of an adaptation of Ricci's diaries by Nicholas Trigault S.J., published in Augsburg in 1615 under the title *De Christiana Expeditione apud Sinas Suscepta ab Societate Jesu*.

Rohwer, Jim, *Asia Rising, How History's Biggest Middle Class Will Change the World* (Butterworth–Heinemann Asia, Singapore, 1995; Nicholas Brealey Publishing, London, 1996).

Salisbury, Harrison E., 'China's CEO', *Success!* 33 (1) (January/February 1986), pp. 72–75.

—— *Tiananmen Diary, Thirteen Days in June* (Unwin Paperbacks, London, Sydney, Wellington, 1989).

Samagalski, Alan, and Buckley, Michael, *China—A Travel Survival Kit* (Lonely Planet Publications, Melbourne, Berkeley, 1984).

Savage-Landor, A. Henry, *China and the Allies* (2 vols.; William Heinemann, London, 1901).

Schell, Orville, *To Get Rich is Glorious, China in the Eighties* (Robin Clark, London, 1985).

Segal, Gerald (ed.), *Chinese Politics and Foreign Policy Reform* (Kegan Paul International, London and New York, for The Royal Institute of International Affairs, London, 1990).

Sitwell, Osbert, *Escape with Me! An Oriental Sketch-Book* (Macmillan, London, 1939; Oxford University Press, Hong Kong, 1983).

Smedley, Agnes, *China's Red Army Marches* (Lawrence and Wishart, London, 1936).

Smith, Adam, *An Inquiry into the Nature and Causes of the Wealth of Nations*, ed. Edwin Cannan (2 vols.; Methuen, London, 1904; 1961).

Smith, A. H., *Chinese Characteristics* (Oliphant Anderson and Ferrier, Edinburgh and London, 5th rev. ed. 1900).

Smolowe, Jill, 'Saving the Orphans', *Time* 4 (22 January 1996), p. 35.

Snow, Edgar, *China's Long Revolution* (Penguin, Harmondsworth, 1974 ed.).

—— *The Other Side of the River, Red China Today* (Random House, New York, 1961, 1962).

—— *Red Star over China* (Victor Gollancz, Great Britain, 1937; Penguin, Harmondsworth, 1972 ed.).

South China Morning Post (Hong Kong).

Stacey, Judith, *Patriarchy and Socialist Revolution in China* (University of California Press, Berkeley, 1983).

Staunton, Sir George Leonard, *An Authentic Account of an Embassy from the King of Great Britain to the Emperor of China* (2 vols.; G. Nicol, London, 1797).

Strong, Anna Louise, *China's Millions: The Revolutionary Struggles from 1925–1935* (Knight Publishing Company, New York, 1935; Foreign Languages Publishing House, Peking, 1965).

—— *The Chinese Conquer China* (Doubleday, New York,1949).

Taylor, Chris, Storey, Robert, and others, *China—A Travel Survival Kit* , 5th ed. (Lonely Planet Publications, Melbourne, Oakland, CA, 1996).

Terzani, Tiziano, *Behind the Forbidden Door, Travels in China* (Allen & Unwin, London, 1986).

Thomson, Robert and Atkin, Renata, *The Chinese Army, An Illustrated History from the Long March to Tiananmen Square* (Weldon Owen Publishing, San Francisco; Australian Broadcasting Corporation, Sydney, 1990).

Times, The (London).

Townsend, James R. and Womack, Brantly, *Politics in China* (Little, Brown and Company, Boston, Toronto, 3rd ed. 1986).

Voltaire, François-Marie Arouet, *Essai sur les mœurs et l'esprit des nations et sur les principaux faits de l'histoire depuis Charlemagne jusqu'à Louis XIII Tome 1* (Éditions Garnier Frères, Paris, 1963 ed.).

Walker, Richard L., *China under Communism, The First Five Years* (George Allen and Unwin, London, 1956).

Wall Street Journal, The.

Walsh, James, 'Red Hot, Flush with Optimism, the Emerging Economic Titan Looks to be Growing Too Far, Too Fast Yet Again', *Time* 7 (15 February 1993), pp. 30–31.

Walsh, James, and others, 'A Leaner, Meaner Fighting Machine', *Time* 19 (10 May 1993), pp. 38–41.

Walsh, James, and others, 'Born to Be Second Class', *Time Australia* 37 (11 September 1995), pp. 52–55.

White, Theodore H., and Jacoby, Analee, *Thunder Out of China* (William Sloane Associates, New York, 1946).

Williams, S. Wells, *The Middle Kingdom, A Survey of the Geography, Government, Education, Social Life, Arts, Religion, &c., of the Chinese Empire and its Inhabitants* (2 vols.; John Wiley, New York, 1851).

—— *The Middle Kingdom, A Survey of the Geography, Government, Literature, Social Life, Arts, and History of the Chinese Empire and its Inhabitants* (2 vols.; Charles Scribner's Sons, New York, 1883). This item is an updated edition of the previous one.

Wilson, Dick, *A Quarter of Mankind, An Anatomy of China Today* (Weidenfeld and Nicolson, London, 1966; Pelican, Harmondsworth, 1968).

Wint, Guy, *Common Sense about China* (Victor Gollancz, London, 1960).

Wolf, Margery, 'Marriage, Family, and the State in Contemporary China', *Pacific Affairs* 57 (2) (Summer 1984), pp. 213–36.

—— *Revolution Postponed: Women in Contemporary China* (Stanford University Press, Stanford, 1985).

Wong, Jan, *Red China Blues, My Long March from Mao to Now* (Doubleday Canada, Toronto, 1996; Doubleday/Anchor, Toronto, New York, London, Sydney, Auckland, 1997).

Wright, Elizabeth, *The Chinese People Stand Up* (BBC Books, London, 1989).

Young, Marilyn B., 'Introduction', *Pacific Affairs* 57 (2) (Summer 1984), pp. 209–12.

Yule, Henry, and Cordier, Henri, *Cathay and the Way Thither, Being a Collection of Medieval Notices of China* (4 vols.; The Hakluyt Society, London, 1913–16).

Zuckerman, Laurence, 'Thrust onto Center Stage', *Time Australia* 23 (5 June 1989), pp. 54–55.

Films

1,2 Miljard, documentary, directed by Pieter Fleury, Diogenes, produced at the end of 1989.

China's Child, documentary, written and produced by Edward Goldwyn, British Broadcasting Corporation, *Horizon*, 1983.

Dreams of Tibet, documentary, directed and produced by Ben Loeterman, written by Ben Loeterman, David Fanning and Orville Schell, Frontline/WGBH Educational Foundation, PBS Online, 1998.

From Mao to Mozart, Isaac Stern in China, documentary, produced by Murray Lerner, Hopewell Foundation production, 1981.

Gate of Heavenly Peace, The, documentary, directed and produced by Richard Gordon and Carma Hinton, written by Richard Gordon, Carma Hinton, and others, broadcast as part of the program TV World, presented by Jeanne Ryckmans, Long Bow Group, 1995.

Good Earth, The, feature, directed by Sidney Franklin, Metro-Goldwyn-Mayer, 1937.

Heart of the Dragon, The, documentary series, produced by Alasdair Clayre, Antelope-Sino-Hawkshead Films Ltd., 1985.

Inside China, documentary series, produced by André Singer and Leslie Woodhead, Granada Television, 1983.

Kundun, feature, directed by Martin Scorsese, Disney/Touchdown Pictures, 1998.

Last Emperor, The, feature, directed by Bernardo Bertolucci, Fox Columbia, 1987.

Love is a Many-Splendored Thing, feature, directed by Henry King, Fox, 1955.

Red Corner, feature, directed by Jon Avnet, Metro-Goldwyn-Mayer Pictures, 1997.

Seven Years in Tibet, feature, directed by Jean-Jacques Annaud, 1997.

Secondary Sources

'A Romance Turns Sour', *Asiaweek*, 9 (13) (1 April 1983), pp. 40–44.

Ch'en, Jerome, *China and the West, Society and Culture 1815–1937* (Hutchinson, London, 1979).

Dawson, Raymond, *The Chinese Chameleon, An Analysis of European Conceptions of Chinese Civilization* (Oxford University Press, London, 1967).

de Rachewiltz, Igor, *Papal Envoys to the Great Khans* (Faber and Faber, London, 1971).

Delfs, Robert, 'Economic Marathon', *Far Eastern Economic Review* 129 (34) (29 August 1985), pp. 50–53.

Forney, Matt, and others, 'Chinese Images, Taiwan is an Easy Sell in Washington; China Isn't', *Far Eastern Economic Review* 161 (9) (26 February 1998), pp. 24–25.

Foucault, Michel, *Power/Knowledge, Selected Interviews and Other Writings 1972–1977, Michel Foucault*, ed. Colin Gordon, trans. Colin Gordon; Leo Marshall; John Mepham; Kate Soper (The Harvester Press, Brighton, 1980).

Franke, Wolfgang, *China and the West*, trans. R. A. Wilson (Basil Blackwell, Oxford, 1967).

Gordon, Colin (ed.), *Power/Knowledge*, see under Foucault, Michel.

Grayson, Benson Lee, (ed.), *The American Image of China* (Frederick Ungar Publishing Co., New York, 1979).

Hollander, Paul, *Political Pilgrims, Travels of Western Intellectuals to the Soviet Union, China and Cuba 1928–1978* (Oxford University Press, New York, 1981).

Hooper, Beverley, '"Real" Chinas in the 1990s', *The China Journal* 39 (January 1998), pp. 83–91.

Hughes, E. R., *The Invasion of China by the Western World* (Adam and Charles Black, London, 1937; 1968).

Humble, Richard, *Marco Polo* (G. P. Putnam's Sons, New York, 1975).

Hunt, Michael H., 'Pearl Buck—Popular Expert on China, 1931–1949', *Modern China, An International Quarterly* 3(1) (January 1977), pp. 33–64.

Isaacs, Harold R., *Scratches on our Minds, American Images of China and India* (John Day, New York, 1958), updated and republished as *Images of Asia, American Views of China and India* (Harper Torchbooks, New York, 1972 ed.).

Jespersen, T. Christopher, *American Images of China, 1931–1949* (Stanford University Press, Stanford, 1996).

Jones, Dorothy B., *The Portrayal of China and India on the American Screen 1896–1955* (MIT Center for International Affairs, Cambridge, Mass., 1955).

Kaminski, Gerd and Unterrieder, Else, *Von Österreichern und Chinesen* (Europaverlag, Vienna, Munich, Zürich, 1980).

Leslie, Donald D., Mackerras, Colin, and Wang Gungwu (eds.), *Essays on the Sources for Chinese History* (Australian National University Press, Canberra, 1973).

Madsen, Axel, *Malraux, A Biography* (William Morrow, New York, 1976).

Morgan, Ted, *Somerset Maugham* (Jonathan Cape, London, 1980).

Rule, Paul, *K'ung-tzu or Confucius? The Jesuit Interpretation of Confucianism* (Allen & Unwin, Sydney, 1986).

Said, Edward W., *Orientalism* (Random House, Vintage Books, New York, 1978; 1979).

Seno, Alexandra A., and Morgan, Peter, 'The Trend Makers', *Asiaweek* 23(8) (6 March 1998), pp. 33–61.

Shambaugh, David, *Beautiful Imperialist: China Perceives America, 1972–1990* (Princeton University Press, Princeton, 1991).

Steele, A. T.,*The American People and China* (McGraw-Hill, New York, 1966).

Strahan, Lachlan, *Australia's China: Changing Perceptions from the 1930s to the 1990s* (Cambridge University Press, New York, 1996).

Strong, Tracy B., and Keyssar, Helene, *Right in her Soul: The Life of Anna Louise Strong* (Random House, New York, 1983).

Varg, Paul, *Missionaries, Chinese, and Diplomats, The American Protestant Missionary Movement in China, 1870–1952* (Princeton University Press, Princeton, 1958).

Wood, Frances, *Did Marco Polo go to China?* (Secker & Warburg, London, 1995).

Young, John D., *Confucianism and Christianity, The First Encounter* (Hong Kong University Press, Hong Kong, 1983).

Zhongguo tongji nianjian 1983 (Chinese Statistical Yearbook 1983) (Chinese Statistical Press, Beijing, 1983).

Index

User's Note: The order of entries is word-by-word. References to end-notes comprise page number followed by the end-note number which is prefixed by the letter 'n'. Titles of films and publications are printed in italics.

Buddhism and Buddhists, 16, 27
Tibetan, 167–9
Bureaucracy (*see also* Mandarins;
Officials), 70, 89, 100, 150, 164
Business people, 6, 66, 76, 143, 174,
175
Butterfield, Fox, 119, 120, 184

CALIFORNIA, UNIVERSITY OF, 173
Cambridge University, 63
Cameron, Clyde, 120, 126
Cannibalism, 113
Cannon, manufacture of, 25
Canterbury, Dean of, 93
Capitalism, 83, 124, 138
Carter, Jimmy, 184
Castration, 29
Cathay, 15
Cathayans (Chinese), 13, 16
Catholicism (*see also* Christianity)
conversion of Chinese to, 24, 26,
178–9
Chai Ling, 144
Chairman Mao: The Last Emperor, 112
Chambers's Encyclopaedia, 54, 55
Chancellor, John, 143
Chang, Jung, 110–11
Chang'an, 14
Change, 40, 56
Ch'en Ta Erh, 73
Chiang Kai-shek, 63, 83, 179
victory in 1927, 68, 73
Chiang Kai-shek, Madame, *see* Song
Meiling
China (*see also* People's Republic of
China)
aggressiveness of, 86, 90, 152
ancient Roman names for, 11
containment of, 152, 154
field research in, 185
future of, 70, 170–4
as model, 37, 84, 177
negative images of, 1949–66, 84–9
positive images of, 1949–66, 90–3
object of images, 3–4, 183
peace-loving, 29, 116, 187
as threat, 85–6, 90, 151–4
under threat, 90

Western relations with, 143, 188,
190–1
China, Alive in the Bitter Sea, 184
China! Inside the People's Republic, 100
China Shall Rise Again, 66
China's Child, 131, 164
China's Millions, 70
China White Paper, 85
Chinese (language), 7, 13, 42, 43, 54,
182
diplomats learn, 48
Jesuits learn, 24–5
Chinese (people)
absence of nerves of, 45
absence of sympathy, 46
artistry, 13, 19, 98, 99
bravery, 77, 99
Brockhaus' view, 55–6
cheats, 36, 41, 45
civility, 41
cleverness, 86
cliquism, 66
conservatism, 45, 64, 72
contentment, 64
courtesy, 51
cowardice, 56
cruelty, 46, 60, 86, 98, 99
deceitful, 44, 56
defeatism, 66
dirtiness, 41, 44, 48, 75
Da Cruz's view, 18–19
Du Halde's view, 31–2
evasion of responsibility, 66
face, 66
hardworking, 13, 19, 56, 77, 98, 99
'Heathen Chinese', 177
honesty, 77, 99
humour, 64
ignorance, 98, 99
inaccuracy, 45, 66
indifference, 64
individualism, negation of, 55, 87
inscrutability, 55, 86
intelligence, 77, 98
lack of self-discipline, 66
Lin Yutang's view, 64
mellowness, 64
mendacity, 44, 48, 53

Sorbonne, 30
Soviet Union (see also Sino-Soviet
relations), 5, 71, 85
Spain, 16, 178
Spratly and Paracel Islands, 153
Stacey, Judith, 129
Stalin, Josef, 87, 101
Standard of living, 138, 178
Stanford University, 132
State Family Planning Commission, 131
State Military Commission, 148
State Statistical Bureau, 93
Staunton, Sir George Leonard, 40, 41
Stein, Sir Aurel, 89
Stern, Isaac, 106
Strong, Anna Louise, 69, 70, 73
Student demonstrations, 138–41, 142
Success!, 118
Sun Yefang, 93
'Supervised liberty', 119
Sweden, 92

TAIPING UPRISING, 49
Taissan, see Taizong, Emperor
Taiwan, 151, 152, 153, 171, 174
Taizong, Emperor, 11
Taugas (Chinese people), 11
Tavris, Carol, 105
Tea, 14, 153
Television, 7, 97, 139, 140
Television documentaries (see also
Films), 7, 106, 112, 164
Terzani, Tiziano, 131, 133
Thailand, 159, 163
Theophylactus Simocatta, 11, 12
Thurman, Uma, 168
Tiananmen Square, 138, 139, 140, 141,
144, 149
Tibet, 4, 31, 144, 147, 151, 166–70,
180, 191
annexation of, 90, 166
independence, 171, 173, 174
travel in, 50, 123
Till Morning Comes, 108, 109
Time, 63, 76, 83, 106, 116, 118, 146,
153, 158, 162, 163, 173
Times, The, 117
Torture, 32, 55

Totalitarianism, 86, 100, 119, 124, 145,
186
Trade, 35
Travellers, 6, 50
Travels in China, 41
Travels of Marco Polo, The, 14
Treatise in which the Things of China
are Related at Great Length, 18
Treaty ports, 66, 127
Trigault, Nicholas, 27, 28
'Truth', as a function of power, 2
Tyler, Patrick, 149

UN FUND FOR POPULATION
ACTIVITIES, 133
United Nations, 86, 131
United Nations World Conference on
Women, 161
United States, 62, 84, 94, 141, 144, 145,
152, 174, 187
as dominant country for images of
China, 4, 59, 94, 184
radical journalism, 69–70
relations with China, 76, 85, 97, 98,
116, 117, 135, 155, 172, 179,
184
study on future of China, 170
visited by Chinese leaders, 150, 154
visited by Song Meiling, 65
US–China Business Council, 175

VALIGNANO, ALESSANDRO, 24
Van der Sprenkel, Otto, 26
Venice, 14
Verbiest, Ferdinand, 25, 26
Vienna, University of, 62
Vietnam, 94, 117, 177–8, 182
Vietnam War, 97, 100, 127
role in changing US view of China,
98
Villagers' Committees, Organic Law on,
191
Virgil, 11
Voltaire, François-Marie Arouet, 31, 33,
36, 37, 41, 177, 181

WADE, T F, 49
Walker, Richard L, 85, 89

Walsh, James, 153
Walt Disney Company, 168
Walter, Richard, 39
Wang Guangmei, 103, 104
Wang Lung (fictional character), 71, 72
War (see also Gulf War; Korean War;
    Vietnam War; World War II)
    against Japan, 65, 76
Wealth of Nations, The, 34
Wei Jingsheng, 144–45
Wei Zhongxian, 29
West, the, 1, 8, 39, 77, 183
    definition, 4–5
    relations with China, 118, 143, 188,
        190
    superiority of, 50, 53, 182
Western images of China, 4, 5, 8, 20,
    40, 54, 97, 116, 134, 135, 138, 190
    Chinese influences on, 63–6
    determinants of, 184–5
    significance of, 187–9
Westernization, 125–7
Wham! (pop group), 125
Whitlam, Gough, 120
Wife-beating, 52
Wild Swans, 110–12, 182
Wilhelm II, Kaiser, 187
Williams, Samuel Wells, 42, 43–5, 47,
    48
Wilson, Dick, 90
Wolf, Margery, 127, 128, 129, 130
Women, 31–2, 55, 129
    discrimination against, 69, 72
    as image-formulators, 59
    images of Fortune, Bishop, and
        Morrison compared, 52–3
    status of, 93, 128, 129, 130, 160,
        161, 162

treatment of, 43, 161–2
Wong, Jan, 112–13, 114
World Bank, 121–2, 130, 163
World Conference on Women, 161
World Health Organization, 160
World Meeting on Women, 161
World War II, 179
Wright, Elizabeth, 164, 165
WuDunn, Sheryl, 160
Wuxi, 123
Wuxuan, 113

XAVIER, FRANCIS, 24
Xenophobia, see Chinese (People);
    Foreigners
Xi'an, 13, 162
Xining, 50
Xinjiang Autonomous Region, 13, 173

YALE COLLEGE, 48
Yalu River, 101
Yan'an, 70, 151
Yangtze River, 50, 160
'Yellow Peril', 177, 187
Yuan Shikai, 50
Yunnan, 50, 123

ZHANG SHUYIN, 162
Zhao Ziyang, 140
Zhaoshi guer, (Orphan of the Zhao
    Family), 36
Zheng Yi, 113
Zhong yong, (Doctrine of the Mean), 30
Zhou Enlai, 91, 97, 101, 103, 104
Zhu Wan, 18
Zhu Rongji, 150, 151, 158–9